CLINICAL RESEARCH REGULATIONS

PRINCIPLES, PRACTICES, AND GLOBAL PERSPECTIVES

PROF. RAJIV DAHIYA, DR. MURALIDHAR RAO AKKALADEVI

Made with ♥ on the Notion Press Platform
www.notionpress.com

Contents

Contents

Clinical Research Regulations: Principles, Practices, And Global Perspectives

Editor
Prof. Rajiv Dahiya
School of Pharmacy, Faculty of Medical Sciences
The University of the West Indies,
St. Augustine, Trinidad & Tobago
Author
Dr. Muralidhar Rao Akkaladevi
Principal,
St. Mary's College of Pharmacy,
Secunderabad, Telangana, India
Published by Notion Press
Notion Press, Inc.
800, West El Camino Real #180,
California, USA 94040
Notion Press Media Pvt Ltd
#7, Red Cross Road,
Egmore, Chennai, Tamil Nadu 600008
Email ID: publish@notionpress.com
Phone Number: +91 44 46315631

Preface

The expanding field of clinical research has become a cornerstone of medical advancement, driving innovations that improve global healthcare outcomes. However, the conduct of clinical trials is bound by rigorous ethical and regulatory standards that vary significantly across regions and research domains. The increasing complexity of clinical research demands that professionals not only understand scientific protocols but also navigate a comprehensive framework of global regulations, making the mastery of both scientific and regulatory knowledge essential.

This book, *Clinical Research Regulations: Principles, Practices, and Global Perspectives*, was conceived to bridge this critical gap by offering a thorough exploration of the diverse regulations governing clinical research. It is designed as a comprehensive reference for students, clinical investigators, regulatory professionals, and healthcare practitioners who are involved in the design, conduct, and oversight of clinical trials. Our primary aim is to provide an integrated understanding of regulatory principles and practices, enabling readers to grasp the full spectrum of clinical research regulations, from ethical considerations to practical implementation.

Structured across **25 detailed chapters**, this book covers the essential phases of clinical research, including early-stage trials, bioequivalence studies, and post-marketing surveillance. In addition, we have included in-depth discussions on ethical frameworks such as the **Declaration of Helsinki**, the **Belmont Report**, and the **ICH-GCP Guidelines**, which serve as the backbone of ethical clinical practice worldwide. By incorporating global perspectives, particularly focusing on regulations from **India**, the **USA**, and the **European Union**, we provide insights into both universal standards and country-specific nuances that influence clinical trial execution.

Each chapter is carefully curated to offer not only regulatory insights but also practical applications, helping the reader connect theoretical knowledge with everyday challenges in clinical research. Special attention is given to critical topics such as **medical device trials**, **research in special populations**, and **biostatistical methods**, making this text invaluable to those engaged in diverse areas of clinical trials.

In writing this book, we wanted to create a resource that is as relevant to those new to clinical research as it is to seasoned professionals. The global regulatory landscape is constantly evolving, and the need for harmonization across different regulatory bodies has never been more important. With that in mind, this book serves as a guide to navigating the complexities of multinational clinical trials, ensuring that ethical and regulatory requirements are met without compromising the integrity of the research.

We are deeply grateful to all the contributors, whose expertise and insights have made this book a rich source of knowledge. Their dedication has been instrumental in shaping the content of this text, and we thank them for their tireless efforts. We also extend our appreciation to the global clinical research community, whose commitment to upholding ethical standards in the pursuit of scientific knowledge continues to inspire and inform the development of safer, more effective healthcare solutions.

It is our sincere hope that this book will become a trusted reference for all those involved in clinical research, providing clarity and guidance as they navigate the ever-evolving regulatory landscape.

Prof. Rajiv Dahiya
Editor

Dr. A. Muralidhar Rao Akkaladevi
Author

Chapter Wise Contents

CHAPTER ONE

Introduction to Clinical Research and Drug Development

1.1 Overview of Clinical Research

Clinical research is a cornerstone of modern medical science, playing a pivotal role in the development of new drugs, medical devices, and treatments. It refers to a systematic investigation designed to evaluate and test the **safety**, **efficacy**, and **effectiveness** of therapeutic interventions in humans. The main goal of clinical research is to generate reliable and valid data that can guide medical decision-making and ensure that healthcare interventions meet the required standards before they are made available for public use. Without rigorous clinical research, new treatments would remain untested, leaving healthcare providers and patients uncertain about their effectiveness or potential risks.

The significance of clinical research lies in its role in protecting patient safety while advancing medical innovation. Before any new **drug**, **vaccine**, or **medical device** can be approved for widespread use, it must go through a series of **clinical trials** to assess its effects on human health. These trials, typically conducted in **multiple phases**, evaluate everything from how the treatment is absorbed and metabolized by the body to its long-term effects on specific patient populations. Through clinical research, healthcare providers can identify **therapeutic benefits**, recognize potential **side effects**, and determine the **optimal dosage** for treatments.

The history of clinical research is marked by several key milestones that have shaped the ethical framework in which modern trials are conducted. One such milestone is the **Nuremberg Code**, established in the aftermath of World War II in response to unethical medical experiments conducted during the war. The code laid the foundation for modern **ethical standards** in clinical research, emphasizing the need for **voluntary participation**, **informed consent**, and the **right to withdraw** from studies at any time. Following this, the establishment of **Good Clinical Practice (GCP)** guidelines further solidified the ethical and scientific framework for conducting clinical trials. GCP ensures that trials are conducted in an ethically sound manner, with the **safety and rights of participants** prioritized throughout the study. These guidelines also ensure that the **data generated** from clinical trials is reliable, allowing for **accurate evaluation** of the intervention being tested.

Clinical research encompasses a wide range of study designs, each contributing uniquely to the body of medical knowledge. **Interventional studies**, such as **randomized controlled trials (RCTs)**, are often considered the gold standard of clinical research. In these studies, participants are randomly assigned to receive either the experimental treatment or a placebo, allowing researchers to determine the treatment's direct effects. Interventional studies are crucial in establishing a treatment's efficacy by controlling variables and reducing bias. On the other hand, **observational studies** involve monitoring participants without manipulating the study environment. These studies are valuable in identifying **long-term effects**, especially for treatments already in use. **Epidemiological studies**, which track patterns, causes, and effects of health conditions in populations, help researchers understand the **risk factors** associated with diseases and the effectiveness of public health interventions. Each type of study design plays a vital role in expanding the **evidence base** that informs clinical practice.

Evidence-based medicine (EBM) is a critical concept that ties into the value of clinical research. EBM refers to the integration of the best available research evidence with clinical expertise and patient values to make informed medical decisions. Clinical research provides the **robust data** necessary to ensure that medical interventions are not based on anecdotal evidence or intuition but rather on well-substantiated findings. Through the results of **clinical trials** and other research, healthcare providers can rely on tested and proven treatments to improve patient outcomes. For example, large-scale trials of medications like **statins** have proven their effectiveness in reducing the risk of **cardiovascular diseases**, which has directly influenced treatment protocols worldwide.

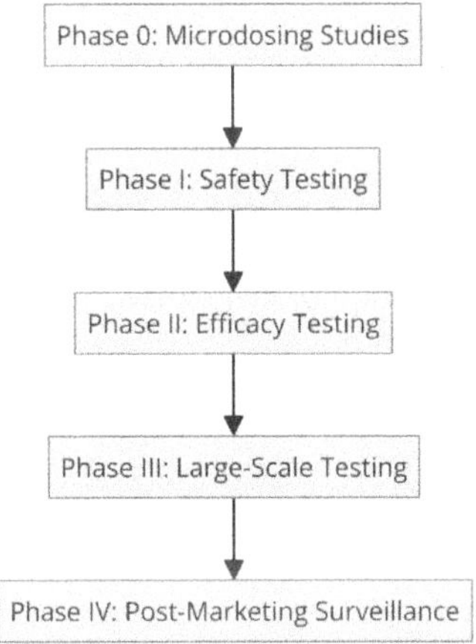

Phases of Clinical Trials

1.2 Drug Development Process

The **drug development process** is a complex and highly regulated journey that begins with the **discovery** of new chemical or biological entities and progresses through various stages of **testing** and **evaluation** before a drug can be approved for public use. This process is designed to ensure that the drug is **safe**, **effective**, and **beneficial** for the target population. The development process typically spans several years, involving a combination of **preclinical testing**, **clinical trials**, and **post-marketing surveillance** to gather comprehensive data about the drug's performance.

The first step in drug development is **discovery**, which involves identifying a promising compound that may have therapeutic potential. Scientists screen hundreds or even thousands of compounds to find candidates that interact with biological targets involved in specific diseases. Once a lead compound is identified, **preclinical testing** begins. Preclinical trials are conducted in **laboratories** and involve both **in vitro (test tube)** and **in vivo (animal)** experiments. The main objective of preclinical testing is to evaluate the compound's **pharmacokinetics (PK)**—how the drug is absorbed, distributed, metabolized, and excreted in the body—and

pharmacodynamics (PD)—how the drug affects the body at the molecular level. Additionally, **toxicology studies** are performed to determine the potential risks and side effects of the compound before it is tested in humans. If the compound shows favorable results, it moves to the next stage: **clinical trials**.

The clinical trial process is divided into **four phases** (Phase 0-IV), each with its specific objectives and regulatory requirements. These trials are designed to gather detailed information about the drug's safety, efficacy, and pharmacological properties in humans.

Phase 0 is the earliest stage of clinical research and involves **microdosing studies** in a very small group of participants (often fewer than 15). The objective of Phase 0 is to gather preliminary **pharmacokinetic (PK)** data to understand how the drug behaves in the human body. Since the doses used are extremely small (typically $1/100^{th}$ of the therapeutic dose), there is little risk to participants. Phase 0 trials provide valuable information about whether the drug is likely to perform as expected in the human body and can help determine if the drug should proceed to larger trials. This phase is not always included in every drug development process but can be crucial in providing early insights into the drug's potential.

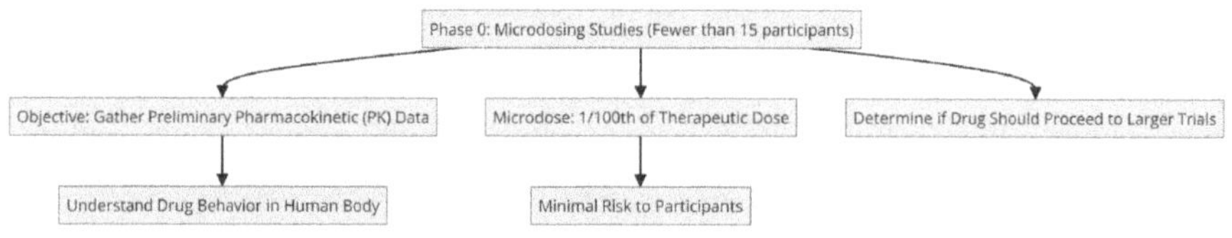

Phase 0 Clinical Trials

Phase I clinical trials are the first phase of drug testing in **human volunteers**. The primary objective of Phase I is to determine the **safety** of the drug and identify the **appropriate dosage** for subsequent trials. These studies typically involve a small group of **healthy participants** (usually 20-100 individuals) who are closely monitored for any **adverse effects**. In addition to assessing safety, researchers also evaluate the **pharmacokinetics** of the drug, including how long it stays in the body and how it is metabolized and excreted. By the end of Phase I, researchers should have a clear understanding of the drug's **safe dosage range** and the potential for any short-term side effects.

Phase II clinical trials are designed to evaluate the **efficacy** of the drug in patients who have the **target condition**. These studies involve a larger group of participants (typically 100-300) and focus on determining whether the drug provides the intended therapeutic effect. Phase II trials also continue to monitor the drug's **safety** profile, but the main goal is to assess how well the drug works in treating or managing the disease. This phase provides the first indication of the drug's effectiveness in a controlled setting, and successful results are necessary to move forward to larger trials. **Pharmacodynamics (PD)** studies are particularly important at this stage, as they help researchers understand the drug's mechanism of action in the body.

Phase III clinical trials are **large-scale studies** involving hundreds or even thousands of patients. The primary goal of Phase III is to confirm the drug's **efficacy** and gather more extensive data on its **safety profile**. These trials are conducted in multiple locations and often involve **randomized, controlled studies** to compare the new drug to existing treatments or placebos. Phase III trials provide the comprehensive data needed to submit the drug for **regulatory approval**. At this stage, researchers continue to monitor the **pharmacokinetics** and **pharmacodynamics** of the drug to ensure that it performs consistently across a diverse patient population. Successful completion of Phase III is crucial, as this is the final step before the drug is submitted to regulatory authorities like the **FDA** or **EMA** for approval.

Phase IV, also known as **post-marketing surveillance**, occurs after the drug has been approved and made available to the public. The goal of Phase IV is to monitor the **long-term effects** of the drug in a much larger and more diverse population. This phase helps identify any **rare side effects** or **long-term risks** that may not have been evident during earlier trials. Phase IV is an essential part of ensuring that the drug remains **safe and effective** throughout its lifecycle. Regulatory agencies require continuous monitoring and reporting of any new **adverse events** to ensure ongoing compliance with safety standards.

The drug development process is heavily regulated by agencies such as the **FDA**, **EMA**, and **CDSCO** to ensure that every phase is conducted with the highest standards of **safety** and **scientific rigor**. Each phase of clinical trials has **strict regulatory requirements**, including the submission of **detailed data** on the drug's performance, safety assessments, and plans for **risk management**. Only after demonstrating **consistent safety and**

efficacy across all phases can a drug be approved for public use, ensuring that it meets the necessary standards to protect patients.

1.3 Medical Device Development Process

The **medical device development process** differs significantly from the drug development process, primarily due to the unique challenges involved in designing and testing devices that interact with the human body in a mechanical or electronic manner. Medical devices range from simple **diagnostic tools** like thermometers to highly complex **therapeutic devices** such as pacemakers and robotic surgical systems. Unlike pharmaceuticals, which rely on chemical interactions within the body, medical devices must account for **mechanical safety**, **design optimization**, and **human factor engineering** to ensure that they function as intended without causing harm to users.

The development of medical devices begins with **concept design** and **prototype development**, where engineers and designers create an initial model of the device. The goal at this stage is to determine how the device will work, how it will be used by healthcare professionals or patients, and how it can be manufactured. Special consideration is given to **human factors engineering**, which ensures that the device is intuitive and easy to use, minimizing the risk of errors during operation. For example, a **blood glucose monitor** designed for diabetic patients must be simple to operate, with clear instructions and user-friendly features. Design optimization also includes ensuring the device can withstand the physical demands of its intended use, such as durability in **implantable devices** or precision in **diagnostic equipment**.

After the prototype is developed, the device undergoes **preclinical testing** to evaluate its **safety** and **functionality** in a controlled environment. This stage is similar to drug preclinical trials but focuses on ensuring that the device performs mechanically and safely under various conditions. For instance, an **artificial heart valve** would be tested in simulated environments to ensure it can withstand the pressure and flow of blood within the body. These tests are essential for identifying potential design flaws and ensuring the device is ready for further evaluation.

Once the device passes preclinical testing, it moves into **clinical investigations**, where it is tested in humans. This phase is regulated by international standards such as **ISO 14155**, which provides guidelines for the design, conduct, and reporting of clinical investigations for medical devices. Clinical investigations for medical devices differ from drug trials in that they often focus on **mechanical performance**, **user safety**, and **device reliability** over time. Devices such as **implantable cardiac devices** or **prosthetics** require thorough clinical testing to ensure they function safely in a real-world setting and meet the intended therapeutic outcomes.

During clinical investigations, the device must comply with stringent **regulatory frameworks** such as the **EU Medical Device Regulation (MDR)**, which governs the approval of medical devices in Europe. The MDR requires manufacturers to provide comprehensive data on the **safety**, **efficacy**, and **quality** of the device, including detailed results from clinical trials. In addition, manufacturers must demonstrate that they have implemented a robust **risk management system** to monitor and address potential device failures or adverse events. Regulatory frameworks like MDR ensure that only devices that meet **high safety standards** are approved for use, protecting patients from potential harm.

After the device is approved for market entry, **post-market surveillance** continues to monitor its performance over time. Post-market surveillance is essential for identifying any **long-term issues** or **unexpected complications** that may arise after the device is widely used. Manufacturers are required to submit periodic safety updates and conduct **post-market clinical follow-ups** to ensure the device continues to meet safety and performance standards. For example, in the case of a new **insulin pump**, post-market surveillance might reveal rare malfunctions that were not detected during clinical investigations. These findings would prompt further investigation or lead to product recalls or design modifications if necessary.

The development of medical devices is a highly regulated and iterative process that requires ongoing evaluation at every stage to ensure **safety**, **effectiveness**, and **patient well-being**. Unlike drugs, which primarily involve chemical interactions, devices must meet stringent **mechanical and usability standards**, ensuring they integrate smoothly into clinical practice without introducing new risks.

1.4 Importance of Regulatory Compliance

Regulatory compliance plays an indispensable role in the development of both drugs and medical devices. It refers to the adherence to a set of rules, guidelines, and regulations established by **national** and **international regulatory bodies** to ensure that products meet **safety**, **efficacy**, and **quality standards** before they are made available to the public. Compliance with these regulations is essential for protecting **patient safety**, maintaining **ethical standards**, and ensuring the **integrity of clinical trial data**. Regulatory bodies such as the **FDA (Food and Drug Administration)** in the United States, **EMA (European Medicines Agency)** in Europe, and **CDSCO (Central Drugs Standard Control Organization)** in India oversee these processes, each playing a critical role in their respective regions to ensure that pharmaceutical products and medical devices are safe for human use.

In clinical trials, **regulatory compliance** ensures that every aspect of the research—from the design of the study to the collection and analysis of data—is conducted according to predefined ethical guidelines. These guidelines emphasize the need for **patient safety**, **informed consent**, and **risk management** throughout the trial. For example, during the development of a new **cancer drug**, the regulatory framework ensures that the trial is designed to minimize potential risks to patients while still generating valuable data on the drug's efficacy and safety. Regulatory compliance also guarantees that all data collected during the clinical trial is **transparent**, **accurate**, and **credible**, which is critical for making informed decisions about the drug's approval.

Various regulatory bodies have specific mandates to oversee the development of drugs and medical devices. In the United States, the **FDA** is responsible for regulating the safety and efficacy of **pharmaceuticals**, **biologics**, and **medical devices**. It ensures that clinical trials meet the strict ethical and scientific standards required for the protection of human subjects and the accuracy of the resulting data. The **EMA** serves a similar function in Europe, ensuring that products entering the European market comply with rigorous **safety** and **performance requirements**. The EMA operates under the **European Union Medical Device Regulation (MDR)** and similar regulations for drugs, requiring manufacturers to provide robust evidence of their product's safety before approval. In India, **CDSCO** is responsible for ensuring that drugs and devices meet the necessary standards for **quality** and **efficacy**, enforcing ethical guidelines for clinical research conducted within the country. Each of these agencies plays a vital role in **regulating clinical trials**, conducting **site inspections**, and reviewing **data submissions** to ensure that products are thoroughly evaluated before being introduced to the market.

Failure to comply with regulatory requirements can have serious consequences for both the development of the product and the overall success of the company involved. Non-compliance can lead to **trial delays**, **fines**, **product recalls**, or even **termination of the trial**. For example, if a pharmaceutical company fails to follow proper **data collection** or **reporting protocols** during a clinical trial, the FDA or EMA may issue a warning or halt the trial until the issue is resolved. In severe cases, such as when patient safety is compromised, regulators may withdraw approval or enforce a product recall, resulting in significant financial losses for the company and potential harm to patients. Additionally, failure to comply with regulatory standards can damage a company's reputation and result in **long-term regulatory scrutiny** for future projects.

For example, in the case of a **medical device recall**, non-compliance with regulatory standards—such as **inadequate safety testing**—can lead to the discovery of previously unreported **adverse effects**, prompting the **FDA** or **EMA** to take regulatory action. This not only affects the company's financial stability but also poses serious risks to the patients who may already be using the device. Thus, adherence to **regulatory guidelines** is essential not only for obtaining initial market approval but also for maintaining long-term product safety and success in the marketplace.

CHAPTER TWO

Types of Clinical Studies

In clinical research, the choice of study design is crucial for producing reliable and interpretable data, which directly impacts medical decision-making. Clinical studies are the foundation for evaluating the safety, efficacy, and overall performance of new treatments, medical devices, or therapies. Different types of study designs are used depending on the research question being addressed, and each type offers distinct advantages and challenges. For example, **Randomized Controlled Trials (RCTs)** are often considered the gold standard in clinical research because they help establish cause-and-effect relationships by randomly assigning participants to treatment or control groups. This randomization reduces bias and provides robust, scientifically rigorous results.

Observational studies, on the other hand, offer insights into the long-term effects of treatments or interventions in real-world settings without manipulating the environment. These studies are valuable for tracking the progression of diseases, monitoring the safety of already approved treatments, and identifying potential **risk factors** for adverse outcomes. In such studies, participants are merely observed, and the outcomes are recorded without any intervention from researchers. This type of design is particularly important in **epidemiology**, where understanding how diseases affect populations over time is critical for shaping public health policies.

Other study designs, such as **crossover trials** and **adaptive trials**, offer flexibility and efficiency in testing treatments. In **crossover studies**, participants receive multiple treatments over different time periods, allowing researchers to compare the effects of each treatment within the same group of individuals. This reduces the variability that comes from differences between participants, offering more precise results. Meanwhile, **adaptive trials** are designed to allow for modifications as the study progresses based on interim data, which can save time and resources. These trials are increasingly used in areas such as **oncology** and **rare diseases**, where adjustments may be needed based on early indications of a treatment's efficacy or safety.

Bioavailability and **bioequivalence studies** are specifically used to compare different formulations of the same drug or between generic and branded versions. These studies focus on the **pharmacokinetics** of the drug—how it is absorbed, distributed, metabolized, and excreted in the body. **Bioequivalence** is crucial for ensuring that generic drugs provide the same therapeutic effects as their branded counterparts, meeting the stringent requirements of regulatory bodies like the **FDA** or **EMA**.

Regulatory significance is a critical aspect of each study design. Regulatory authorities such as the **FDA** in the USA, the **EMA** in Europe, and the **CDSCO** in India, require specific types of studies to approve new treatments or devices. For example, for a new drug to receive approval, **Randomized Controlled Trials** are typically mandatory to prove the drug's efficacy compared to existing treatments or placebos. **Observational studies** are often used in post-marketing surveillance to monitor the long-term safety of treatments after they have been approved and released to the market. **Crossover trials** may be used when comparing two closely related treatments, particularly in cases where patient populations are small, and the same individuals need to be tested for multiple interventions. **Bioequivalence studies** are required for the approval of **generic drugs**, ensuring they perform similarly to their branded versions.

Choosing the right study design depends on a number of factors, including the **objectives** of the trial, the **available resources**, and the **ethical considerations** involved. For example, an RCT may not be ethically feasible if it involves withholding a life-saving treatment from participants, making **observational studies** a better choice in such cases. Similarly, crossover trials may be preferred when the study population is limited, as it allows each participant to serve as their own control, improving the statistical power of the study without increasing the sample size. Understanding the strengths and limitations of each design is essential for selecting the most appropriate method to answer the research question effectively and ensure reliable outcomes.

2.1 Randomized Controlled Trials (RCTs)

Randomized Controlled Trials (RCTs) are widely regarded as the **gold standard** in clinical research due to their ability to generate reliable and high-quality evidence regarding the efficacy and safety of new treatments, therapies, or interventions. The defining feature of RCTs is the process of **randomization**, which ensures that participants are assigned to either the **treatment group** or the **control group** entirely by chance. This randomness eliminates **selection bias**, where researchers or participants might influence who receives the treatment, thus ensuring that the two groups are comparable in all respects except for the intervention being studied.

The process of **randomization** is crucial because it ensures that the **treatment group**, which receives the experimental therapy, and the **control group**, which typically receives a placebo or standard treatment, are equivalent at the start of the trial. By doing so, researchers can attribute any differences in outcomes between the groups to the intervention itself, rather than to other confounding factors. For example, in a trial testing a new medication for hypertension, randomization ensures that factors such as **age**, **gender**, or **existing health conditions** are evenly distributed across both groups, thus reducing the risk that these variables could skew the results. This is particularly important in large-scale trials where even small imbalances could significantly affect the interpretation of the data.

Another essential feature of RCTs is the use of **blinding**, which further reduces bias. In a **single-blind trial**, the participants do not know whether they are receiving the treatment or a placebo, while in a **double-blind trial**, neither the participants nor the investigators know which group is receiving the treatment. This helps to ensure that the results are not influenced by **expectations** or **placebo effects**. For instance, if participants believe they are receiving a new, potentially life-changing treatment, they may report improvements even if they are only receiving a placebo. Similarly, investigators may unconsciously interpret results more favorably if they know which participants are receiving the active treatment. **Double-blinding** is therefore considered the most rigorous form of blinding in clinical trials, as it helps eliminate both **participant** and **investigator bias**, ensuring that the outcomes reflect the true efficacy of the intervention.

The **statistical significance** of RCTs is often enhanced by the use of **large sample sizes**, which allow researchers to detect even small differences in treatment effects with greater accuracy. Larger trials generally produce more **precise** and **reliable** estimates of treatment efficacy because they reduce the influence of random variation. For example, in a small trial, the results could be skewed by the presence of a few outliers—individuals whose response to the treatment is markedly different from the rest of the participants. However, in a large trial, the effect of these outliers is minimized, resulting in a more accurate reflection of the treatment's overall efficacy. Large sample sizes are also necessary to ensure that the trial is adequately powered to detect differences between treatment and control groups, reducing the risk of **false negatives** (failing to detect a true effect) or **false positives** (detecting an effect where none exists).

RCTs are not only scientifically rigorous but are also a **regulatory requirement** for the approval of new drugs and medical devices. Regulatory bodies such as the **FDA (Food and Drug Administration)** in the United States and the **EMA (European Medicines Agency)** in Europe require that new treatments undergo thorough testing in **well-designed RCTs** before they can be approved for use in clinical practice. These trials must demonstrate that the new intervention is not only effective but also safe for the target population. For example, in the approval process for a new **cancer treatment**, the FDA would require evidence from several phases of RCTs, showing that the treatment provides a **significant benefit** over existing therapies without introducing unacceptable risks. RCTs are therefore essential for ensuring that new interventions meet the **highest standards of safety and efficacy** before they are made available to the public.

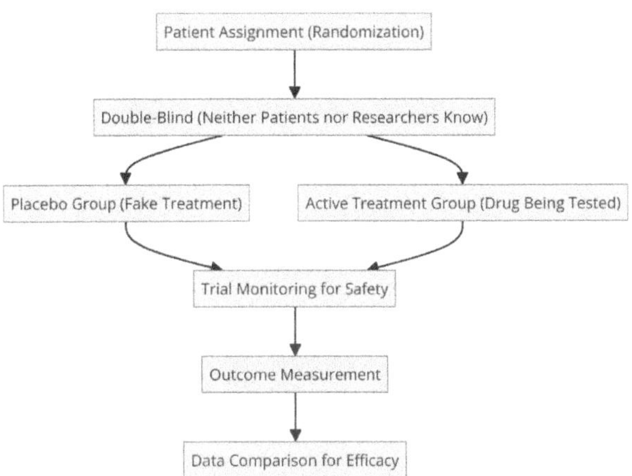

Comparison between Placebo-Controlled Trials and Active Treatment Groups

2.2 Observational Studies

Observational studies play a crucial role in clinical research by providing valuable insights into **real-world outcomes** and the **long-term**

effects of interventions without manipulating the study environment. Unlike **Randomized Controlled Trials (RCTs)**, which are designed to test the efficacy of treatments under controlled conditions, observational studies focus on **monitoring participants** in their natural settings. This allows researchers to gather data on how treatments or diseases progress over time, often in large, diverse populations. Because observational studies do not require randomization or intervention, they are particularly useful for studying **chronic diseases** and evaluating how treatments perform in **everyday clinical practice**.

There are several types of observational studies, each with its own methodology and purpose. **Cohort studies** are one of the most widely used types. In a cohort study, researchers follow a group of individuals (the cohort) over time, observing their exposure to certain risk factors or treatments and tracking the development of outcomes, such as disease progression or recovery. For instance, in a cohort study investigating the long-term effects of **smoking**, researchers might track a group of smokers and non-smokers over several decades to compare the incidence of **lung cancer** or **heart disease** between the two groups. This type of study provides **prospective data**, as researchers observe the cohort in real-time as events unfold.

Another common type of observational study is the **case-control study**, which is retrospective in nature. In this design, researchers select individuals who have already developed a particular outcome or disease (cases) and compare them to individuals who have not (controls). The goal is to look back in time to determine what **risk factors** or exposures might have contributed to the development of the disease. For example, a case-control study might be used to investigate the potential causes of **type 2 diabetes**, comparing patients with diabetes (cases) to those without (controls) to identify lifestyle or genetic factors that might be associated with the condition. Case-control studies are useful for studying **rare diseases** or outcomes that take a long time to develop, as they allow researchers to quickly gather data without the need for long-term follow-up.

Cross-sectional studies provide a snapshot of a population at a single point in time. In these studies, researchers collect data on both **exposure** and **outcome** simultaneously, making them useful for identifying associations between variables, such as the prevalence of a disease and its potential risk factors. Cross-sectional studies are often used in **epidemiology** to assess the **prevalence** of diseases or conditions within a population. For example, a cross-sectional study might be conducted to assess the percentage of a population affected by **hypertension** and to identify potential correlations with factors such as age, diet, or physical activity levels. While cross-sectional studies are relatively quick and inexpensive to conduct, they cannot establish cause-and-effect relationships because the data is collected at a single point in time, making it impossible to determine whether the exposure preceded the outcome.

One of the key advantages of observational studies is their ability to provide insights into **natural disease progression** and **treatment outcomes** in real-world settings. For chronic conditions like **diabetes**, **hypertension**, or **rheumatoid arthritis**, observational studies can track how patients respond to treatments over time, allowing researchers to observe the long-term effects of interventions that may not be fully captured in the controlled environment of an RCT. Additionally, observational studies often include a more **diverse** patient population than RCTs, which may have strict inclusion criteria. This diversity allows for a better understanding of how treatments perform in various subgroups, such as older adults or individuals with comorbidities, who may be underrepresented in clinical trials.

Another critical role of observational studies is in identifying **risk factors** for diseases and conditions. For instance, long-term **cohort studies** have been instrumental in identifying risk factors for diseases such as **cardiovascular disease** (e.g., high cholesterol, smoking) and **cancer** (e.g., exposure to carcinogens). By observing large populations over time, researchers can identify patterns that may point to specific risk factors associated with disease development, providing valuable information for **preventive medicine**.

Observational studies are also essential for tracking the **safety profile** of treatments **post-approval**. After a drug or medical device has been approved and is in widespread use, observational studies can monitor its performance in the general population, identifying any **adverse effects** or **complications** that may not have been apparent during the initial clinical trials. This is especially important for detecting rare side effects that may only occur in a small subset of patients. For example, an observational study might reveal that a medication used to treat high blood pressure is associated with a rare but serious side effect, such as **kidney damage**, prompting further investigation and regulatory action.

2.3 Crossover Studies

Crossover studies are a unique type of clinical trial design in which participants receive multiple treatments, one after the other, with each participant experiencing both the **treatment** and **control** (or another treatment) phases. This design is particularly advantageous because it allows each participant to serve as their own **control**, reducing the variability that might arise between participants. As a result, crossover studies are highly efficient for comparing treatments in a smaller group of participants, as they eliminate the **between-subject variability** that can confound the results in parallel-group studies.

In a **crossover design**, participants are randomly assigned to receive **Treatment A** first and then **Treatment B**, or vice versa. This approach helps ensure that any differences observed between the treatments are due to the intervention itself, rather than individual differences among participants. For example, in a crossover study comparing two different drugs for managing **blood pressure**, each participant would receive both drugs at different times, allowing the researchers to compare the effects of each drug in the same person. This minimizes the variability that might result from differences in baseline characteristics like **age**, **gender**, or **comorbid conditions**, making the results more reliable.

One of the critical elements of a crossover study is the inclusion of a **washout period** between treatments. The washout period is designed to ensure that the effects of the first treatment do not carry over into the second treatment phase. Without a sufficient washout period, the lingering effects of the first treatment could influence the outcomes observed during the second treatment, confounding the results. The length of the washout period depends on the pharmacokinetics and pharmacodynamics of the treatments being studied. For example, if a drug has a **long half-life**, meaning it stays in the body for an extended period, a longer washout period would be necessary to ensure that it is completely cleared from the participant's system before the second treatment begins. Washout periods are crucial in **bioequivalence studies**, where even small residual effects of a drug could affect the comparison between formulations.

Crossover studies are particularly useful for evaluating **short-term outcomes** and are commonly used in studies where the treatments are expected to have **immediate or reversible effects**. Because participants receive both treatments, fewer subjects are needed to achieve **statistical power** than in a traditional parallel-group design, where each participant would receive only one treatment. This makes crossover studies ideal for situations where **sample sizes** are small, such as in early-phase trials or **bioequivalence studies**, where researchers compare the pharmacokinetic profiles of two different formulations of the same drug. For example, a bioequivalence study might use a crossover design to compare the absorption of a **generic drug** to its **branded counterpart**, ensuring that both formulations provide the same therapeutic effect. By using a crossover design, researchers can determine whether the two drugs are **bioequivalent** within the same participants, reducing the number of participants needed and improving the precision of the results.

Overall, crossover studies offer several advantages, including reduced variability, smaller sample sizes, and the ability to make direct comparisons between treatments within the same participants. However, they are best suited for conditions or treatments with **short-term** or **reversible effects**, as the design relies on the ability to eliminate the effects of the first treatment before moving on to the second.

2.4 Adaptive Clinical Trials

Adaptive Clinical Trials represent a significant advancement in trial design by offering a degree of **flexibility** not seen in traditional fixed designs. In an adaptive trial, modifications can be made to the study protocol based on **interim data** without compromising the integrity or validity of the trial. This ability to adapt during the course of the trial allows researchers to make **data-driven decisions** that can optimize the study and improve outcomes for participants. The key feature of adaptive trials is that they allow changes to elements like **sample size**, **dosage levels**, and **inclusion criteria** based on early findings, thereby making the process more efficient and potentially accelerating the path to regulatory approval.

One of the primary advantages of **adaptive designs** is the ability to adjust **sample sizes** mid-trial if initial results suggest that the current sample may be insufficient to detect meaningful differences between treatments. For example, if interim data indicate that the effect size of a new cancer drug is smaller than expected, the researchers can increase the sample size to ensure that the study is adequately powered to detect significant results. Similarly, if early data show a particular dosage level to be more effective or safer than others, adaptive trials allow for adjustments to the **dosage regimens**, enabling researchers to explore **optimal dosing** strategies in real-time. Adaptive trials may also involve changes to **inclusion or exclusion criteria** if interim data suggest that certain subgroups of patients respond better to the treatment. This flexibility ensures that the trial remains

dynamic and responsive to emerging data, allowing researchers to focus on the most promising outcomes while minimizing the time and resources spent on less effective strategies.

While adaptive clinical trials offer many benefits, they also come with **regulatory requirements** and **statistical challenges**. To maintain **statistical integrity**, the trial must be designed from the outset with pre-specified **decision rules** that govern how and when changes can be made. These rules must be carefully designed to prevent **bias** and ensure that the trial remains valid and reliable, even after modifications. For example, if interim data indicate that the trial should expand the sample size, the rules for when and how that expansion occurs must be predefined to avoid introducing **selection bias** or **data skewing**. Regulatory agencies such as the **FDA** and **EMA** have strict guidelines for adaptive trial designs, ensuring that mid-trial modifications are made in a **scientifically sound** manner. Researchers must submit detailed protocols outlining how interim analyses will be conducted, how decisions will be made, and how the integrity of the study will be preserved.

Adaptive trials can significantly **save time and resources**, particularly in **fast-paced fields** like **oncology** or **rare diseases**, where the need for efficient and effective trials is paramount. In oncology, for instance, treatments are often tested on patients with rapidly progressing diseases, where traditional trial timelines may not be fast enough to meet urgent needs. Adaptive trials allow researchers to stop the trial early if **preliminary results** show that the treatment is highly effective, enabling the therapy to reach patients faster. Conversely, if early results indicate that the treatment is unlikely to provide a significant benefit, the trial can be stopped early to avoid wasting resources on a **non-viable** intervention. In the case of **rare diseases**, where the patient population is small, adaptive designs can help maximize the efficiency of the study by adjusting the trial based on interim results, ensuring that every data point is used optimally.

Adaptive clinical trials provide a **flexible, efficient**, and **innovative** approach to clinical research, allowing researchers to adapt their strategies based on real-time data while maintaining the **scientific rigor** necessary for regulatory approval. Their ability to **reduce trial timelines**, **optimize resource allocation**, and focus on the most promising outcomes makes them particularly valuable in areas of medical research where speed and efficiency are critical.

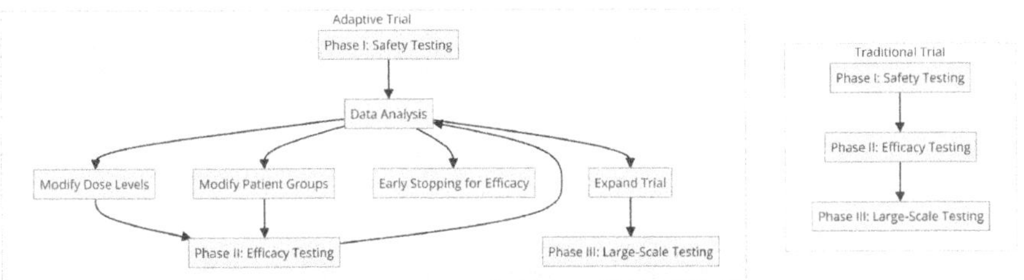

Traditional Clinical Trials and Adaptive Clinical Trials

2.5 Bioavailability and Bioequivalence Studies

Bioavailability and **Bioequivalence Studies** are essential components of drug development, particularly when evaluating the **efficacy** and **safety** of both new formulations and generic drugs. These studies focus on how a drug is absorbed into the bloodstream, distributed throughout the body, metabolized by the liver or other organs, and ultimately excreted. The goal of bioavailability studies is to measure the **proportion** of a drug that reaches the **systemic circulation** in an **active form**, which directly impacts the **dosage** needed to achieve therapeutic effects. For example, a drug with low bioavailability may require a higher dose to achieve the desired effect, whereas a drug with high bioavailability may be administered at a lower dose.

Bioavailability is typically expressed as a **percentage** and refers to the fraction of the administered dose that reaches the bloodstream and is available to produce a therapeutic effect. For example, if 50% of a drug is absorbed into the bloodstream after oral administration, its bioavailability would be 50%. **Intravenous (IV) administration** generally has 100% bioavailability since the drug is delivered directly into the bloodstream, bypassing the digestive system. However, for drugs administered via oral, topical, or inhalation routes, the bioavailability is often lower due to factors like **first-pass metabolism** (the breakdown of the drug by the liver before it reaches systemic circulation), **solubility**, and **stability** in the digestive tract.

Bioequivalence studies are particularly important in the context of **generic drug approval**, as they are designed to ensure that the **generic version** of a drug performs in the same way as the **branded innovator** product. A generic drug must demonstrate that it has **similar bioavailability** to the branded product, meaning that the **rate** and **extent** of absorption into the bloodstream are comparable. This is critical to ensure that the generic drug provides the same **therapeutic effect** as the branded drug, allowing healthcare providers and patients to use it with confidence that it will work as intended.

In a typical bioequivalence study, researchers administer the **generic** and **innovator drugs** to participants in a **crossover design**, where each participant receives both formulations in different sequences, allowing direct comparison of how the two drugs are absorbed and metabolized. The primary parameters measured are the **maximum concentration (Cmax)** of the drug in the blood, the **time to reach maximum concentration (Tmax)**, and the **area under the curve (AUC)**, which represents the total drug exposure over time. For a generic drug to be considered **bioequivalent** to a branded drug, the **90% confidence interval** for the **ratio of the AUC and Cmax** between the two formulations must fall within a range of **80% to 125%**. This range ensures that the generic drug's bioavailability is not significantly different from the branded drug and that it will have the same **therapeutic effect** at the same dosage.

Regulatory bodies such as the **FDA** and **EMA** have strict requirements for demonstrating bioequivalence. Before a generic drug can be approved for market release, manufacturers must submit data from bioequivalence studies showing that their product meets these criteria. The FDA and EMA evaluate these studies to ensure that the generic drug is **therapeutically equivalent** to the branded version, meaning that it will provide the same **clinical benefit** with no significant differences in safety or efficacy. Failure to demonstrate bioequivalence can result in the generic drug being denied approval, as regulatory agencies prioritize patient safety and the consistent performance of medications.

These studies are particularly important in the development of **generic drugs**, as they ensure that patients can use lower-cost alternatives to branded medications without sacrificing efficacy or safety. For instance, when a patent expires on a blockbuster drug, generic manufacturers must conduct bioequivalence studies to prove that their versions meet the same rigorous standards. This ensures that patients can access affordable medications without compromising on quality or therapeutic outcomes.

CHAPTER THREE

Phase 0 Clinical Trials

Phase 0 clinical trials, also known as **exploratory IND studies** or **microdosing trials**, represent the very first stage of clinical research in humans. These trials are conducted before the more extensive **Phase I trials** and are designed to provide **early pharmacokinetic (PK)** and **pharmacodynamic (PD)** data on a drug candidate. The primary objective of Phase 0 trials is to evaluate how the investigational drug behaves in the human body, focusing on its absorption, distribution, metabolism, and excretion (ADME) at **subtherapeutic doses**. These studies are typically small in scale, involving a limited number of participants—often fewer than 15—and are intended to minimize the risks to volunteers while gathering critical early-stage data.

The main purpose of **Phase 0 trials** is not to determine the therapeutic efficacy of a drug, but rather to assess its **pharmacokinetic profile**. By administering **microdoses**, researchers can observe how the drug is processed by the body without exposing participants to the higher doses used in later phases. This approach helps identify whether the drug exhibits favorable PK properties that would warrant further investigation in **Phase I trials**, where the focus shifts to safety and dosing. For example, a microdosing study may reveal that the drug is rapidly cleared from the body or has poor bioavailability, which could indicate that it may not be viable for further development. In this way, Phase 0 trials help researchers make early decisions about whether a drug candidate should continue through the development pipeline.

One of the key advantages of conducting **Phase 0 trials** is the potential to **reduce both time and cost** in the drug development process. By screening out **non-viable drug candidates** early on, pharmaceutical companies can avoid the expense of conducting larger-scale Phase I trials on compounds that are unlikely to succeed. This early filtering process can streamline drug development, allowing researchers to focus their resources on drug candidates that show the most promise. For instance, if a drug demonstrates poor pharmacokinetics in a Phase 0 trial, it may be abandoned, saving the time and money that would have been spent on more extensive testing in later phases.

Another defining feature of Phase 0 trials is the use of **microdosing**, where doses are typically set at **1/100th** of the level expected to produce a therapeutic effect. This ensures that participants are exposed to only minimal amounts of the drug, significantly reducing the risk of adverse effects. Microdosing is particularly useful for gathering early data on **pharmacokinetics** and **pharmacodynamics**, as even small doses can provide valuable information on how the drug interacts with its target in the body. For example, microdosing may help researchers determine whether the drug reaches its intended site of action or if it is rapidly metabolized and excreted without having the desired effect. This information is critical for making informed decisions about whether to proceed to higher doses in **Phase I trials.**

Phase 0 trials also contribute to the ethical considerations of drug development, as they allow for early data collection with minimal risk to participants. Since the doses administered are far below therapeutic levels, the likelihood of experiencing **serious adverse effects** is reduced, making Phase 0 trials a safer starting point for first-in-human studies. Furthermore, these trials often involve extensive **preclinical data** to support the use of microdosing, ensuring that any potential risks to participants are carefully managed and justified. By providing early insights into drug behavior, Phase 0 trials play a critical role in determining whether a drug candidate is suitable for further development, ultimately shaping the direction of the entire clinical research process.

3.1 Microdosing Studies

Microdosing studies form the core of **Phase 0 clinical trials**, offering a way to gather valuable early-stage data on a drug's behavior in the human body without exposing participants to therapeutic doses. In these studies, participants receive **subtherapeutic doses**, typically **1/100th** of the expected therapeutic dose. This small dosage is designed to be well below the level at which any **clinical effects** are expected, ensuring that participants are at minimal risk. The primary goal of microdosing is to assess how the drug is **absorbed**, **distributed**, **metabolized**, and **excreted** (ADME) within the body, providing early insights into its pharmacokinetics.

The **pharmacokinetics (PK)** of a drug—how it moves through the body—is crucial for understanding whether it behaves as predicted from **preclinical studies** conducted in animals. By administering such small doses, researchers can collect data on the drug's **half-life**, **bioavailability**, and **elimination pathways** without introducing the risks associated with full-dose trials. For example, a drug administered in a microdosing study might reveal **rapid metabolism**, meaning it is broken down by the body too quickly to be effective, or show poor absorption in the gut, indicating that it may not reach the bloodstream in sufficient concentrations to have a therapeutic effect. These findings can help researchers make early decisions about whether to proceed to **Phase I trials**, where higher doses and more participants are involved.

Microdosing studies are typically conducted with a small number of participants, usually **fewer than 15**, and take place over a short duration. The small sample size is sufficient for gathering early **PK data** because the goal is not to establish efficacy but to confirm whether the drug's **pharmacokinetics** are suitable for continued development. For example, a microdosing study might take just a few days, during which participants receive the subtherapeutic dose and provide **blood** or **urine samples** at regular intervals. These samples are then analyzed to determine the concentration of the drug and its metabolites in the body, giving researchers a clear picture of how the drug is processed.

One of the key advantages of microdosing is that it allows researchers to **screen out non-viable drug candidates** early in the process, potentially saving significant time and resources. If a drug shows unfavorable pharmacokinetics at the microdose level—such as being poorly absorbed or rapidly eliminated—it may be abandoned before larger and more expensive trials are conducted. This early filtering can significantly reduce the **financial risk** associated with drug development, allowing companies to focus their efforts on more promising candidates.

Microdosing also provides valuable insights into a drug's behavior in **humans**, which can sometimes differ significantly from its behavior in **animal models**. For instance, a drug might demonstrate excellent pharmacokinetics in preclinical studies but fail to exhibit the same properties in human trials due to differences in metabolism between species. By providing an early look at how the drug performs in humans, microdosing studies help ensure that only drugs with favorable **PK profiles** proceed to the next phase of development, where larger groups of participants will be exposed to higher doses in **Phase I trials**.

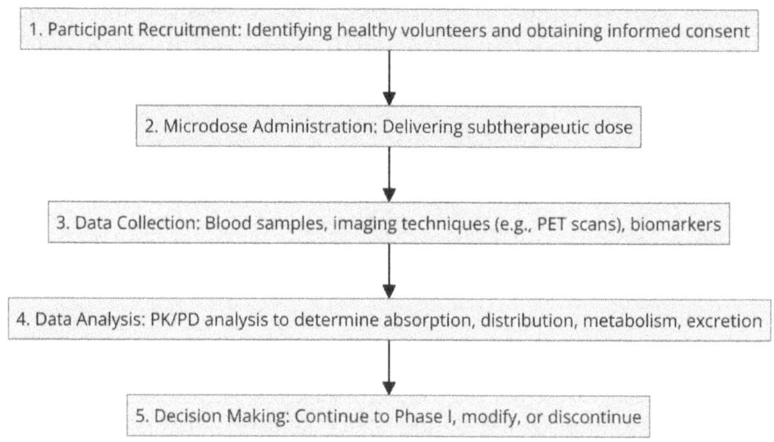

Step-by-Step Process of a Phase 0 Microdosing Study

3.2 Objectives and Methodology

Phase 0 trials have distinct objectives, setting them apart from later-phase clinical trials, which focus on safety and efficacy. The primary goals of these trials are to gather **pharmacokinetic (PK)** and **pharmacodynamic (PD)** data, providing an early understanding of the drug's behavior in the human body without aiming for therapeutic efficacy. These studies are critical in determining whether a drug candidate is worth pursuing into **Phase I trials**, where the safety and dosing range are established.

The first and most important **objective** of Phase 0 trials is to collect early **pharmacokinetic (PK) data**, which includes how the drug is absorbed, distributed, metabolized, and excreted. Understanding these properties helps predict the drug's behavior in the human body, and can provide insight into potential issues such as **poor bioavailability**, **rapid elimination**, or **slow metabolism**. For example, in a microdosing study, researchers may observe that a drug is metabolized too quickly to maintain therapeutic levels in the bloodstream, signaling that it may not be a viable candidate for further development. This information is crucial in determining whether to proceed to later-phase trials where higher doses and larger participant groups are tested.

The second **objective** is to gather preliminary **pharmacodynamic (PD) data**, which involves assessing the drug's interaction with its **biological target**. Phase 0 trials, although conducted at subtherapeutic doses, may still provide valuable information about whether the drug reaches its intended target and initiates the expected biochemical or molecular interactions. For example, a drug designed to bind to a specific **receptor** may show measurable engagement with that receptor in a microdosing study, even though it does not produce a therapeutic effect. This can help guide decisions about the drug's **mechanism of action** and its potential efficacy at higher doses.

The third **objective** of Phase 0 trials is to inform decisions about **dose selection** for later phases of development, particularly **Phase I trials**. The data collected from Phase 0 studies help researchers estimate the doses required to achieve therapeutic effects in humans while maintaining safety. By understanding how the drug behaves at very low doses, researchers can make more informed decisions about **starting doses** in Phase I, ensuring that the higher doses administered are both safe and effective. This step is critical for avoiding **toxicity** or **inefficacy** during the initial trials in humans.

In terms of **methodology**, **microdosing** studies are designed to administer very small doses—typically **1/100th** of the dose expected to produce therapeutic effects. These studies usually involve fewer than 15 participants, and the trial duration is short, often spanning just a few days. Participants are carefully selected, and the study protocol ensures that each individual receives a dose that is unlikely to produce any adverse effects due to its minimal strength.

Non-invasive techniques play a crucial role in data collection during Phase 0 trials. The use of **blood sampling**, **urine analysis**, and **imaging** allows researchers to gather the necessary PK and PD data without introducing significant discomfort or risk to participants. For instance, frequent **blood draws** can track the concentration of the drug and its metabolites over time, providing insight into how quickly the drug is absorbed and eliminated. **Urine analysis** offers additional data on how the drug is excreted, while advanced imaging techniques, such as **PET scans**, can visually demonstrate how the drug interacts with its target or distributes thr **mittees** and **regulatory bodies** play a crucial role in overseeing Phase 0 trials to ensure that the trials meet strict ethical standards and minimize risks to participants. Before a Phase 0 trial can begin, it must be reviewed and approved by an **Institutional Review Board**

(IRB) or an **Ethics Committee (EC)**. These committees ensure that the trial protocol adheres to ethical guidelines, including participant safety and risk minimization. Regulatory bodies like the **FDA** or **EMA** also evaluate the scientific and ethical justifications for conducting a Phase 0 trial, ensuring that the potential benefits of gathering early data outweigh the minimal risks to participants. For example, if a drug has shown promise in **preclinical trials**, but its pharmacokinetics in humans remain unknown, a Phase 0 trial might be justified to gather this early data with minimal exposure.

Despite the minimal risks associated with **microdosing**, these trials are not without ethical challenges. Researchers must balance the potential benefits of gathering valuable early data with the ethical responsibility to protect participants from harm. While the doses administered in Phase 0 trials are too low to produce therapeutic effects, they are also designed to be low enough to minimize the likelihood of **adverse effects**. Nonetheless, participants are still exposed to a new investigational drug, and it is essential to ensure that the risks, though small, are communicated clearly and ethically managed. The potential benefit of these trials is not for the individual participant but for future drug development, which could accelerate the path to **Phase I trials** and ultimately bring new treatments to market faster.

Another important ethical aspect is the consideration of **vulnerable populations**. Phase 0 trials must ensure that vulnerable individuals—such as those who are economically disadvantaged or those with limited access to healthcare—are not disproportionately enrolled in these trials without a full understanding of their purpose. The selection of participants must be fair, and additional safeguards must be in place to protect those who might not fully grasp the nature of their involvement.

CHAPTER FOUR

Phase I Clinical Trials

Phase I clinical trials mark the first stage of testing a new investigational drug in humans. These trials are critical in determining the **safety**, **tolerability**, **pharmacokinetics (PK)**, and, in some cases, the **pharmacodynamics (PD)** of the drug. Phase I trials are generally small in scale, involving a limited number of **healthy volunteers** or, in some cases, **patients** with the target condition. The primary objective is to evaluate the **safety profile** of the drug, including identifying any **adverse effects**, and to determine how the drug is absorbed, distributed, metabolized, and excreted by the body. Phase I trials also provide an opportunity to assess **dose-response relationships**, helping researchers identify the appropriate dose range for subsequent trials.

Typically, Phase I trials are divided into **Single Ascending Dose (SAD)** and **Multiple Ascending Dose (MAD)** studies, which allow researchers to escalate doses to determine the **maximum tolerated dose (MTD)** and identify the **optimum dose** for further development. These studies are vital in determining whether the drug is safe to continue into **Phase II trials**, where efficacy is further explored.

In addition to dose escalation studies, Phase I trials also investigate other important aspects of the drug, such as how food affects drug absorption (**Food Effect Studies**) and how the drug interacts with other medications (**Drug-Drug Interaction Studies**). By gathering early data on **pharmacokinetic endpoints** and determining the **safety and tolerability** of the drug, Phase I trials provide the foundation for continued drug development, ensuring that the drug can move into larger and more comprehensive **Phase II** and **Phase III** trials with a better understanding of its safety and pharmacological profile.

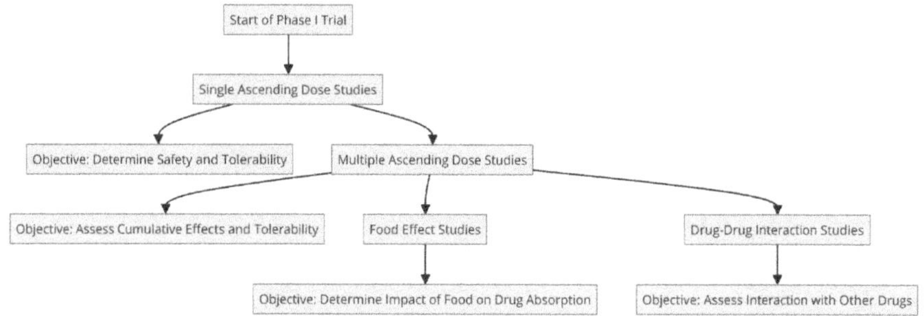

Progression of a Phase I trial

4.1 Single Ascending Dose (SAD)

Single Ascending Dose (SAD) studies are an essential part of early clinical drug development, especially in Phase I clinical trials. These studies primarily focus on the safety, tolerability, and pharmacokinetics (PK) of a new investigational drug. SAD studies are designed to assess how the human body responds to the drug when administered in increasing doses. The concept of **SAD studies** revolves around administering a single dose of the drug to participants, with each subsequent group of participants receiving a slightly higher dose. This structured approach allows researchers to evaluate the body's reaction to varying dose levels while closely monitoring for any adverse effects.

The primary **objective of SAD studies** is to determine the **maximum tolerated dose (MTD)**. The MTD is the highest dose at which the drug can be safely administered without causing unacceptable side effects. Identifying the MTD is crucial because it helps establish the dose limits for future clinical studies, particularly Phase II trials. The point at which participants experience severe or intolerable side effects provides valuable information regarding the drug's safety margin and potential therapeutic window.

Typically, SAD trials involve **healthy volunteers** rather than patients with the targeted condition, as the goal is to evaluate safety before moving on to efficacy studies. These trials are small in scale, generally involving **6 to 8 participants per group**, also referred to as cohorts. The number of cohorts depends on how many dose levels are being tested. For example, a SAD trial might include **4-6 cohorts**, each receiving a progressively higher dose of the drug. To minimize risk, doses are escalated cautiously, often with close monitoring and a decision-making process to determine whether it is safe to proceed to the next dose level.

Another critical aspect of **SAD studies** is the collection of **pharmacokinetic (PK) data**. PK data help researchers understand how the drug behaves within the body, including how it is absorbed, distributed, metabolized, and excreted. Parameters such as **half-life (t1/2), maximum concentration (Cmax)**, and **area under the curve (AUC)** are assessed to gain insights into the drug's profile. PK data from SAD studies are vital for determining the optimal dosing regimen for later phases of clinical trials. For example, the **AUC** provides information about the total drug exposure over time, while **Cmax** reveals the peak concentration of the drug in the bloodstream.

The metabolism of the drug is also carefully monitored to identify any potentially harmful byproducts. Researchers track how long the drug and its metabolites remain in the body and evaluate whether the drug's elimination is within a safe range. **Liver enzymes**, such as **ALT** and **AST**, are also monitored to detect any signs of hepatotoxicity, while other organ functions, such as kidney clearance rates, are assessed through **creatinine** and **blood urea nitrogen (BUN)** levels.

Overall, SAD studies represent a critical milestone in the drug development process. The data collected during these trials provide a foundational understanding of the drug's safety and guide future studies. If a drug shows a favorable safety profile and acceptable PK parameters in SAD studies, it moves on to more complex trials, including multiple-dose studies, efficacy testing, and studies in patient populations.

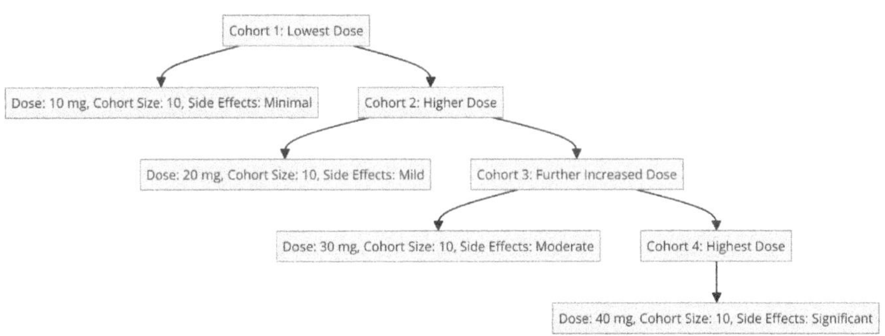

Progressive Dose Escalation in Single Ascending Dose (SAD) Studies: Monitoring Safety and Tolerability

4.2 Multiple Ascending Dose (MAD)

Multiple Ascending Dose (MAD) studies are a natural progression from Single Ascending Dose (SAD) studies and play a crucial role in the early stages of drug development, particularly in **Phase I clinical trials.** While SAD studies focus on the safety and tolerability of a single dose of a drug, MAD studies are designed to assess how the drug behaves in the body when administered repeatedly over a specified period. This approach allows researchers to evaluate the cumulative effects of the drug and to observe any adverse reactions that might emerge with repeated dosing. The findings from MAD studies help in understanding the longer-term safety profile of the drug and provide insight into its pharmacokinetic (PK) behavior over time.

The primary **objective of MAD studies** is to observe whether repeated doses of the drug result in different or more severe side effects than those seen in SAD studies. By administering the drug multiple times, researchers can determine if the **cumulative effect** of the drug leads to toxicity or other adverse events. This is particularly important for drugs that are intended to be administered over extended periods, as they may accumulate in the body, potentially causing side effects that were not evident after a single dose.

MAD trials typically involve participants receiving multiple doses of the drug over a period of **days or weeks**. For example, a participant might receive a dose every 24 hours for **7 to 14 days**. Just like in SAD studies, the participants in MAD studies are usually divided into cohorts, with each cohort receiving a progressively higher dose. **Cohort sizes are typically small**, often consisting of **6 to 10 participants** per group, and the trials usually involve several cohorts. Each cohort begins with a lower dose, which is increased for subsequent groups once it is deemed safe. This stepwise approach allows researchers to carefully monitor the participants for any side effects before deciding to escalate the dose.

A key element of **MAD studies** is understanding the drug's **steady-state concentration**. The steady-state concentration is the point at which the rate of drug administration equals the rate of drug elimination, resulting in a stable concentration of the drug in the bloodstream. Determining the steady-state is essential for drugs intended for long-term use, as it provides valuable information about the appropriate dosing frequency and amount. For example, if a drug reaches its steady state after **4 to 5 doses** administered every **12 hours**, this helps establish the dosing schedule for future clinical trials and for potential therapeutic use.

In addition, **MAD studies** help researchers evaluate the **elimination half-life** of the drug over time. The half-life is a measure of how long it takes for the concentration of the drug in the blood to decrease by half. For drugs that are administered repeatedly, it is critical to understand whether the half-life changes with multiple doses, as this can affect the drug's accumulation in the body. For instance, if the half-life of the drug is found to increase with repeated dosing, this might indicate that the drug is accumulating, which could lead to higher risks of toxicity.

Another important outcome of MAD studies is the ability to detect any **dose-dependent pharmacokinetics**, which means that the drug's behavior in the body may change at higher doses. For example, a drug might be metabolized more slowly at higher doses due to saturation of metabolic pathways. This can lead to higher-than-expected drug levels in the bloodstream, increasing the risk of adverse effects. By identifying these patterns in MAD studies, researchers can make informed decisions about the appropriate dose range for future clinical trials.

Overall, **MAD studies** provide critical information on the drug's safety, tolerability, and pharmacokinetic profile when administered repeatedly over time. These studies guide the design of later-stage clinical trials and help determine the long-term viability of the drug.

4.3 Dose Escalation Methods

In Phase I clinical trials, determining the **maximum tolerated dose (MTD)** is critical to ensuring the safety of participants and the success of the drug development process. To achieve this, researchers employ various **dose escalation methods**, which involve gradually increasing the dose of a drug to assess its safety, tolerability, and potential side effects. The dose escalation process is essential because it allows for the identification of the optimal dose that maximizes therapeutic benefits while minimizing adverse reactions. Several strategies are used to achieve this goal, each with its advantages and limitations.

One of the most common methods used in early-phase trials is the **fixed-dose escalation method.** In this approach, participants are assigned to cohorts, with each group receiving a predefined dose increment of the drug. For example, the starting dose might be set at **10 mg**, and subsequent groups might receive **20 mg, 40 mg, and 80 mg** doses. The increments are decided before the trial begins and remain consistent throughout the study. The advantage of this method is its simplicity and ease of implementation.

By using fixed increments, researchers can clearly define dose levels and quickly evaluate the safety profile at each stage. However, a major limitation of this method is the potential for **underestimation** or **overestimation** of the optimal dose. Fixed increments do not account for individual variability in drug response, which may result in missing the most effective dose or exposing participants to unnecessary risks if the dose increments are too large.

In contrast, the **adaptive dose escalation method** provides greater flexibility by adjusting the dose increments based on participant responses. In this method, each dose level is determined after evaluating the safety and tolerability data from the previous group. If the participants in the current cohort tolerate the drug well with minimal side effects, the dose can be increased more aggressively in the next cohort. On the other hand, if participants exhibit significant adverse reactions, the escalation can be slowed, or the dose increments can be reduced. This adaptive approach allows for a more **customized dosing regimen**, which can improve the chances of finding the MTD without unnecessarily exposing participants to high doses. One disadvantage, however, is the increased **complexity** in trial design and management. Adaptive trials require real-time monitoring of participant data and may require frequent adjustments to the dosing schedule, which can extend the trial duration.

Another approach is the **Bayesian model-based dose escalation method**, which uses prior data and statistical models to guide dose escalation decisions. In this approach, the trial begins with a certain amount of prior knowledge, such as data from preclinical studies or earlier trials. As the trial progresses, the model is continuously updated with new data from participants, and dose escalation decisions are made in real-time based on this evolving information. The **Bayesian model** uses probabilistic techniques to estimate the likelihood of different outcomes at various dose levels, such as the probability of observing adverse effects or achieving therapeutic benefits. This method offers a highly efficient way to explore the dose-response relationship while minimizing the risk to participants. By using data-driven predictions, the Bayesian approach can potentially reduce the number of participants required to identify the MTD. However, it is also more **resource-intensive** and requires sophisticated statistical expertise, making it less commonly used in early-phase trials compared to simpler methods.

Each of these dose escalation methods has its own strengths and weaknesses, and the choice of method depends on the specific goals of the trial, the nature of the drug being tested, and the available resources. While **fixed-dose escalation** is straightforward and easy to manage, it lacks flexibility. The **adaptive dose escalation** method offers greater responsiveness to participant safety but can be more complex to implement. The **Bayesian model** provides a more refined and predictive approach but demands more extensive statistical support and prior knowledge.

4.4 Food Effect Studies

Food Effect Studies are an integral part of Phase I clinical trials and are designed to assess how the presence of food in the digestive system influences the absorption, bioavailability, and overall pharmacokinetic (PK) profile of a drug. These studies are particularly important because food can significantly alter how a drug is processed in the body, affecting its efficacy and safety. Understanding the impact of food on a drug's behavior is essential for developing appropriate dosing recommendations and for ensuring that the drug performs consistently in both fed and fasted states.

In **Food Effect Studies**, participants are typically administered the drug under two conditions: in a **fasted state** and in a **fed state**. The fasted state refers to when the participant has not eaten for a set period, often **8 to 12 hours** before taking the drug. In the fed state, participants are given a standardized meal—usually high in fat and calories—before receiving the drug. This comparison allows researchers to observe how food influences the drug's absorption and whether the drug's bioavailability changes significantly when taken with food. For example, a participant might receive the drug after consuming a meal containing **800 to 1000 calories**, with a substantial portion coming from fat, to simulate how the drug would behave in real-world conditions.

The **rate of absorption** and the **extent of absorption** are two critical parameters measured in these studies. Food can have varying effects on different drugs. In some cases, food might delay the absorption of the drug, reducing the **maximum concentration (Cmax)** achieved in the bloodstream. This occurs because food slows gastric emptying, meaning the drug takes longer to move from the stomach to the intestines, where absorption primarily occurs. In other cases, food can enhance absorption by increasing **bile flow**, which helps dissolve fat-soluble drugs, leading to a higher **Cmax** and **area under the curve (AUC)**, which represents total drug exposure. For example, some drugs may see their bioavailability increase by **30-50%** when taken with food, while others may experience reduced absorption by a similar percentage.

Understanding how food affects the absorption of a drug is crucial for determining **dosage recommendations**. Drugs that are heavily influenced by food may require specific instructions, such as "take on an empty stomach" or "take with food," to ensure optimal therapeutic outcomes. For instance, certain medications might need to be taken with a meal to enhance absorption, especially if they are poorly soluble in water. On the other hand, drugs whose absorption is significantly reduced by food may be recommended for administration in a fasted state to ensure sufficient bioavailability.

Moreover, **Food Effect Studies** help identify potential **drug-food interactions** that could pose safety risks. Some drugs, for example, may become toxic if food increases their bioavailability too much. Alternatively, if food drastically reduces absorption, the drug may fail to reach therapeutic levels, rendering it ineffective. By conducting these studies early in Phase I, researchers can provide clear guidance to patients and healthcare providers on how to take the drug in relation to food.

4.5 Drug-Drug Interaction (DDI) Studies

Drug-Drug Interaction (DDI) Studies are an integral part of Phase I clinical trials, designed to investigate how an experimental drug interacts with other commonly prescribed medications. These studies are crucial because many patients, particularly those with chronic conditions, often take multiple medications simultaneously. Understanding potential interactions between drugs ensures that the new drug can be safely used alongside other treatments and helps avoid harmful or unexpected effects.

The primary goal of **DDI studies** is to determine whether the new drug alters the **metabolism, efficacy**, or **safety profile** of other drugs, or if other medications influence the experimental drug's behavior in the body. This interaction can occur through several mechanisms. For example, one drug might accelerate or inhibit the metabolism of another, leading to changes in drug levels in the bloodstream. Such changes could reduce the effectiveness of the medications or increase the risk of toxicity. For instance, a drug that speeds up the metabolism of another medication might reduce its therapeutic effect, while a drug that inhibits metabolism could cause the other drug to accumulate to harmful levels.

A key focus of **DDI studies** is the role of **cytochrome P450 (CYP) enzymes** in drug metabolism. The **CYP450** family of enzymes is responsible for metabolizing a large percentage of drugs, and many DDIs occur because one drug either induces or inhibits these enzymes. For example, if a new drug inhibits a particular CYP enzyme, it may prevent the metabolism of another drug that relies on that enzyme, leading to increased concentrations of the second drug in the body. A well-known example of this is the interaction between **warfarin** (an anticoagulant) and certain drugs that inhibit **CYP2C9**, which can lead to dangerously elevated levels of warfarin and an increased risk of bleeding. Conversely, drugs that induce CYP enzymes may accelerate the breakdown of other medications, reducing their effectiveness.

DDI studies are critical for identifying potential **contraindications** or **necessary dose adjustments** when the experimental drug is used in combination with other medications. For example, if a new drug is found to significantly increase the levels of another medication by inhibiting its metabolism, it may be necessary to reduce the dose of the affected medication to avoid toxicity. Similarly, if the new drug induces the metabolism of another drug, it may be necessary to increase the dose of the affected drug to maintain therapeutic efficacy.

To conduct a DDI study, participants are typically divided into groups where they receive the experimental drug alone, the other medication alone, and both drugs together. Researchers then compare how the drugs are metabolized and how their pharmacokinetics (PK) profiles change when administered in combination. Parameters such as **Cmax**, **AUC**, and **half-life** are closely monitored to determine if there are any significant changes in drug levels. Additionally, side effects and adverse reactions are tracked to ensure that combining the drugs does not result in unexpected toxicities.

By identifying drug interactions early in clinical development, **DDI studies** provide essential data that inform **product labeling** and help healthcare providers make informed decisions about prescribing the drug in combination with other therapies. These studies play a critical role in preventing harmful drug interactions that could compromise patient safety or treatment efficacy.

4.6 Pharmacokinetic Endpoints

In **Phase I clinical trials**, the measurement of **pharmacokinetic (PK) endpoints** is crucial for understanding how a drug behaves within the body. These endpoints provide detailed information about the drug's absorption, distribution, metabolism, and elimination (ADME), all of which are essential for determining the optimal dosing regimen for later phases of clinical trials. By analyzing these PK parameters, researchers can ensure that the drug is both safe and effective at the appropriate dosage.

One of the most important PK endpoints is **Cmax**, or the **maximum concentration** of the drug in the bloodstream. This value indicates the peak level of the drug after it has been administered and absorbed into the system. Cmax is critical for assessing the drug's therapeutic potential, as well as for evaluating any potential toxicity that may occur at high concentrations. For instance, if the Cmax exceeds a certain threshold, it could lead to adverse effects, making it necessary to adjust the dose. In contrast, if the Cmax is too low, the drug may not reach the therapeutic concentration required to produce its intended effect.

Another key endpoint is **Tmax**, which refers to the **time it takes to reach Cmax**. Tmax provides insight into the **rate of absorption** of the drug. A shorter Tmax indicates rapid absorption, which may be desirable for medications that need to act quickly, such as pain relievers or emergency treatments. Conversely, a longer Tmax suggests slower absorption, which may be beneficial for sustained-release formulations. For example, a drug with a Tmax of **1 hour** would be absorbed more rapidly than a drug with a Tmax of **4 hours**, influencing the decision on how frequently the drug should be administered.

The **area under the curve (AUC)** is another critical PK endpoint. The AUC represents the **total drug exposure** over time and is calculated by measuring the concentration of the drug in the bloodstream at various time points after administration. A larger AUC indicates that the body is exposed to more of the drug, while a smaller AUC suggests less exposure. The AUC is particularly useful for comparing the bioavailability of different formulations of the same drug or for evaluating how food or other factors might influence drug absorption. For instance, if the AUC of a drug increases by **50%** when taken with food, this could affect dosing recommendations for patients.

In addition to these endpoints, the **half-life (t1/2)** of the drug is another important parameter. The half-life measures how long it takes for the concentration of the drug in the blood to decrease by **50%**. This value helps determine how long the drug remains active in the body. Drugs with a short half-life may need to be administered more frequently, while those with a long half-life may be suitable for less frequent dosing. For example, a drug with a half-life of **2 hours** would require multiple doses throughout the day, while a drug with a half-life of **24 hours** might only need to be taken once daily. The half-life also plays a role in determining how long it takes for the drug to reach a steady-state concentration when administered repeatedly.

Clearance is another vital PK endpoint, reflecting how quickly the drug is removed from the body. Clearance is measured in terms of volume per unit of time (e.g., **mL/min** or **L/hr**) and gives an indication of how efficiently the body can eliminate the drug. High clearance suggests rapid elimination, which may require more frequent dosing to maintain therapeutic levels, while low clearance indicates slower elimination, which could lead to drug accumulation and possible toxicity. For instance, a drug with a clearance rate of **100 mL/min** is eliminated more quickly than a drug with a clearance rate of **20 mL/min**, and this difference directly impacts the dosing schedule.

The combination of these PK endpoints—Cmax, Tmax, AUC, half-life, and clearance—provides a comprehensive understanding of the drug's behavior in the human body. These endpoints help researchers determine the **optimal dosing regimen** for future trials, ensuring that the drug reaches therapeutic levels without causing toxicity. By carefully analyzing these PK parameters in Phase I trials, researchers can make informed decisions about how to proceed with further testing and eventually how to prescribe the drug for safe and effective use in patients.

4.7 Safety and Tolerability

The assessment of **safety and tolerability** is a fundamental objective of **Phase I clinical trials**. These early-stage trials are primarily designed to evaluate the **side effects** of a drug in a small group of participants and to establish the **maximum tolerated dose (MTD)**. Ensuring the safety of participants is the top priority in clinical research, especially during Phase I, as this is the first time the drug is being tested in humans. Understanding how the body reacts to the drug, identifying any adverse effects, and determining the drug's tolerability are essential for moving forward with larger and more comprehensive clinical trials.

An essential aspect of safety evaluation in Phase I trials is the monitoring and reporting of **adverse events (AEs)** and **serious adverse events (SAEs)**. An **adverse event** is any unwanted medical occurrence experienced by a participant after receiving the drug, regardless of whether the event is directly related to the drug itself. **AEs** can range from mild side effects like headaches or nausea to more severe symptoms such as dizziness or allergic reactions. **Serious adverse events (SAEs)**, on the other hand, are more severe and can include life-threatening conditions, hospitalizations, permanent disability, or even death. SAEs are critical in determining the safety profile of a drug and are closely monitored throughout the trial.

The process of monitoring **AEs** and **SAEs** involves careful observation of participants during and after drug administration. Researchers track **vital signs** such as heart rate, blood pressure, temperature, and respiratory rate, as these can indicate early signs of a drug-related adverse effect. In addition, **laboratory tests** are routinely conducted to assess organ function, including liver and kidney health, as well as blood counts. For instance, elevated levels of **liver enzymes** like ALT and AST may indicate hepatotoxicity, while abnormal **creatinine levels** can signal kidney damage. These lab results provide valuable data on the drug's impact on critical physiological systems.

Beyond physical assessments, researchers also monitor for any **psychological effects** the drug may induce, such as mood changes, anxiety, or depression. Psychological side effects are particularly important to track for drugs that target the central nervous system or interact with neurotransmitters. All adverse events, whether physical or psychological, are carefully documented and reported according to regulatory guidelines. Any serious or unexpected AEs must be reported immediately to the appropriate regulatory authorities, such as the **US Food and Drug Administration (FDA)** or the **European Medicines Agency (EMA)**, to ensure participant safety.

The assessment of **tolerability** is equally important in Phase I trials. **Tolerability** refers to how well participants can endure the side effects of the drug without experiencing intolerable discomfort or harm. While some degree of side effects may be acceptable in clinical research, determining the limits of what is tolerable is critical for setting safe dosage levels. If participants experience severe side effects or are unable to tolerate higher doses, the drug dose must be reduced, or the trial may need to be halted altogether. The goal is to find a dose that achieves the desired therapeutic effect while minimizing side effects, which is typically referred to as the **maximum tolerated dose (MTD)**.

Once the MTD is established, it becomes the basis for dosing in subsequent trials, ensuring that future participants are not exposed to harmful levels of the drug. For example, if the MTD is determined to be **100 mg** based on tolerability assessments, this dose would be used as the upper limit for dosing in later-phase trials.

Safety assessments in Phase I trials also include regular review meetings where the trial data is analyzed to identify any trends or patterns in adverse events. These meetings help researchers and regulatory authorities make informed decisions about whether it is safe to continue the trial, adjust the dosing regimen, or modify the study protocol.

CHAPTER FIVE

Phase II Clinical Trials

Introduction to Phase II Clinical Trials

Phase II clinical trials represent a critical step in the drug development process, where the focus shifts from purely evaluating safety and tolerability, as in Phase I, to assessing the drug's **efficacy** in a patient population. While Phase I trials involve healthy volunteers and are primarily concerned with determining the safe dosage range and identifying potential side effects, Phase II trials mark the beginning of testing the drug in **patients who have the disease or condition** the drug is intended to treat. This phase is crucial for determining whether the drug shows real therapeutic potential, which is essential for advancing to larger and more expensive trials in **Phase III**.

The primary purpose of Phase II trials is to gather further **safety data** while confirming the drug's **efficacy** in a controlled setting. These trials are typically conducted with **100 to 300 patients**, a larger group than Phase I but still relatively small compared to later phases. This stage is often referred to as the "**therapeutic exploratory phase**" because it provides preliminary evidence that the drug can work in real-world conditions, although in a controlled and limited patient population. The trials are generally **randomized** and may include **placebo-controlled** groups to ensure that the observed effects are truly due to the drug and not a result of other factors.

One of the key differences between **Phase I** and **Phase II** trials lies in the **objectives**. In Phase I, the main goal is to determine the drug's safety profile, including how it is absorbed, distributed, metabolized, and excreted (pharmacokinetics), as well as identifying any potential adverse effects. In contrast, Phase II trials are designed to assess both **efficacy** and **safety** in a patient population, making it a pivotal stage in the drug development process. **Efficacy** refers to the ability of the drug to produce the intended therapeutic effect, while safety remains an ongoing concern, with adverse events being closely monitored throughout the trial.

Phase II trials also play a vital role in **dose optimization**. Researchers aim to identify the **optimal dose** that achieves the best balance between efficacy and safety. This involves determining the **minimum effective dose** and the **maximum tolerated dose**. The data collected during this phase help refine the dosing strategy for **Phase III**, where a larger patient population will be tested.

The significance of **Phase II** lies in its ability to confirm early signals of efficacy that were identified in preclinical studies or during Phase I trials. Successful Phase II trials provide a clear **proof of concept (PoC)**—a demonstration that the drug has the potential to be effective in treating the target condition. These trials also set the stage for the much larger and more rigorous **Phase III trials**, where the focus will be on confirming efficacy and safety in a broader and more diverse patient population. In cases where a drug fails to show sufficient efficacy or safety in Phase II, development may be halted, preventing the further investment of resources into a drug with limited therapeutic potential.

5.1 Proof of Concept (PoC) Studies

Proof of Concept (PoC) studies are an essential part of **Phase II clinical trials**, designed to determine whether the investigational drug shows **preliminary efficacy** in treating the target condition. These studies focus on providing early evidence that the drug has a beneficial effect on patients who suffer from the specific disease or condition for which the drug was developed. Unlike **Phase I trials**, which are conducted on healthy volunteers to assess safety, PoC studies are the first step in testing the drug on actual patients, making them a critical milestone in the drug development process.

PoC studies typically involve patients with the target disease and are usually **randomized** and **placebo-controlled**. Randomization ensures that participants are assigned to different treatment groups by chance, reducing bias and ensuring that the results are statistically reliable. A placebo-controlled design means that one group of patients receives the investigational drug, while another group receives a placebo—a substance with no therapeutic effect. This comparison helps researchers understand whether the effects observed in the treatment group are truly due to the drug and not the result of psychological or external factors.

PoC studies often involve relatively **small patient populations**, typically ranging from **50 to 200 participants**, depending on the disease being studied. These small-scale studies allow researchers to gather initial data on the drug's **therapeutic effect** without exposing large numbers of patients to potential risks. The results from PoC studies provide early signals about whether the drug can produce meaningful clinical outcomes, such as symptom relief, disease stabilization, or biomarker changes that indicate a response to treatment.

The specific **outcomes measured** in PoC studies can vary depending on the nature of the disease being treated. For example, in a trial for an anti-inflammatory drug, the primary outcome might be a reduction in **inflammation markers** such as **C-reactive protein (CRP)** or a decrease in swelling and pain. In a cancer trial, the key outcomes could include **tumor size reduction** or improvements in **survival rates**. For diseases like diabetes, researchers might measure changes in **blood glucose levels** or **HbA1c**, a biomarker that indicates long-term glucose control. These outcomes provide valuable information about whether the drug is having the desired therapeutic effect and can guide decisions about whether to proceed to larger-scale efficacy trials in **Phase III**.

Another important aspect of PoC studies is the use of **biomarkers**, which are measurable indicators of biological processes or treatment responses. Biomarkers can provide early and objective evidence of the drug's impact on the disease, often before clinical symptoms are noticeably improved. For example, in a cardiovascular study, researchers might track **blood pressure** or **cholesterol levels** as biomarkers, while in a cancer trial, changes in specific proteins or genes associated with tumor growth could serve as biomarkers.

Successful PoC studies provide the confidence needed to move forward with drug development, while a lack of efficacy at this stage might lead to modifications in the drug's formulation or dosage, or even a decision to halt development. These studies are crucial in ensuring that only promising drugs progress to the more extensive and resource-intensive trials that follow in Phase III.

5.2 Dose-Response Studies

Dose-response studies play a crucial role in **Phase II clinical trials** by determining the optimal dose of an investigational drug that provides the best balance between **efficacy** and **safety**. The primary objective of these studies is to establish the **dose-response relationship**, which is the correlation between the dose of a drug and the magnitude of its therapeutic effect. This relationship helps researchers identify the minimum effective dose that achieves the desired therapeutic outcome and the **maximum tolerated dose (MTD)**, where the side effects become unacceptable.

In a **dose-response study**, various doses of the drug are administered to different groups of patients. For instance, patients might be randomly assigned to receive doses such as **10 mg, 50 mg, or 100 mg**. The study is designed to assess how these different doses affect both the **therapeutic efficacy** and the **side effect profile**. This approach allows researchers to observe how increasing the dose impacts the drug's effectiveness and whether higher doses lead to a greater therapeutic benefit or an increase in adverse effects.

The **dose-response curve** is a graphical representation of the relationship between drug dose and therapeutic response. Typically, the curve shows that as the dose increases, the efficacy of the drug also increases up to a certain point. Beyond this optimal dose, further increases may not lead to additional benefits and might even result in adverse effects. The curve helps identify the **optimal dose**—the dose that provides the maximum therapeutic benefit with minimal side effects. Additionally, it helps determine the MTD, which is the highest dose that can be administered without causing unacceptable side effects.

Dose-response studies are crucial for guiding decisions about dosing in **Phase III trials**. By understanding how different doses affect efficacy and safety, researchers can select the most appropriate dose for larger and more comprehensive studies. This ensures that the drug is administered at a dose that maximizes its benefits while minimizing risks to patients.

In the design of these studies, researchers carefully monitor and analyze both **therapeutic effects** and **side effects**. This includes evaluating clinical outcomes such as symptom relief, disease progression, or biomarker changes, alongside any adverse reactions reported by the participants. The goal is to find the balance where the drug is effective but still well-tolerated by the patient population.

5.3 Safety and Efficacy Evaluation

Safety and efficacy evaluation is a pivotal aspect of **Phase II clinical trials**, where the focus is on determining both the **safety** and **therapeutic benefit** of an investigational drug. This phase is designed to ensure that the drug not only has the desired therapeutic effect but also does not pose significant risks to patients.

Safety Assessments are crucial in this phase. Researchers closely monitor participants for **adverse events (AEs)** and **serious adverse events (SAEs)**. Adverse events are any undesirable experiences or side effects that occur after drug administration, which might or might not be related to the drug. Serious adverse events are those that are life-threatening, require hospitalization, or result in significant disability or death. Alongside monitoring these events, researchers also review **laboratory test results** to detect any changes in health indicators that might suggest potential safety concerns. This comprehensive safety monitoring ensures that any risks associated with the drug are promptly identified and addressed.

Efficacy Assessments focus on measuring the drug's effectiveness in treating the target condition. Key aspects of efficacy evaluation include assessing **clinical endpoints** such as symptom relief, reduction in disease progression, and changes in biomarkers. For instance, in a trial for a new antihypertensive drug, efficacy might be measured by the reduction in blood pressure readings. In oncology, it could involve tumor size reduction or improvements in survival rates. Biomarker changes, such as alterations in blood glucose levels or inflammatory markers, are also crucial in evaluating how well the drug works.

The **dual evaluation** of safety and efficacy in Phase II trials helps researchers confirm that the drug is not only effective but also safe for patient use. This phase provides a balance between assessing the drug's potential benefits and understanding its safety profile. The results from these studies guide decisions about whether to advance the drug to **Phase III trials**, which involve a larger patient population and further validation of the drug's therapeutic benefits and risks.

5.4 Patient Population Selection

Patient population selection is a fundamental aspect of **Phase II clinical trials**, crucial for ensuring that the results are both reliable and relevant. The aim of this phase is to evaluate the drug's efficacy and safety in a population that closely represents the target patient group for which the drug is intended. Selecting the appropriate patient population helps in accurately measuring the drug's effects and understanding how it performs in real-world conditions.

The **selection process** involves the use of **inclusion** and **exclusion criteria**, which are set to define who can and cannot participate in the trial. **Inclusion criteria** specify the characteristics that participants must have to be eligible for the study. These may include aspects such as **disease**

severity, **age**, **gender**, and **coexisting conditions**. For example, a trial for a new asthma medication might include patients with a specific level of asthma severity, aged 18 to 65, to ensure that the drug is tested on individuals who would benefit from it and are representative of the target demographic.

Conversely, **exclusion criteria** outline the conditions or characteristics that disqualify potential participants from the trial. These criteria help prevent confounding variables that could affect the study's outcomes. For instance, individuals with certain comorbidities or those taking specific medications that might interfere with the study drug could be excluded to avoid skewing the results.

Careful patient selection is crucial because it ensures that the drug's effects are measured accurately. By defining a patient population that closely matches the intended use of the drug, researchers can reduce variability in responses and obtain more precise data. If the selected population is too broad, it might include individuals who do not fully represent the target group, leading to diluted or inconsistent results. Conversely, if the population is too narrow, it might not capture the full range of the drug's effects and potential side effects, limiting the generalizability of the findings.

5.6 Challenges and Outcomes in Phase II Trials

Phase II clinical trials are pivotal in the drug development process, but they come with their own set of **challenges** and **expected outcomes**. Understanding these aspects is essential for interpreting the results and making informed decisions about the future of the drug.

Challenges in Phase II trials often include:

1. **Patient Recruitment**: Recruiting the right patients for the trial can be challenging. This process requires identifying and enrolling participants who meet the inclusion criteria and are willing to comply with the study protocol. Recruitment difficulties can arise from factors such as the rarity of the disease, stringent inclusion and exclusion criteria, or competition with other trials.
2. **Variability in Responses**: Patient responses to the drug can vary widely. Factors such as genetic differences, concurrent medications, and variations in disease severity can influence how individuals respond to treatment. This variability can complicate the interpretation of results and make it challenging to determine the drug's true efficacy and safety.

3. **Balancing Efficacy with Safety**: One of the primary goals of Phase II trials is to find a balance between achieving therapeutic efficacy and minimizing side effects. Determining the optimal dose that provides the best therapeutic benefit without causing unacceptable adverse effects requires careful analysis and adjustment throughout the trial.

Outcomes of Phase II trials are critical in guiding the next steps in drug development:

1. **Proof of Concept**: Successful Phase II trials demonstrate that the drug has the desired therapeutic effect on the target condition. This proof of concept is essential for justifying further investment in the drug and progressing to Phase III trials.
2. **Groundwork for Phase III**: If Phase II results are positive, they lay the foundation for Phase III trials, which are larger and more definitive. These results help define the final study design for Phase III, including the dosing regimen, patient population, and outcome measures.
3. **Decision-Making Points**: Based on the Phase II data, several critical decisions must be made:

    - **Continue to Phase III**: If the drug shows promising efficacy and acceptable safety, the development may proceed to larger, more comprehensive trials.
    - **Modify the Drug**: If the results indicate that the drug is not performing as expected, modifications might be necessary. This could involve adjusting the dose, changing the formulation, or refining the study protocol.
    - **Terminate Development**: If the drug fails to demonstrate sufficient efficacy or shows significant safety concerns, further development may be halted. This decision is based on a thorough analysis of the trial data and the potential for future success.

CHAPTER SIX

Phase III Clinical Trials

6.1 Introduction to Phase III Clinical Trials

Phase III clinical trials represent a crucial stage in the drug development process, marking the transition from exploratory research to comprehensive evaluation. These trials are designed to confirm the drug's efficacy, monitor its side effects, and gather data from a larger patient population. This stage is pivotal for determining whether the drug should be approved for widespread use.

Transition from Phase II to Phase III: Phase III trials follow successful Phase II trials, where preliminary efficacy and safety data are established in smaller, controlled settings. While Phase II trials focus on determining whether the drug works in a specific population and setting, Phase III trials aim to validate these findings on a much larger scale. This phase involves multiple sites and often diverse patient groups, providing a broader understanding of the drug's effectiveness and safety profile. The transition to Phase III signifies that the drug has shown promising results in earlier stages and is ready for rigorous testing to confirm its therapeutic value.

Importance of Large-Scale Testing: Large-scale testing in Phase III trials is essential for several reasons:

- **Confirmation of Efficacy**: Phase III trials aim to confirm the drug's effectiveness by testing it in a larger, more diverse population. This helps verify whether the observed benefits in Phase II are consistently replicated in different settings and among various patient groups.
- **Safety Monitoring**: With a larger sample size, Phase III trials can better detect rare or unexpected side effects that may not have been evident in earlier trials. This comprehensive safety evaluation ensures that the drug's risk profile is well understood.

- **Regulatory Approval**: Data from Phase III trials form the basis for regulatory submissions and approvals. The extensive data collected helps regulatory agencies make informed decisions about the drug's safety and efficacy for public use.

6.1 Multinational Clinical Trials

Multinational clinical trials play a critical role in Phase III studies, offering several key advantages while also presenting unique challenges. These trials involve conducting research across multiple countries and regions, which can significantly impact the drug development process.

Benefits of Conducting Multinational Trials:

1. **Diverse Patient Populations**: One of the main benefits of multinational trials is the access to a diverse range of patient populations. Testing the drug in various geographic locations allows researchers to evaluate how different groups respond to the treatment. This diversity can help ensure that the drug is effective across different genetic backgrounds, environmental factors, and lifestyle conditions. It also increases the generalizability of the results, making them more applicable to the global population.
2. **Regulatory Advantages**: Conducting trials in multiple countries can also facilitate faster regulatory approval. By gathering data from various regions, pharmaceutical companies can address the requirements of different regulatory agencies simultaneously. This approach can streamline the approval process and potentially shorten the time to market for the drug.

Challenges of Multinational Trials:

1. **Logistical Issues**: Managing a multinational trial involves complex logistics. Coordinating between different countries requires careful planning and execution to ensure consistency in data collection, treatment administration, and patient monitoring. Time zone differences, language barriers, and varying healthcare systems can further complicate the process.
2. **Cultural Differences**: Cultural differences can affect patient recruitment and adherence to the study protocol. Different attitudes toward healthcare and varying levels of patient engagement can influence how

patients participate in the trial. It is important to consider these factors when designing the study and interpreting the results.

3. **Regulatory Compliance**: Each country has its own regulatory requirements and guidelines for clinical trials. Ensuring compliance with these regulations across multiple countries can be challenging. It requires thorough knowledge of each country's rules and effective communication between regulatory bodies and the trial sponsors.

6.2 Global Registration Studies

Global registration studies are a critical component of the drug approval process, designed to provide comprehensive data to regulatory authorities across different countries. These studies are essential for gaining approval for a new drug in multiple markets and ensuring that it meets the necessary standards for safety and efficacy worldwide.

Purpose of Global Registration Studies:

1. **Comprehensive Data Collection**: Global registration studies aim to gather extensive data on the drug's safety and efficacy from diverse populations. This data is crucial for demonstrating to regulatory agencies that the drug performs well across various geographic regions and patient demographics. By including data from different countries, these studies help to build a robust case for the drug's approval.
2. **Meeting Regulatory Requirements**: Different countries have different regulatory requirements for drug approval. Global registration studies are designed to address these varying requirements by collecting data that satisfies the criteria of multiple regulatory agencies. This approach helps streamline the approval process and facilitates a smoother entry into international markets.

Harmonizing Clinical Trial Protocols:

1. **Standardization of Protocols**: To ensure that the data collected in global registration studies is consistent and reliable, it is essential to harmonize clinical trial protocols across different countries. This means designing studies with standardized procedures, measurement methods, and endpoints. Harmonization helps to minimize variability in the data and ensures that results are comparable across different regions.

2. **Addressing Regulatory Variations**: While harmonization is important, it is also necessary to account for specific regulatory requirements in each country. This may involve adapting protocols to meet local guidelines while still maintaining overall consistency. Effective communication with regulatory agencies and a thorough understanding of their requirements are crucial for successful global registration.

6.3 Sample Size and Statistical Analysis

Sample size and statistical analysis are fundamental elements in the design and interpretation of Phase III clinical trials. Proper determination of sample size and application of appropriate statistical methods ensure that the study can reliably assess the drug's efficacy and safety.

Sample Size Determination:

1. **Calculation Based on Effect Size**: The sample size for a Phase III trial is calculated based on the expected effect size, which is the magnitude of the drug's effect compared to a control. The larger the expected effect, the smaller the sample size needed to detect it. Conversely, a smaller effect size requires a larger sample to achieve reliable results.
2. **Variability and Power**: Sample size also depends on the variability of the outcome measures. Greater variability in the data typically requires a larger sample size to accurately detect treatment effects. Additionally, the desired power of the study—usually set at 80% or 90%—affects the sample size. Higher power means a greater likelihood of detecting a true effect if it exists, which translates to a larger sample size.

Statistical Methods:

1. **Intent-to-Treat Analysis**: This method involves including all participants in the groups to which they were initially assigned, regardless of whether they completed the study or adhered to the treatment protocol. It helps to avoid biases and provides a more realistic assessment of the drug's effectiveness in a real-world setting.
2. **Per-Protocol Analysis**: In contrast, per-protocol analysis includes only those participants who strictly adhere to the study protocol. This approach can provide insights into the drug's efficacy under optimal conditions but may introduce biases if dropouts or non-compliance are not properly accounted for.

3. **Statistical Significance**: Statistical significance is crucial in determining the drug's efficacy. It is assessed using p-values, which indicate whether the observed effects are likely due to chance. A p-value of less than 0.05 is commonly used as a threshold to declare statistical significance.

6.4 Regulatory Considerations

Regulatory considerations are a crucial aspect of Phase III clinical trials, ensuring that the trial adheres to established guidelines and meets the requirements for drug approval. This phase involves comprehensive interactions with regulatory agencies and thorough documentation of trial results.

Role of Regulatory Agencies:

1. **Oversight by Regulatory Authorities**: Regulatory agencies, such as the U.S. Food and Drug Administration (FDA) and the European Medicines Agency (EMA), play a pivotal role in overseeing Phase III clinical trials. These agencies review trial protocols, monitor trial conduct, and assess the safety and efficacy data submitted by the sponsor. Their primary objective is to ensure that the drug meets the necessary safety and effectiveness standards before it can be approved for widespread use.
2. **Approval and Guidance**: Regulatory authorities provide guidance on trial design, including recommendations on endpoints, statistical methods, and safety monitoring. They also review and approve the final data package before granting marketing authorization. Their feedback is essential for aligning the trial with regulatory expectations and ensuring compliance with legal and ethical standards.

Good Clinical Practice (GCP) and Ethical Standards:

1. **Adherence to GCP Guidelines**: Good Clinical Practice (GCP) guidelines are international standards for conducting clinical trials. These guidelines ensure that trials are conducted ethically, data is reliable, and participant rights are protected. Adhering to GCP involves proper documentation, informed consent, and rigorous monitoring of trial procedures.
2. **Ethical Considerations**: Ethical standards in clinical trials involve ensuring that the study is designed to benefit participants and minimize harm. This includes obtaining informed consent, maintaining participant

confidentiality, and ensuring that the trial is conducted with scientific integrity and respect for participants.

Compiling Data for Submission:

1. **Data Compilation:** After the completion of Phase III trials, the sponsor must compile a comprehensive data package for submission to regulatory authorities. This package includes clinical trial results, safety data, efficacy outcomes, and any relevant supplementary information. It must be meticulously prepared to address all aspects of the trial and demonstrate the drug's benefit-risk profile.
2. **Submission Process:** The submission process involves presenting the data in a structured format, often through a regulatory submission dossier. This dossier is reviewed by regulatory agencies, who may request additional information or clarifications before making a final decision on drug approval.

6.5 Multicenter Trials

Multicenter trials are an integral component of Phase III clinical studies, designed to enhance the robustness and generalizability of the data by involving multiple research sites.

Definition and Purpose:

1. **Multicenter Trials:** These are clinical trials conducted at multiple locations or centers simultaneously. The primary purpose of multicenter trials is to gather data from a diverse patient population across different geographic areas. This diversity helps to ensure that the findings are applicable to a broader segment of the population and not just limited to a specific region or demographic.
2. **Increasing Sample Diversity:** By including participants from various locations, multicenter trials enhance the representativeness of the study sample. This diversity helps in assessing the drug's efficacy and safety across different populations and settings, thereby improving the generalizability of the results.

Logistical Challenges:

1. **Coordination Between Sites**: One of the main challenges in multicenter trials is coordinating between different research sites. Each site may have its own procedures, practices, and resources, which can create variability in data collection and management. Ensuring that all sites adhere to a standardized protocol is crucial for maintaining data integrity and consistency.
2. **Consistency in Data Collection**: To address variability, it's essential to implement strict guidelines and training for all participating sites. This includes standardizing data collection methods, reporting procedures, and adherence to trial protocols. Regular monitoring and audits are necessary to ensure that all sites follow the established procedures.

Role of a Central Coordinating Team:

1. **Central Coordination**: A central coordinating team manages the overall conduct of the multicenter trial. This team is responsible for overseeing site operations, ensuring compliance with the trial protocol, and resolving any issues that arise during the study. The coordinating team also handles the collection, analysis, and reporting of data from all sites.
2. **Management and Communication**: Effective communication between the central coordinating team and individual sites is vital. The team provides support, guidance, and updates to ensure that all sites are aligned with the trial objectives and procedures. They also facilitate the sharing of information and best practices among sites to enhance trial efficiency and effectiveness.

6.7 Conclusion of Phase III Trials

Phase III trials are the final and most critical stage in the drug development process, playing a decisive role in determining whether a new drug can be approved for widespread use.

Importance of Demonstrating Efficacy and Safety:

1. **Confirming Efficacy**: The primary objective of Phase III trials is to confirm the drug's efficacy demonstrated in earlier phases. These trials are designed to provide comprehensive evidence that the drug works as intended for the target condition across a broad population. The large sample sizes and rigorous testing ensure that the drug's benefits are well-established before it is approved for public use.

2. **Ensuring Safety**: Alongside efficacy, Phase III trials also focus on verifying the drug's safety profile. By monitoring a large number of participants over extended periods, these trials help identify any rare or long-term adverse effects that may not have been detected in earlier phases. Demonstrating a favorable benefit-risk ratio is crucial for obtaining regulatory approval.

Impact on Regulatory Approval and Treatment Guidelines:

1. **Regulatory Approval**: Successful Phase III trials provide the evidence needed for regulatory authorities to assess the drug's safety and efficacy. Positive results can lead to the submission of a New Drug Application (NDA) or Marketing Authorization Application (MAA). Regulatory bodies, such as the FDA and EMA, review the trial data to make an informed decision on whether to grant approval for the drug to enter the market.
2. **Influencing Treatment Guidelines**: Once approved, the drug's Phase III trial results influence treatment guidelines and clinical practices. Health authorities and medical societies often update their recommendations based on new evidence from these trials, impacting how the drug is used in clinical settings and its role in managing specific conditions.

CHAPTER SEVEN

Phase IV Clinical Trials

7.1 Post-Marketing Studies

Phase IV clinical trials, also known as **post-marketing studies**, are conducted after a drug has received FDA approval and is available to the public. While pre-approval trials (Phases I-III) are essential for establishing a drug's safety and efficacy in controlled environments, they often involve relatively small and homogenous patient populations. Once the drug reaches the market, it is used by a much larger and more diverse population, potentially revealing safety concerns or efficacy variations that were not detected in earlier trials. Post-marketing studies play a critical role in this context, as they provide ongoing assessment of the drug's **long-term safety**, **effectiveness**, and **potential risks**. These studies can involve observational research, registries, or even additional randomized trials, depending on the regulatory requirements and the safety profile of the drug.

The main **objectives of post-marketing studies** include monitoring for **rare adverse effects** that may not have been detected in pre-approval trials due to the limited sample sizes. For example, serious side effects that occur in 1 in 10,000 patients may not be apparent in a trial of 1,000 participants but could become a significant issue once the drug is used by millions of people. Post-marketing studies also aim to assess the drug's **performance in diverse patient populations**, including those with varying demographics such as age, gender, ethnicity, and underlying health conditions. These studies are especially important for understanding how the drug behaves in populations that may not have been adequately represented in pre-approval clinical trials, such as elderly patients or individuals with multiple comorbidities. By observing the drug's real-world use, researchers can determine if the drug remains effective and safe across these different groups.

Another key objective is to evaluate the **comparative effectiveness** of the drug when used alongside or against other treatments. Post-marketing studies can help establish how well the drug performs compared to existing therapies, and whether it offers any significant advantages or disadvantages in terms of efficacy or safety. This information is crucial for healthcare providers making treatment decisions, as it helps them understand how the new drug fits into the broader treatment landscape.

Several **examples and case studies** highlight the importance of post-marketing studies. One well-known case is the pain reliever **rofecoxib (Vioxx)**, a COX-2 inhibitor initially approved for treating arthritis. Post-marketing surveillance revealed that patients taking Vioxx had an increased risk of heart attacks and strokes, risks that were not apparent in the pre-approval trials. As a result, the drug was voluntarily withdrawn from the market in 2004, highlighting how critical post-marketing studies are in identifying severe, rare adverse effects that only emerge when a drug is used by a broader population.

Another example is the diabetes drug **rosiglitazone (Avandia)**, which was initially approved for controlling blood sugar levels in patients with type 2 diabetes. Post-marketing studies linked the drug to an elevated risk of cardiovascular events, including heart attacks. Following these findings, the FDA added strict warning labels to the drug, significantly limiting its use and recommending that it be prescribed only to patients who could not be treated with other medications.

These examples demonstrate that post-marketing studies are an integral part of ensuring that drugs remain safe and effective after they have been approved for public use. They help identify previously unknown risks and allow regulatory agencies to take action, such as modifying drug labels, restricting usage, or, in severe cases, withdrawing the drug from the market to protect public health.

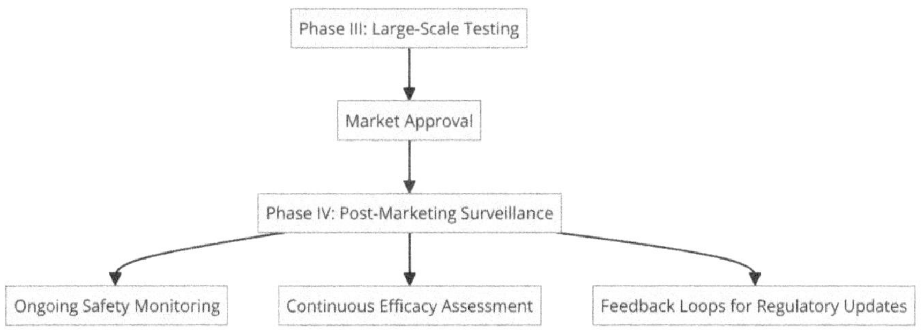

Transition from Phase III to Phase IV in clinical trials

7.2 Long-Term Safety Monitoring

Long-term safety monitoring is a critical aspect of **Phase IV clinical trials**, designed to ensure that the safety profile of a drug remains acceptable as its use expands to larger and more diverse patient populations. While pre-market clinical trials provide valuable information on a drug's short-term safety, it is only through long-term monitoring that rare, delayed, or cumulative adverse effects can be identified. This process involves continuous observation of patients who are taking the drug over extended periods, often for years, to assess how the treatment impacts their health over time. The necessity of long-term safety monitoring becomes even more significant in cases where the drug is intended for chronic conditions, such as **hypertension**, **diabetes**, or **arthritis**, where patients are expected to take the medication daily for the rest of their lives.

Long-term safety monitoring uses a range of **surveillance methods**, including **registries**, **observational studies**, and **pharmacoepidemiological studies**, to collect real-world data on the drug's performance and safety. Registries, for instance, track patient outcomes by maintaining large databases of patients who are taking the drug. This allows researchers to identify patterns, such as an increase in certain adverse events over time or in specific subpopulations. Additionally, **active surveillance systems** monitor reports of adverse events in real-time, enabling faster identification of potential safety concerns. These systems are supported by the reporting of adverse events through programs like the FDA's **MedWatch**, which encourages healthcare professionals and patients to report any unexpected side effects or safety issues they encounter.

One of the major objectives of long-term safety monitoring is to detect **rare adverse events** that may not have been observed during pre-market trials due to the relatively small sample sizes used in those trials. For example, **hepatotoxicity** (liver damage) might not emerge until a drug has been used by thousands of patients over several years, and long-term safety monitoring is essential to identifying such risks. A well-known example involves the diabetes drug **troglitazone**, which was initially approved and widely prescribed. However, post-market data and long-term safety monitoring revealed that the drug could cause severe liver damage in a small percentage of patients, leading to its eventual withdrawal from the market.

Long-term safety monitoring also plays a crucial role in refining and updating the **risk-benefit profile** of a drug. As data from long-term use accumulate, the balance between the therapeutic benefits and potential risks may shift, prompting regulatory agencies to take actions such as updating the drug's labeling, restricting its use to certain populations, or even recalling the drug. In some cases, long-term safety monitoring has resulted in the introduction of "**black box warnings**"—the FDA's strictest warning for prescription drugs—on the drug label, signaling serious safety risks that patients and healthcare providers must be aware of.

7.3 Periodic Safety Update Reports (PSUR)

Periodic Safety Update Reports (PSURs) are an essential regulatory requirement in Phase IV clinical trials, aimed at providing a comprehensive assessment of the drug's safety profile during its post-marketing phase. These reports are submitted at regular intervals to regulatory authorities, such as the FDA and the European Medicines Agency (EMA), and serve to update them on any new safety data that has emerged since the drug's approval. The goal of PSURs is to ensure that the benefit-risk balance of the drug remains favorable and to identify any new or previously unrecognized risks that could impact patient safety. PSURs are critical because they help regulators maintain an ongoing overview of a drug's performance in real-world settings, which may differ significantly from controlled clinical trials.

A typical PSUR contains several key elements. One of the main components is a **cumulative summary of adverse events** reported since the last PSUR or since the drug's approval. This summary includes any adverse reactions, ranging from mild side effects to serious adverse events (SAEs), such as hospitalization or life-threatening conditions. The report also includes a detailed **analysis of these events**, assessing whether there are any patterns or trends that suggest new safety concerns or changes in the severity of known risks. In addition, the PSUR will provide updates on any **ongoing clinical studies** or **post-marketing surveillance programs** that are still in progress, along with data from these studies that could affect the drug's safety profile. Furthermore, manufacturers are required to conduct a **benefit-risk assessment**, reassessing whether the therapeutic benefits of the drug continue to outweigh its potential risks in the light of new data.

The **frequency of PSUR submissions** varies depending on the stage of the drug's lifecycle and the requirements set by the regulatory authorities. Typically, PSURs are required to be submitted **annually** for the first several years after a drug's approval, after which the frequency may be reduced to every **two or three years.** However, if significant safety concerns arise or if the drug is used in high-risk populations, the regulatory body may request more frequent updates. The continuous submission of PSURs allows for **proactive risk management**, ensuring that any emerging safety concerns are identified and addressed before they escalate into more serious issues.

A notable example of the impact of PSURs can be seen with the anticoagulant drug **dabigatran**, which was initially approved for preventing stroke in patients with atrial fibrillation. Post-marketing data, compiled through PSURs, revealed a higher-than-expected incidence of serious bleeding events. Based on this new safety information, regulators updated the drug's labeling to include stronger warnings about bleeding risks and issued new guidelines for dosing in certain patient populations. This highlights the importance of PSURs in enabling regulators to react quickly to new safety data and implement changes that protect public health.

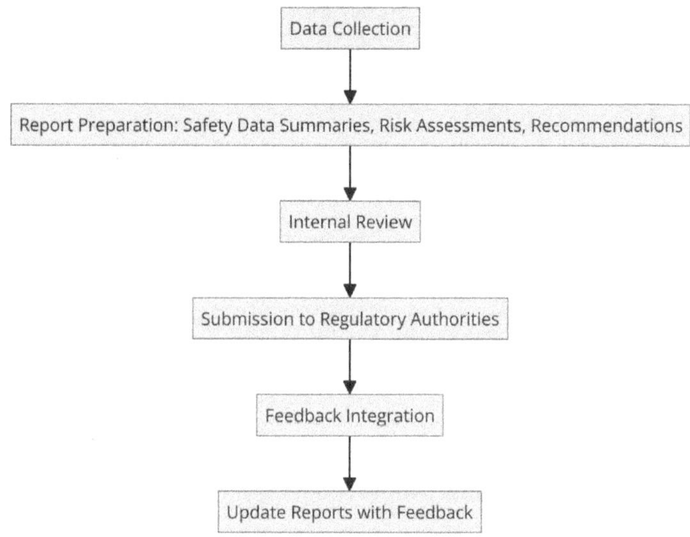

PSUR Preparation and Submission proces

7.4 Risk Management Plans (RMPs)

Risk Management Plans (RMPs) are a critical part of the post-marketing surveillance strategy in Phase IV clinical trials, designed to ensure that any risks associated with a drug are identified, assessed, and managed effectively throughout its lifecycle. An RMP is a comprehensive document that outlines how a pharmaceutical company intends to monitor and mitigate potential risks linked to the use of a drug after it has been approved and is available to the public. The RMP is not only a requirement for obtaining regulatory approval in many regions but also serves as a proactive tool to manage the long-term safety of the drug as new data become available from its widespread use in the real world.

The primary goal of an RMP is to **identify risks** that were either known before the drug was approved or may emerge as the drug is used by a larger and more diverse population. These risks can include **adverse reactions** that were detected in clinical trials, such as mild side effects, as well as potential serious events that might occur infrequently or only after long-term exposure. The RMP provides a framework for continuously monitoring these risks and developing strategies to minimize their impact on patients. For example, the RMP will often include specific **risk**

minimization measures, such as educational materials for healthcare providers, special dosing instructions, or additional warnings on the product label to ensure that the drug is used safely and effectively.

A key component of an RMP is the **risk assessment strategy**, which involves ongoing data collection from post-marketing studies, observational research, and adverse event reporting systems. These strategies are essential for evaluating the frequency and severity of any newly identified risks. In cases where risks are identified, the RMP will specify appropriate actions to mitigate these risks, such as revising the drug's labeling, modifying the dosing regimen, or restricting its use to specific patient populations. The plan also includes steps for communicating risks to healthcare providers and patients, ensuring that they are well-informed about potential safety concerns and how to manage them.

RMPs also encompass **Risk Evaluation and Mitigation Strategies (REMS)**, which are specific to high-risk drugs in the United States. REMS programs often require additional safety measures, such as limiting the distribution of the drug to certified healthcare providers or requiring that patients undergo regular monitoring while using the drug. For example, **isotretinoin**, a drug used to treat severe acne, is subject to a REMS program due to its high risk of causing birth defects. As part of the RMP, women of childbearing potential must use contraception and undergo regular pregnancy tests while taking the drug, and prescribers must be certified through the REMS program to prescribe it.

An example of the importance of RMPs can be seen with the multiple sclerosis drug **natalizumab**, which was linked to a rare but serious brain infection called **progressive multifocal leukoencephalopathy (PML)**. The risk of PML was identified after the drug had already been approved, prompting the development of a comprehensive RMP. The plan included measures such as heightened patient monitoring, restricted distribution, and educational initiatives for healthcare providers to ensure that the drug's benefits continued to outweigh its risks.

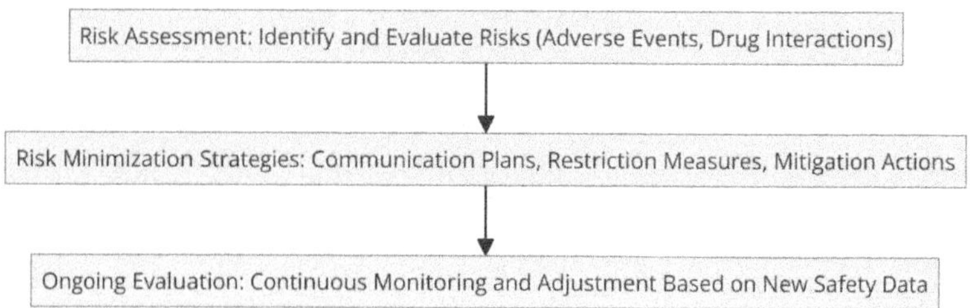

Components of a Risk Management Plan (RMP)

7.5 Pharmacoepidemiological Studies

Pharmacoepidemiological studies are a cornerstone of Phase IV clinical trials, providing essential insights into the use, safety, and effectiveness of drugs in real-world settings. These studies apply **epidemiological methods** to investigate the patterns, causes, and effects of drug use across large populations, helping to uncover long-term outcomes and rare adverse events that may not have been evident during pre-approval clinical trials. Unlike controlled clinical trials, which are conducted under strict protocols with selected patient groups, pharmacoepidemiological studies assess how drugs perform in the broader and more varied population that uses them after approval. This real-world data is crucial for identifying **unexpected side effects**, drug interactions, and variations in effectiveness among different demographic groups.

There are several types of pharmacoepidemiological studies commonly used in post-marketing surveillance. **Cohort studies** are one of the most frequently employed methods, where large groups of patients who use the drug are followed over time to observe any health outcomes. These studies allow researchers to track long-term safety and effectiveness, particularly for drugs that are intended for chronic conditions, such as hypertension or diabetes. Another common study design is the **case-control study**, which compares patients who experience an adverse event (the cases) with those who do not (the controls) to identify risk factors associated with the drug. These studies are especially useful for investigating **rare adverse events**, such as serious allergic reactions or organ toxicity, that may only become apparent after the drug has been widely used.

Pharmacoepidemiological studies are also valuable for detecting potential **drug-drug interactions** or risks associated with specific subpopulations. For instance, elderly patients, children, and those with comorbid conditions may respond differently to a drug compared to the general population. These studies help in identifying such differential effects, allowing regulators and healthcare providers to adjust treatment guidelines accordingly. An example of the importance of pharmacoepidemiology can be seen with the drug **rosiglitazone**, used to treat type 2 diabetes. Post-marketing studies revealed an increased risk of cardiovascular events, including heart attacks, among certain patient groups. As a result, regulators imposed strict usage guidelines and warnings, ensuring that the drug was prescribed only to patients who were not at high risk for these adverse outcomes.

Another significant application of pharmacoepidemiological studies is in assessing **drug utilization** patterns, which helps to ensure that drugs are being used as intended. These studies analyze how often, for how long, and by whom a drug is being used. For example, studies might reveal that a drug approved for short-term use is being prescribed for longer durations than recommended, leading to the identification of potential safety issues associated with overuse. This data is critical for making regulatory decisions, such as updating dosing guidelines or issuing safety communications to healthcare professionals.

CHAPTER EIGHT

Clinical Investigation and Evaluation of Medical Devices

8.1 Introduction to Medical Devices and In-Vitro Diagnostics (IVDs)

Medical devices and **in-vitro diagnostics (IVDs)** play a crucial role in modern healthcare by enabling both the treatment and diagnosis of a wide range of medical conditions. **Medical devices** refer to instruments, machines, implants, or other similar products that are used to diagnose, prevent, or treat diseases or conditions in humans. These devices vary widely in their complexity, ranging from simple tools like thermometers and bandages to highly sophisticated machines like MRI scanners and implantable pacemakers. In contrast, **in-vitro diagnostics (IVDs)** are tests performed on samples taken from the body, such as blood, urine, or tissue, to provide critical information regarding a patient's health. IVDs are essential for diagnosing diseases, monitoring medical treatments, and predicting patient outcomes.

Unlike **pharmaceuticals**, which involve chemical or biological substances that act within the body to achieve a therapeutic effect, medical devices and IVDs do not rely on metabolic processes for their function. Pharmaceuticals generally treat or prevent diseases through biochemical interactions, whereas medical devices often rely on physical or mechanical means. For instance, a drug like insulin helps regulate blood sugar by directly interacting with the body's metabolism, while a **blood glucose monitor** (an IVD) provides information about a patient's blood sugar levels but does not physically alter those levels.

In recent years, there has been a growing reliance on medical devices and diagnostics in healthcare, with advancements in technology driving the development of more complex and integrated solutions. For example, **wearable devices** that monitor vital signs in real-time, such as heart rate monitors or continuous glucose monitors, have become commonplace in managing chronic diseases. These innovations reflect the increasing importance of medical devices and IVDs in personalizing healthcare and improving patient outcomes.

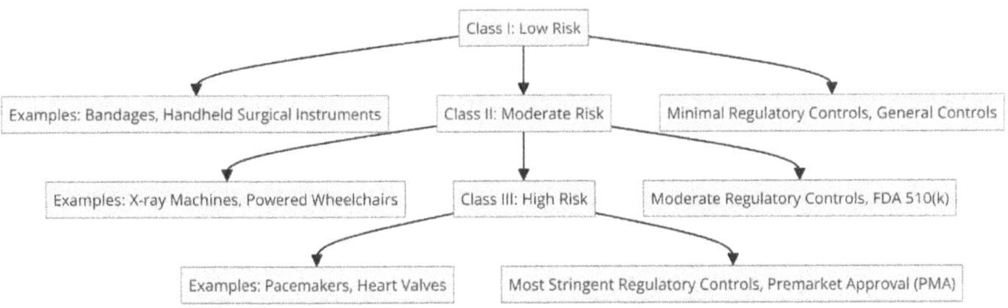

Classification of medical devices (Class I, II, III) based on risk factors

Regulatory definitions and classifications for medical devices and IVDs are critical to ensuring their safety and effectiveness. In many regulatory systems, medical devices are classified based on their **risk levels**, which reflect the potential harm to patients if the device fails or malfunctions. These classifications influence the **clinical evaluation process**, including the level of scrutiny during regulatory approval and post-market monitoring requirements. For instance, in the United States, the **FDA** classifies medical devices into **three classes**:

- **Class I devices** are considered low-risk and are subject to the least regulatory control. Examples include simple devices like bandages or manual wheelchairs. These devices typically do not require extensive clinical testing before market approval.
- **Class II devices** present moderate risk and require more stringent regulatory controls. Examples include **blood pressure monitors** and **infusion pumps**. For Class II devices, manufacturers often need to submit **510(k) premarket notifications** to the FDA, demonstrating that the device is substantially equivalent to a legally marketed device.
- **Class III devices** are high-risk devices that sustain or support life, are implanted, or pose a significant risk to the patient. Examples include **implantable pacemakers** and **heart valves**. Class III devices require **premarket approval (PMA)**, which involves rigorous clinical testing to ensure their safety and effectiveness.

Similarly, **IVDs** are also classified according to risk. For example, low-risk IVDs like **pregnancy tests** are classified as Class I, while higher-risk IVDs, such as those used for **genetic testing**, may fall under Class III. The risk classification of a device or IVD determines the amount of clinical data required for approval and influences the regulatory oversight throughout the product's lifecycle.

In-vitro diagnostics (IVDs) play a pivotal role in healthcare by providing critical information that informs the diagnosis and management of diseases. These diagnostics are used in a wide array of applications, from detecting infections and monitoring chronic conditions to screening for genetic disorders and guiding treatment decisions. **Blood glucose monitors**, for instance, are commonly used by diabetic patients to track their blood sugar levels, allowing them to make informed decisions about their insulin use. Similarly, **pregnancy tests** are one of the most widely recognized IVDs, used to detect the presence of the hormone **human chorionic gonadotropin (hCG)** in urine, indicating pregnancy.

During the **COVID-19 pandemic**, the importance of IVDs became even more evident with the widespread use of **COVID-19 test kits**, both for detecting active infections through **PCR testing** and for identifying antibodies in individuals who had recovered from the virus. These diagnostics provided essential data for managing public health responses and guiding individual treatment decisions. The rapid development and deployment of IVDs during the pandemic highlighted their essential role in modern healthcare, where timely and accurate diagnosis is critical for managing disease spread and improving patient outcomes.

8.2 Types of Studies for Devices

Clinical studies for medical devices can broadly be categorized into **pre-market studies** and **post-market studies**, each serving a distinct purpose in evaluating the safety, efficacy, and performance of the device. These studies are essential in ensuring that medical devices not only meet the necessary regulatory requirements before being introduced to the market but also continue to function safely and effectively after approval.

Pre-market studies are conducted before the device is approved for commercial use. Their primary objective is to generate clinical data that demonstrates the safety, effectiveness, and performance of the device under controlled conditions. These studies are critical in the **regulatory approval process**, providing the necessary evidence that the device works as intended and does not pose undue risks to patients. The outcomes of pre-market studies guide regulatory agencies in determining whether a device can be made available for widespread use. These studies are particularly important for high-risk devices, such as **implantable cardiac devices** or **prosthetic heart valves**, where any failure could have life-threatening consequences.

On the other hand, **post-market studies** are conducted after a device has been approved and is already in use by patients. These studies aim to assess the **long-term safety** and **effectiveness** of the device under real-world conditions, where larger and more diverse populations use the device. Post-market studies are crucial because they help identify rare adverse events or complications that may not have been detected during the pre-market phase due to smaller study populations or shorter follow-up periods. For example, after the introduction of certain **metal-on-metal hip implants**, post-market studies revealed unexpected rates of failure and adverse reactions, leading to safety alerts and product recalls. Thus, post-market studies play a key role in maintaining patient safety and ensuring the continued performance of medical devices.

Within pre-market studies, two important types of clinical trials are **feasibility studies** and **pivotal studies**. **Feasibility studies** are typically conducted in the early stages of device development. These studies are designed to assess the **initial safety** and **performance** of the device, often with a small number of participants. The main goal is to determine whether the device functions as expected and whether it is safe enough to proceed to larger, more definitive trials. For example, a feasibility study for a new type of **minimally invasive surgical tool** might involve testing its effectiveness in a small number of surgeries to ensure that it can be used safely and that it achieves the desired outcomes.

Once a device has demonstrated safety and performance in feasibility studies, it proceeds to **pivotal studies**. These are larger trials that provide the primary data needed for regulatory approval. Pivotal studies are designed to rigorously assess the device's **efficacy**, **safety**, and **clinical benefit** compared to existing alternatives or standard care. These trials typically involve a larger, more diverse patient population and longer follow-up periods. For example, a pivotal study for a new **implantable pacemaker** would involve hundreds of patients and follow them for a significant period to evaluate both the short-term and long-term safety and efficacy of the device. The data generated from pivotal studies are submitted to regulatory agencies, such as the **FDA** or **European Medicines Agency**

(EMA), as part of the application for marketing approval.

In addition to pre-market studies, **post-market surveillance** is an essential component of the clinical evaluation of medical devices. Post-market surveillance includes the ongoing monitoring of the device once it has been introduced to the market. This monitoring is necessary because some adverse events or complications may only become apparent after the device has been used by a larger and more diverse population over an extended period. For example, a device that performed well in a controlled trial might exhibit different performance characteristics when used by patients with comorbid conditions or when subjected to routine wear and tear over time. Post-market surveillance helps identify these issues early and allows regulatory authorities to take action, such as updating the device's labeling, issuing safety warnings, or in extreme cases, recalling the device.

A notable example of the importance of post-market surveillance is the case of **transvaginal mesh implants**, which were used in the treatment of pelvic organ prolapse. Initially approved based on pre-market studies showing promising results, post-market surveillance revealed a significant number of adverse events, including **pain**, **infection**, and **organ damage**, leading to multiple recalls and lawsuits. These findings underscore the need for robust post-market monitoring, especially for high-risk devices.

8.3 Clinical Evaluation Process for Devices

The clinical evaluation process for medical devices involves a structured approach to assess the safety, effectiveness, and performance of the device before it can be approved for public use. Unlike pharmaceuticals, the evaluation of medical devices must account for not only their interaction with human physiology but also the mechanical and functional aspects of the device itself. This process generally begins with preclinical testing and extends through multiple stages of clinical trials in humans.

The first stage of clinical evaluation typically involves **preclinical testing**, which includes **in vitro** (laboratory) studies and **animal testing**. During these stages, the device is tested in controlled environments to evaluate its basic functionality and ensure that it poses no immediate risks. For example, **in vitro testing** may involve evaluating the device's material for **biocompatibility** to ensure that it will not cause adverse reactions when implanted in the human body. Similarly, **animal studies** may be used to assess the device's performance and safety in a living system before moving on to human trials. These studies are essential for identifying potential issues before clinical trials begin.

Once the device has passed preclinical testing, it moves into **clinical trials in humans**. This stage often begins with **pilot studies**, which are small-scale trials designed to assess the initial safety and functionality of the device in a limited number of human subjects. The goal of pilot studies is to ensure that the device operates as intended and does not present any unforeseen risks. For example, a **new orthopedic implant** might undergo a pilot study to ensure that it can be safely inserted and integrated into bone tissue without causing adverse reactions.

After the pilot studies, the device moves into larger, more definitive **pivotal trials**. These trials provide the primary data needed to demonstrate the device's **safety**, **effectiveness**, and overall **clinical benefit**. Pivotal trials are often conducted with a larger and more diverse patient population and are designed to generate robust data that can be used for regulatory approval. For instance, a pivotal trial for an **implantable defibrillator** would involve a large number of patients with cardiac conditions, and the study would assess not only the device's ability to prevent arrhythmias but also the overall survival rate and quality of life improvements for patients. The data from pivotal trials are typically submitted to regulatory agencies such as the **FDA** or **EMA** as part of the approval process.

Device-specific challenges often arise during the clinical evaluation of medical devices that are distinct from those faced in drug trials. One major challenge is the **variability in device performance**. Unlike pharmaceuticals, which have a relatively uniform effect once administered, medical devices may perform differently depending on how they are used or the physical condition of the patient. For instance, the success of a **surgical robot** depends not only on the technology itself but also on the skill and experience of the surgeon operating it. Variations in user experience and technique can significantly influence the outcomes of the clinical trial, making it more challenging to isolate the device's performance from external factors.

Another challenge is the **learning curve** associated with the use of new devices. Many devices, particularly complex ones like **implantable neurostimulators** or **robotic surgical systems**, require healthcare providers to undergo specialized training before they can use them effectively. The initial results of a trial may reflect the learning phase of the users rather than the actual performance of the device. Over time, as users become more proficient, the device's performance may improve, complicating the interpretation of trial results. This challenge makes it essential to monitor device outcomes over extended periods to account for changes in user expertise.

Additionally, **device design** plays a significant role in determining clinical outcomes. Minor variations in the design of the device can lead to substantial differences in safety and effectiveness. For instance, a slight modification in the shape of an **intracoronary stent** could affect how well it integrates with the surrounding blood vessels, potentially leading to complications such as **restenosis** (re-narrowing of the artery). These design factors must be carefully evaluated during clinical trials to ensure that the final product performs as intended in real-world settings.

In terms of **data collection and outcome measures**, medical device trials differ from drug trials in several key ways. One of the primary data points in device trials is the **device failure rate**, which tracks how often the device malfunctions or does not perform as expected. For example, in a trial for a **hip replacement device**, the failure rate might refer to the number of cases where the implant loosens or fails to bond properly with the bone, requiring revision surgery.

In addition to failure rates, **performance metrics** are critical in device trials. These metrics might include specific functional outcomes, such as the **accuracy of a diagnostic tool**, the **durability of an implant**, or the **precision of a surgical instrument**. These performance measures are essential for determining whether the device meets the predefined success criteria.

Another important component of data collection in device trials is **patient-reported outcomes**. These outcomes reflect the patient's perspective on the effectiveness of the device in improving their quality of life, alleviating symptoms, or enhancing their overall health. For example, in a trial for a **spinal cord stimulator** used to treat chronic pain, patient-reported outcomes might focus on how much pain relief the device provides and whether it improves daily functioning. These subjective measures are critical because they provide insights that may not be captured through technical performance metrics alone.

8.4 Key Concepts in Medical Device Clinical Investigation

Medical device clinical investigations require a structured approach that addresses unique challenges compared to pharmaceutical trials. Among the most critical concepts in these investigations are **risk-benefit analysis**, **human factors and usability**, and the identification of appropriate **clinical endpoints**. Each of these factors plays a significant role in evaluating whether a medical device is safe and effective for its intended purpose.

Risk-Benefit Analysis is a cornerstone of medical device clinical trials, particularly for high-risk devices. It involves weighing the potential risks of using the device against the expected therapeutic or diagnostic benefits it offers to patients. Unlike pharmaceuticals, where adverse effects are typically biological reactions to chemical substances, medical devices may carry risks associated with **mechanical failure**, **invasiveness**, or **long-term wear and tear** on the body. The purpose of risk-benefit analysis is to determine whether the advantages of the device, such as symptom relief or life extension, justify any associated risks, including serious adverse events.

For example, devices like **implantable pacemakers** and **ventricular assist devices (VADs)** carry inherent risks due to their invasive nature and dependence on long-term functionality. A pacemaker regulates heart rhythm and is a life-saving device for patients with severe arrhythmias, but the risks include infection at the implantation site, device malfunction, or lead displacement. The benefit of preventing life-threatening arrhythmias typically outweighs these risks, but the balance must be carefully evaluated in clinical trials. Similarly, **VADs**, which help patients with heart failure pump blood, can improve survival and quality of life but also pose risks such as blood clots, stroke, or device failure. The regulatory approval process for such devices heavily depends on demonstrating through clinical trials that the potential benefits—such as extended life expectancy and improved cardiac function—outweigh these risks.

Human Factors and Usability play a critical role in the overall success or failure of medical devices. Medical devices are often designed for use by healthcare professionals, patients, or caregivers, and their effectiveness depends not only on their technical performance but also on how well they can be used safely and correctly. **Usability testing** is therefore a crucial component of device development and evaluation. It ensures that the device's design, interface, and operating instructions are intuitive and reduce the likelihood of user errors that could compromise patient safety.

For example, **insulin pumps** used by diabetic patients must be easy to program and operate to ensure accurate insulin dosing. During usability testing, manufacturers assess whether patients or healthcare providers can use the device correctly under real-world conditions. If users struggle with understanding how to set the correct dosage or misinterpret the device's alarms, the risk of insulin overdose or underdose increases, leading to potential hypoglycemia or hyperglycemia. Similarly, **surgical robots** designed to assist surgeons during procedures must undergo usability testing to ensure that the controls are responsive and that the interface provides accurate feedback to the surgeon. Even a slight delay in response time or a poorly designed user interface could lead to surgical errors.

Another example is **automatic external defibrillators (AEDs)**, which are designed for use by laypeople in emergencies. Usability testing of AEDs focuses on ensuring that the instructions are clear and that the device guides the user step by step, minimizing confusion during a high-stress situation. By prioritizing human factors in the design and testing phases, manufacturers can help prevent errors in both clinical and home settings, thereby enhancing the safety and effectiveness of the device.

Clinical Endpoints and Performance are central to evaluating the success of a medical device in a clinical trial. **Clinical endpoints** refer to specific, measurable outcomes that indicate whether the device achieves its intended purpose. These endpoints can vary widely depending on the type of device being tested. For example, for a **coronary stent**, a key clinical endpoint might be the **rate of restenosis**, or re-narrowing of the artery, over a specified follow-up period. For a **joint replacement implant**, endpoints could include **patient-reported pain reduction**, **improved mobility**, or the **durability of the implant** over several years.

Other important clinical endpoints include the **device success rate**, which measures how often the device functions as intended without complications or failure. For instance, in trials for **cochlear implants**, the device success rate may be measured by the percentage of patients who experience significant improvement in hearing acuity after the device is activated. Additionally, clinical endpoints may focus on **patient condition improvement** or **symptom reduction**, such as a decrease in the frequency of seizures in patients using a **vagus nerve stimulator** for epilepsy.

Patient-reported outcomes (PROs) are another important endpoint in medical device trials, as they reflect the patient's perspective on how well the device improves their quality of life. For example, in trials for **spinal cord stimulators** used to treat chronic pain, patients might report changes in their pain levels, overall physical function, and ability to return to daily activities. These subjective outcomes are important because they provide insight into how the device impacts the patient's day-to-day life, beyond the technical performance metrics.

8.5 Regulatory Requirements for Medical Device Trials

The regulatory requirements for medical device trials are designed to ensure that medical devices are safe and effective before being made available to the public. Different regulatory pathways exist depending on the risk classification of the device, the country in which it is being tested, and its intended use. Meeting these regulatory requirements is a crucial step for manufacturers, as it allows for the legal distribution of the device and ensures ongoing post-market surveillance.

Overview of Regulatory Pathways: Medical devices are typically subject to different regulatory pathways based on their **risk classification**. High-risk devices, such as **implantable defibrillators** and **prosthetic heart valves**, undergo the most rigorous scrutiny, while low- to moderate-risk devices, like **blood pressure cuffs** or **digital thermometers**, may have a more streamlined approval process.

One of the key pathways for high-risk devices is the **Premarket Approval (PMA)** process, which is required for devices classified as **Class III** in the United States. The PMA process involves extensive clinical trials, preclinical data, and laboratory testing to demonstrate that the device is both safe and effective for its intended use. The FDA thoroughly reviews the submitted data, and the timeline for PMA approval can range from **6 months to over a year**, depending on the complexity of the device and the amount of data required. For example, devices like **pacemakers** and **ventricular assist devices (VADs)**, which support or sustain life, must undergo this stringent approval process to ensure that they meet the highest standards of safety and reliability.

For moderate-risk devices, which fall under **Class II**, the **510(k) clearance process** is typically required. In this pathway, manufacturers must demonstrate that their device is **substantially equivalent** to a legally marketed device (predicate device) that has already received FDA approval. The 510(k) process is less time-consuming and less costly than the PMA process, and it typically takes about **90 days** for approval. However, the FDA still requires performance data and other supporting information to ensure that the device is safe and effective. Devices like **syringes**, **wheelchairs**, and **blood glucose monitors** often go through the 510(k) pathway. Although the requirements are less burdensome than those for Class III devices, the manufacturer must still meet important regulatory standards.

In addition to these pathways, there are also **Investigational Device Exemptions (IDEs)**, which allow for the use of a new medical device in a clinical study to collect the data needed for PMA or 510(k) approval. IDEs are essential for testing new devices in real-world settings before they are made available to the public.

Regulatory Bodies and Guidelines: Several key regulatory bodies oversee the approval and monitoring of medical devices globally. The **U.S. Food and Drug Administration (FDA)** is one of the most well-known regulatory bodies and is responsible for reviewing and approving medical devices in the United States. The FDA's **Center for Devices and Radiological Health (CDRH)** evaluates the safety and effectiveness of devices through the PMA and 510(k) processes, as well as post-market surveillance once the device is approved. The FDA also conducts regular audits and inspections to ensure ongoing compliance with regulatory requirements.

In Europe, medical devices are regulated by the **European Medicines Agency (EMA)** and the **European Commission** through the **Medical Devices Regulation (MDR)**, which replaced the previous directives. The MDR sets stringent standards for the clinical investigation and approval of devices and requires manufacturers to undergo conformity assessments, often in collaboration with **Notified Bodies**. Devices sold in the European Union must meet the **CE marking** requirements, indicating that they conform to health, safety, and environmental protection standards. The MDR also places a strong emphasis on post-market surveillance and **vigilance reporting** for adverse events.

In India, the **Central Drugs Standard Control Organization (CDSCO)** is responsible for regulating medical devices. The **Medical Device Rules 2017** classify devices into four categories based on risk, and manufacturers must submit clinical trial data to CDSCO for approval of new devices. The CDSCO oversees both **pre-market** and **post-market** activities, ensuring that devices meet safety and efficacy standards. Like the FDA, CDSCO monitors adverse events and requires manufacturers to report any device-related safety issues.

Ethical and Safety Considerations: Ethical considerations are paramount in medical device trials, particularly when devices are tested on human subjects. The **informed consent** process is a key ethical requirement, ensuring that participants understand the potential risks and benefits of participating in the trial. Informed consent must be obtained before any trial-related procedures begin, and it must be voluntary, meaning that participants have the right to withdraw from the trial at any time without facing any penalties.

Patient safety is the primary concern during clinical trials. Devices must be tested rigorously to ensure that they do not pose unnecessary risks to participants. Regulatory bodies such as the FDA, EMA, and CDSCO require that clinical trial protocols include detailed **safety monitoring plans**, specifying how adverse events will be tracked and reported. For example, in trials involving **implantable medical devices**, any malfunction or unexpected device-related complication must be immediately reported to the regulatory authority to determine whether the trial should be paused or modified. The **Data Safety Monitoring Boards (DSMBs)**, often set up to oversee clinical trials, play a key role in ensuring that patient safety is maintained throughout the study.

Finally, **reporting of adverse events** is a critical component of medical device trials. Manufacturers must report all serious adverse events to regulatory authorities in a timely manner. These events include any malfunction of the device that leads to death, serious injury, or the need for additional medical intervention. Failure to report adverse events can result in regulatory action, including fines, recalls, or the suspension of the clinical trial. Post-market surveillance also plays an essential role in monitoring the long-term safety of medical devices after they have been approved and widely used by the public.

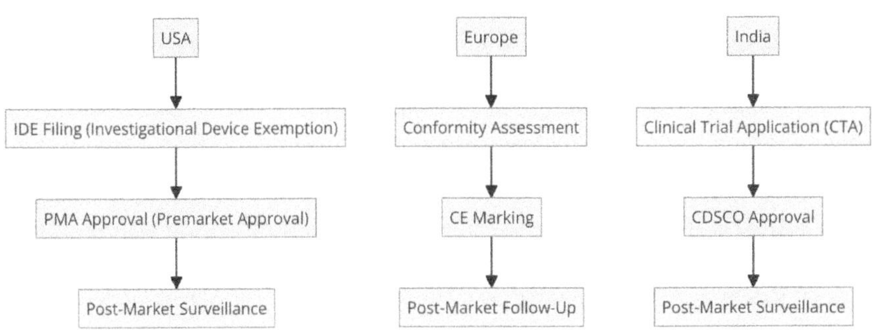

Medical Device Regulatory Approval Process in USA, Europe, and India

CHAPTER NINE

Historical Perspectives in Clinical Research Ethics

In the realm of clinical research, the ethical treatment of participants has evolved through a series of historical events and landmark decisions that have shaped modern research ethics. Chapter 9 delves into significant historical episodes that underscore the critical importance of ethical standards in clinical research. These pivotal moments not only highlight past transgressions but also serve as profound lessons that have driven the development of current ethical guidelines and regulatory frameworks.

The chapter begins with an exploration of the **Nuremberg Code**, a foundational document that emerged from the aftermath of World War II. The Code was born out of the harrowing revelations of human rights abuses committed during the Nazi regime, setting forth essential principles for conducting ethical research. Following this, the chapter examines the **Thalidomide Study**, a tragic episode in pharmaceutical history that exposed the dire consequences of inadequate drug safety testing and led to substantial reforms in drug approval processes.

Further, the chapter addresses the **Nazi Trials**, which brought to light the horrific medical experiments conducted by Nazi physicians. These trials not only sought justice but also significantly influenced the establishment of ethical standards for clinical research. The **Tuskegee Syphilis Study** is also scrutinized for its egregious ethical violations, shedding light on racial and ethical misconduct in research.

The chapter then explores the **Belmont Report**, a crucial document that formalized ethical principles and guidelines for research involving human subjects. Lastly, it delves into the **Declaration of Helsinki**, which represents a global commitment to maintaining ethical standards in clinical research, particularly in the context of international research practices.

Through this chapter, readers will gain a comprehensive understanding of how historical injustices and ethical breaches have shaped contemporary research ethics, ensuring that such violations are not repeated. Each section provides a detailed examination of these historical events, highlighting their impact on the evolution of ethical guidelines and the protection of research participants.

9.1 The Nuremberg Code

Historical Context

The **Nuremberg Code** emerged from the harrowing revelations of human rights abuses committed during World War II. In the aftermath of the war, the Allied powers sought to bring Nazi war criminals to justice through the Nuremberg Trials. These trials, held in Nuremberg, Germany, from 1945 to 1946, uncovered a series of unethical medical experiments conducted by Nazi doctors on concentration camp prisoners. These experiments, conducted without the subjects' consent and often resulting in extreme suffering or death, were marked by profound violations of human dignity and ethical standards.

The trials revealed that many of these experiments were conducted under conditions of extreme coercion and without any consideration for the well-being of the participants. The inhumane nature of these experiments, which included forced exposure to diseases, surgical procedures without anesthesia, and other cruel practices, shocked the international community and highlighted the urgent need for ethical standards in research involving human subjects. In response, the Nuremberg Code was established to address these violations and ensure that future research adhered to principles of respect for human dignity and ethical conduct.

Principles of the Code

The **Nuremberg Code** consists of ten key principles designed to protect research participants and ensure ethical standards in clinical research. These principles include:

1. **Voluntary Consent**: The Code mandates that participants must give their informed consent voluntarily, without any form of coercion or undue influence. This means participants should be fully aware of the nature, purpose, and potential risks of the research.
2. **Right to Withdraw**: Participants have the right to withdraw from the study at any time without facing any negative consequences. This

principle ensures that participation is entirely voluntary and that individuals are not forced to continue if they wish to leave.

3. **Beneficial Results for Society**: The Code stipulates that experiments should be conducted to yield valuable results that benefit society. The research should contribute to knowledge that improves human health and welfare, rather than serving merely as a scientific curiosity.
4. **Risk Minimization**: The research should avoid unnecessary physical and mental suffering and injury. The potential benefits of the study must outweigh the risks, and steps should be taken to minimize any harm to participants.
5. **Scientific Validity**: Experiments must be conducted based on scientific principles and prior knowledge. The study should be designed to achieve its objectives through well-established scientific methods.
6. **Qualified Personnel**: Research should be conducted by individuals with the necessary qualifications and expertise. Only those with appropriate training and experience should undertake experiments involving human subjects.
7. **Proper Supervision**: The research should be conducted under appropriate supervision to ensure adherence to ethical standards and to address any issues that arise during the study.
8. **Ethical Review**: The study should be subject to ethical review by an independent committee to assess the research protocol and ensure that it meets ethical standards.
9. **Protection from Harm**: Researchers must provide adequate protection against potential risks and harm, ensuring the safety and well-being of participants throughout the study.
10. **Honesty and Integrity**: Researchers should conduct themselves with honesty and integrity, reporting their findings accurately and without fabrication or falsification.

10 Principles of the Nuremberg Code

Impact and Legacy

The **Nuremberg Code** has had a profound impact on the field of medical research and ethics. It set the groundwork for modern ethical standards by emphasizing the need for voluntary consent and the protection of participants' rights. The principles outlined in the Code influenced the development of subsequent ethical guidelines and regulations, such as the Declaration of Helsinki and the Belmont Report, which continue to shape research practices globally.

The Code's legacy is evident in the rigorous ethical standards applied in clinical research today, including the requirement for Institutional Review Boards (IRBs) to review research proposals and ensure that they meet ethical criteria. The principles of the Nuremberg Code serve as a constant reminder of the importance of ethical considerations in research and the need to safeguard human dignity and rights.

9.2 The Thalidomide Study

Background

The **Thalidomide tragedy** represents one of the most significant ethical failures in the history of clinical research. In the late 1950s, Thalidomide was marketed as a safe and effective treatment for morning sickness in pregnant women. The drug, originally developed by the German pharmaceutical company Chemie Grünenthal, was promoted as a wonder drug for alleviating nausea and anxiety. It was soon widely prescribed in various countries, including Germany, the UK, and Canada.

However, the optimism surrounding Thalidomide quickly turned to horror as reports emerged of severe birth defects among babies born to women who had taken the drug during pregnancy. These defects included limb malformations, such as missing or shortened limbs, as well as other serious conditions affecting the eyes, ears, and internal organs. By the early 1960s, it became apparent that Thalidomide was a major teratogen, a substance that caused developmental abnormalities in the fetus. The drug's use led to thousands of affected infants, highlighting a devastating failure in drug safety and regulation.

Ethical Failures

The Thalidomide tragedy was marked by several profound ethical lapses in the drug's study and approval process. **Inadequate pre-marketing testing** played a crucial role in the disaster. The drug had not undergone sufficient testing for its effects on pregnant women or its potential to cause birth defects. Animal studies, which could have identified the teratogenic effects of Thalidomide, were either not conducted or inadequately interpreted.

Lack of sufficient safety monitoring further compounded the problem. Once the drug was on the market, there was inadequate surveillance of its effects, and the regulatory agencies of the time failed to act promptly upon emerging reports of adverse effects. The approval process was not robust enough to catch such critical issues before the drug was widely distributed.

Regulatory Changes

The Thalidomide crisis led to a fundamental overhaul of drug approval processes. One of the most significant outcomes was the introduction of more rigorous safety and efficacy testing for new drugs. In the United States, this led to the passage of the **1962 Kefauver-Harris Amendments** to the Federal Food, Drug, and Cosmetic Act. These amendments mandated that drug manufacturers provide substantial evidence of both safety and effectiveness before a drug could be approved for use. The amendments also introduced more stringent requirements for the informed consent of research participants and for the monitoring of clinical trials.

In Europe and other regions, similar reforms were enacted to ensure that the mistakes of the Thalidomide era would not be repeated. Regulatory agencies began to require more comprehensive pre-clinical and clinical testing, including long-term safety studies, and improved post-marketing surveillance to detect and address potential issues more rapidly.

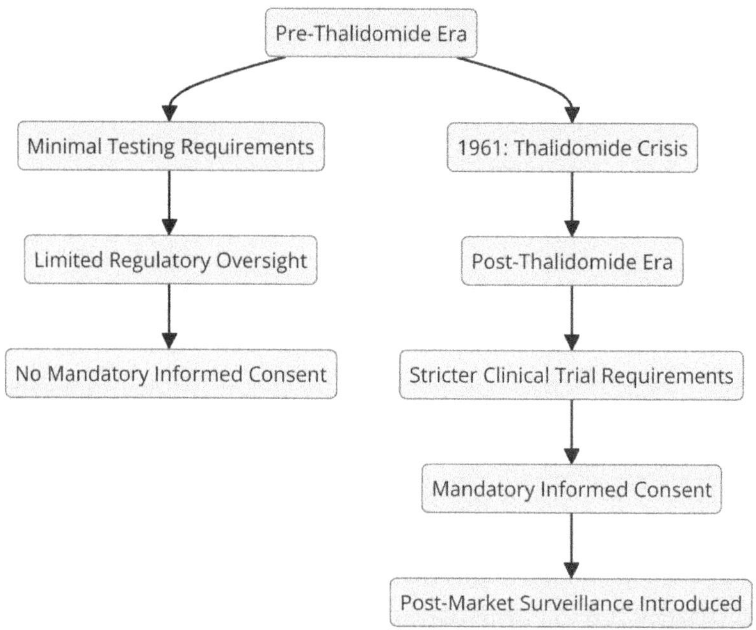

Evolution of Drug Regulation Pre- and Post-Thalidomide:

9.3 Nazi Trials

Overview of the Trials

The **Nazi medical experiments** during World War II stand as some of the most horrific examples of unethical research in history. These experiments were conducted in concentration camps and involved extreme and brutal methods, including forced sterilizations, high-altitude experiments, and exposure to infectious diseases. Notorious experiments included:

- **Forced Sterilizations:** Nazi doctors conducted forced sterilizations on individuals deemed "unfit" or "inferior" according to the regime's eugenic policies. These procedures were performed without consent and often led to severe physical and psychological trauma.
- **High-Altitude Experiments:** These experiments aimed to simulate the conditions of high-altitude flights to test the limits of human endurance. Subjects, including prisoners, were subjected to extreme pressure changes and hypoxia, often resulting in death or permanent injury.

- **Infectious Disease Studies:** Prisoners were deliberately infected with diseases such as typhus, tuberculosis, and malaria to study the effects of these diseases and test potential treatments, often resulting in severe suffering and death.

These heinous acts were brought to international attention during the **Nuremberg Trials** held after World War II. The trials sought to prosecute the Nazi doctors and scientists responsible for these atrocities. The defendants were charged with crimes against humanity, war crimes, and violations of medical ethics.

Legal and Ethical Implications

The **Nuremberg Trials** had profound legal and ethical implications. They were pivotal in the establishment of the **Nuremberg Code**, which set forth fundamental principles for conducting ethical research. The Code emphasized:

- **Voluntary Consent:** Participants must voluntarily consent to research without any form of coercion or undue influence.
- **Beneficial Outcomes:** Research must be conducted for the benefit of society and must have the potential to yield valuable knowledge.
- **Minimization of Harm:** Risks to participants must be minimized, and the experiment should avoid unnecessary physical or mental suffering.

The trials also established important legal precedents for prosecuting medical crimes against humanity. The principles outlined in the Nuremberg Code became foundational in the development of modern research ethics and provided a framework for the ethical treatment of research subjects.

Significance

The significance of the Nazi Trials extends beyond their immediate legal outcomes. They played a critical role in shaping the ethical standards in clinical research and reinforced the importance of **human rights**. The trials underscored the necessity of ethical review processes and rigorous oversight to prevent the recurrence of such atrocities. They also highlighted the global commitment to safeguarding the rights and welfare of research participants, influencing ethical guidelines and regulatory practices worldwide.

9.4 Tuskegee Syphilis Study

Study Background

The **Tuskegee Syphilis Study** is a notorious example of unethical medical research conducted in the United States. The study began in **1932** and continued for **40 years**, involving **399 African American men** with **syphilis** in **Macon County, Alabama**. The study's official aim was to observe the natural progression of untreated syphilis. However, participants were not informed about the true nature of the study or the fact that effective treatment was available.

Initially, the study was presented as a "study of bad blood," and the participants were misled into believing that they were receiving treatment for their condition. In reality, they were deliberately denied access to **penicillin**, which became widely available as a cure for syphilis in the 1940s. The men were subjected to regular physical exams, but the results were never communicated to them, and they were not treated for their disease. The study continued for decades, even as the ethical standards for medical research evolved and as new treatments became available.

Ethical Violations

The Tuskegee Syphilis Study is marked by several major **ethical violations**:

- **Lack of Informed Consent:** Participants were never properly informed about the nature of the study or their right to withdraw. They were misled about their diagnosis and the nature of the research.
- **Failure to Provide Treatment:** Despite the availability of **penicillin**, an effective treatment for syphilis, participants were denied this medication. The study aimed to observe the progression of the disease without intervening to alleviate suffering or improve health outcomes.
- **Racial Exploitation:** The study exploited a vulnerable African American population, reflecting broader patterns of racial injustice and discrimination. The researchers took advantage of the participants' socio-economic status and lack of access to healthcare.

These ethical breaches resulted in significant harm to the participants, including progression of the disease, related health complications, and deaths that could have been prevented.

Consequences and Reforms

The exposure of the **Tuskegee Syphilis Study** in **1972** led to widespread public outrage and condemnation. The ethical violations prompted a significant re-evaluation of research practices in the U.S. and led to several important reforms:

- **Informed Consent:** The study underscored the necessity of obtaining informed consent from all research participants. This principle became a cornerstone of ethical research practices.
- **Ethical Guidelines:** The Public Health Service's Office of Protection from Research Risks was established to oversee the ethical conduct of research involving human subjects. This led to the creation of stricter ethical guidelines and regulations to ensure the protection of research participants.
- **The Belmont Report:** The principles of **respect for persons**, **beneficence**, and **justice** were emphasized in the Belmont Report (1979), which provided a framework for ethical research practices.

9.5 The Belmont Report

Introduction and Context

The **Belmont Report**, published in **1979**, was a significant response to the growing ethical concerns regarding research involving human subjects, notably highlighted by cases such as the **Tuskegee Syphilis Study**. Commissioned by the National Commission for the Protection of Human Subjects of Biomedical and Behavioral Research, the Belmont Report aimed to establish a clear and comprehensive set of ethical principles and guidelines to govern research practices. The document was crafted to address the need for rigorous ethical standards and to safeguard the welfare of research participants, ensuring that future studies adhered to high moral and ethical standards.

Key Principles

The Belmont Report articulates three core principles that have become fundamental to ethical research involving human subjects:

1. **Respect for Persons:** This principle emphasizes the need to acknowledge the autonomy of individuals and to obtain informed consent. Respect for persons involves recognizing the rights of individuals to make their own decisions regarding participation in research. This principle necessitates that researchers provide participants with comprehensive information about the study, including its purpose, procedures, risks, and benefits, and ensure that consent is given voluntarily without coercion. For those who may lack full autonomy, such as children or individuals with

impaired decision-making capacity, additional protections and considerations must be in place.

2. **Beneficence:** The principle of beneficence focuses on the obligation of researchers to maximize benefits and minimize harm to participants. It requires that the potential benefits of the research outweigh the risks involved. Researchers must conduct studies in a way that promotes the well-being of participants and ensures their safety throughout the research process. This principle mandates rigorous risk assessment and ongoing monitoring to prevent harm and address any issues that arise during the study.
3. **Justice:** Justice pertains to the fair distribution of the benefits and burdens of research. This principle ensures that no group of people is unfairly burdened by the risks of research, while others benefit disproportionately from the outcomes. It calls for equitable selection of participants, so that vulnerable or marginalized groups are not exploited and that the benefits of research are shared fairly across different populations. Justice also involves considering the societal and ethical implications of research findings and ensuring that they contribute positively to public good.

Impact on Research Ethics

The Belmont Report has had a profound impact on the field of research ethics. Its principles have been incorporated into numerous regulations and guidelines governing research practices, including the **Common Rule** (45 CFR 46), which sets forth federal regulations for human subjects research in the United States. The Report has played a critical role in shaping the way Institutional Review Boards (IRBs) and Ethics Committees (ECs) review and oversee research proposals, ensuring that studies are conducted with a strong ethical foundation. By establishing clear ethical guidelines, the Belmont Report has helped to build trust in the research process and improve the protection of research participants.

9.6 The Declaration of Helsinki

Historical Development

The **Declaration of Helsinki** was first adopted by the **World Medical Association (WMA)** in **1964** as a set of ethical principles to guide medical research involving human subjects. This landmark document emerged in response to growing concerns about the ethical standards of clinical research, particularly in the wake of unethical practices such as those observed in the **Nuremberg Trials** and the **Tuskegee Syphilis Study**. The Declaration aimed to address these issues by establishing comprehensive guidelines to ensure that research conducted by physicians upholds the highest ethical standards. Over time, the Declaration has undergone numerous revisions, reflecting evolving ethical considerations and advancements in medical research practices.

Core Elements

The Declaration of Helsinki is structured around several core elements designed to ensure ethical conduct in clinical research:

1. **Informed Consent:** The Declaration mandates that researchers obtain voluntary, informed consent from all participants. This involves providing participants with sufficient information about the study's purpose, procedures, risks, and benefits, allowing them to make an informed decision about their participation. Informed consent must be obtained without coercion, and participants should be able to withdraw from the study at any time without penalty.
2. **Ethical Review:** The Declaration emphasizes the necessity of ethical review by independent committees, known as **Ethics Committees (ECs)** or **Institutional Review Boards (IRBs)**. These bodies are responsible for evaluating the ethical aspects of research protocols to ensure that they comply with established ethical standards. The review process is intended to safeguard the rights and welfare of participants by scrutinizing the potential risks and benefits of the research.
3. **Scientific and Ethical Rigor:** The Declaration underscores the importance of scientific and ethical rigor in the design and conduct of clinical trials. Researchers are required to ensure that their studies are scientifically sound and that the research methodology adheres to the highest standards of ethical practice. This includes the obligation to conduct research that is relevant and likely to provide valuable knowledge while minimizing risks to participants.

Global Influence

The Declaration of Helsinki has had a profound impact on global research ethics, influencing the development of ethical guidelines and regulations worldwide. It has been adopted and adapted by various countries and organizations, becoming a cornerstone of ethical research practices across the globe. The Declaration's principles have been integrated into national regulations and institutional policies, shaping how clinical research is conducted and ensuring that ethical standards are maintained. Its influence extends beyond medical research to encompass broader issues of human rights and ethical conduct in research.

CHAPTER TEN

ICH-GCP Guidelines and International Ethics

10.1 Introduction to the International Conference on Harmonization (ICH)

History and Purpose of the International Conference on Harmonization (ICH)

The **International Conference on Harmonization (ICH)** was established in **1990** as a collaborative effort between regulatory authorities and the pharmaceutical industry in **Europe, Japan, and the United States**. The primary objective of the ICH was to harmonize the **technical requirements for drug development and registration** across different regions. Prior to the establishment of the ICH, there were significant differences in regulatory guidelines for drug approval, which resulted in inefficiencies, increased costs, and delays in bringing new drugs to the market.

The ICH was formed to create a **common regulatory framework** that could be adopted by multiple regions, thereby improving the efficiency of the **drug development process**. By harmonizing guidelines, the ICH aimed to reduce the need for duplicative testing, streamline clinical trials, and ensure that drugs were safe, effective, and of high quality, regardless of the region in which they were developed or marketed.

Challenges and the Need for Global Standards

Before the ICH, the pharmaceutical industry faced significant challenges due to the **variations in regulatory requirements** across different regions. For example, a drug approved in the **United States** might require additional testing or meet different criteria for approval in **Japan** or **Europe**. This not only slowed down the process of drug development but also increased the cost of bringing new treatments to patients. These discrepancies in regulatory standards created **barriers to innovation** and posed challenges in conducting **global clinical trials**, as trials had to be tailored to meet the specific requirements of each region.

The **need for a global standard** became apparent as pharmaceutical companies sought to bring new therapies to international markets. Harmonizing the **regulatory frameworks** across regions would allow companies to conduct **multinational clinical trials** more efficiently, share data across borders, and avoid repeating costly and time-consuming studies. The ICH addressed this need by developing guidelines that established a unified set of criteria for the approval of drugs, covering everything from clinical trial design and conduct to safety and efficacy evaluations.

Global Membership of ICH

The ICH has grown significantly since its inception in 1990. Initially formed as a collaboration between **regulatory authorities** and the **pharmaceutical industry** from **Europe, Japan, and the USA**, the organization has expanded to include representatives from more than **35 countries** and international organizations. Today, the ICH's membership spans across all major regions of the world, including countries like **India, China, Brazil, and Canada.** This broad membership base ensures that the **ICH guidelines** are globally relevant and can be applied to drug development and approval processes in diverse regulatory environments.

Countries and organizations involved in the ICH are classified into **regulatory members, industry members, and observers**. Regulatory members represent government agencies responsible for drug approval, while industry members represent the pharmaceutical industry, and observers include other global health organizations like the **World Health Organization (WHO)**. This collaboration ensures that the ICH guidelines are informed by both regulatory and industry perspectives, promoting a balance between **public health needs** and **industry innovation**.

10.2 Good Clinical Practice (ICH-GCP) Guidelines

Introduction to Good Clinical Practice (ICH-GCP) Guidelines

The **Good Clinical Practice (GCP)** guidelines were developed under the framework of the **International Conference on Harmonization (ICH)** to ensure that **clinical trials involving human subjects** are conducted ethically, with **scientific rigor**, and in compliance with **regulatory standards**. GCP guidelines provide a comprehensive set of standards for the **design, conduct, monitoring**, and **reporting** of clinical trials, ensuring that the rights, safety, and well-being of trial participants are protected, while also ensuring the reliability and integrity of the data generated from these trials.

GCP serves as a **universal standard** for clinical research, harmonizing ethical and scientific practices across different regions, which is crucial in today's globalized pharmaceutical landscape. The guidelines apply to all parties involved in clinical trials, including investigators, sponsors, and ethics committees, ensuring that trials are performed consistently and transparently worldwide.

Core Principles of ICH-GCP

1. **Ethical Conduct**
   One of the fundamental principles of ICH-GCP is that **clinical trials must be conducted ethically**, adhering to the principles outlined in the **Declaration of Helsinki** and complying with **regulatory requirements** in each region where the trial is conducted. This means that the **well-being of the participants** should always be the top priority, and the trial must be designed to minimize risks and ensure that potential benefits outweigh the risks. Ethical review by **Institutional Review Boards (IRBs)** or **Ethics Committees** is mandatory before trials can commence, ensuring independent oversight.
2. **Informed Consent**
   Informed consent is a critical requirement in all clinical trials governed by GCP. Participants must be provided with **comprehensive information** about the study, including its purpose, procedures, potential risks, and benefits, in a language they can understand. They must voluntarily agree to participate without any form of coercion. The process of obtaining informed consent must be thoroughly documented, ensuring that participants have the **right to withdraw** from the trial at any point without penalty. This principle protects the **autonomy and dignity of participants**.
3. **Data Integrity**
   Ensuring the accuracy and **integrity of data** is essential in clinical trials. ICH-GCP mandates that all data collected during the trial must be **accurately recorded, verifiable**, and capable of being validated through audits. This includes proper **documentation practices**, ensuring that records are kept meticulously and can be reviewed by **regulatory authorities** if necessary. By maintaining strict data integrity, researchers can ensure the **reliability of trial outcomes**, enabling regulatory agencies to make informed decisions regarding drug approval.

4. **Confidentiality**

   Another key principle of GCP is the protection of **participant confidentiality**. All **personal health information** and other data collected during the trial must be handled in accordance with local and international privacy laws, such as **HIPAA (Health Insurance Portability and Accountability Act)** in the United States and **GDPR (General Data Protection Regulation)** in Europe. Researchers are responsible for maintaining the **anonymity of participants**, ensuring that identifiable information is not disclosed without consent. This principle helps build **trust** between participants and researchers, promoting greater participation in clinical trials.

Global Influence of ICH-GCP Guidelines

The implementation of **ICH-GCP** guidelines has significantly influenced the way clinical trials are conducted globally. According to estimates, over **90% of clinical trials** in major pharmaceutical markets—including **the United States, Europe, Japan, and India**—now adhere to these guidelines. This widespread adoption has helped standardize clinical research, reducing **discrepancies** across regions and ensuring that trial results can be trusted regardless of where they are conducted.

The consistent application of GCP guidelines has also improved the **quality of data** submitted to regulatory bodies like the **FDA (Food and Drug Administration)** in the United States and the **EMA (European Medicines Agency)** in Europe. This has expedited the approval process for new drugs and treatments by reducing the need for **duplicative trials** and enabling the sharing of data across borders.

Moreover, GCP guidelines have increased **patient protection** by ensuring that the ethical treatment of participants is non-negotiable. With independent **ethical reviews** and **monitoring** in place, clinical trials are now held to higher standards than ever before, preventing many of the ethical violations seen in past studies.

10.3 Ethical Guidelines for Clinical Trials

Broader Ethical Guidelines for Clinical Trials

Clinical trials are governed by a set of **ethical guidelines** designed to protect the **dignity, safety, and well-being** of human subjects involved in research. These guidelines emphasize the importance of **respect for individuals**, ensuring that participants are treated fairly and are not subjected to unnecessary risks. One of the most influential ethical documents guiding clinical research is the **Declaration of Helsinki**, developed by the **World Medical Association (WMA)**. First adopted in **1964**, it provides a framework for ensuring that research involving human subjects adheres to **ethical standards**. The Declaration of Helsinki complements the **ICH-GCP (Good Clinical Practice)** guidelines by focusing on the **ethical foundations** that should govern all aspects of clinical research, from trial design to participant recruitment.

The **Declaration of Helsinki** highlights several key ethical principles, such as **informed consent**, the need for **scientific validity** in research, and the obligation to **prioritize the well-being of participants** over the interests of science or society. Together with ICH-GCP, these guidelines ensure that clinical trials are conducted with both **ethical integrity** and **scientific rigor**.

Specific Guidelines in Ethical Clinical Trials

1. **Vulnerable Populations**

   Special considerations must be made when enrolling **vulnerable populations** in clinical trials. These populations include **children, the elderly, pregnant women**, and individuals with **cognitive impairments** or **limited decision-making capacity**. Vulnerable populations are at a higher risk of exploitation, and their inclusion in trials requires **additional safeguards** to protect their rights and well-being. For example, trials involving children often require **assent from the child** (when possible) in addition to **informed consent from parents or guardians**. Ethical guidelines mandate that clinical trials involving these populations must be carefully reviewed to ensure that they are **necessary** and that there are **minimal risks** to participants.
2. **Risk-Benefit Analysis**

   A fundamental ethical requirement for all clinical trials is that they must only proceed if a **rigorous risk-benefit analysis** demonstrates that the potential **benefits of the research outweigh the risks**. The **Declaration of Helsinki** and ICH-GCP guidelines both stress that participants must not be exposed to **unnecessary harm**. Clinical trials are reviewed by **Ethics Committees** or **Institutional Review Boards (IRBs)** to evaluate whether the risks are justified by the potential benefits, not only to the individual participants but also to society as a whole. For example, a trial testing a new cancer treatment must show that the treatment has the potential to offer significant therapeutic benefits while minimizing adverse effects. Trials that pose **high risks** with **limited potential**

benefits are deemed unethical and are not approved.

3. **Compensation for Injury**

   Another key element of ethical guidelines is the obligation to provide **compensation for injuries** sustained during clinical trials. Sponsors of clinical trials must take responsibility for **any adverse events** or harm caused by the trial. This includes providing **medical treatment and financial compensation** to participants who experience **trial-related injuries**. The compensation process is particularly important in high-risk trials where participants may be exposed to experimental therapies with unknown effects. In many countries, including **India**, the **United States**, and **Europe**, regulatory frameworks now require that sponsors have **insurance** or other financial mechanisms in place to compensate participants for **trial-related injuries**. This obligation protects participants from bearing the **burden of medical expenses** caused by their participation in the trial.

Global Adoption of Ethical Guidelines

The ethical guidelines discussed above have been incorporated into the national frameworks of many countries, ensuring that clinical trials are conducted under **uniform ethical standards**. According to data from global health organizations, over **100 countries** worldwide now mandate adherence to ethical guidelines, such as the **Declaration of Helsinki** and **ICH-GCP** guidelines, in clinical research. This widespread adoption has harmonized ethical standards in clinical trials globally, ensuring that **participants are protected** regardless of where a trial is conducted.

Countries like the **United States, the United Kingdom, India**, and **Japan** have stringent ethical regulations in place, requiring all clinical trials to be reviewed by **IRBs** or **Ethics Committees**. In some countries, national health authorities also play a role in ensuring compliance with ethical standards, further reinforcing the importance of **protecting human subjects** in research. The growing trend of **international clinical trials** has made it essential to have **globally recognized ethical guidelines** that apply across borders, helping to safeguard participants in **multinational studies**.

10.4 International Perspectives on Ethics in Clinical Research

Interpretation and Implementation of Ethical Standards in Different Regions

Ethical standards in clinical research vary across regions, with each country or regulatory body adopting guidelines to ensure that **clinical trials are**

conducted ethically and that **participant rights are protected**. Regulatory frameworks in major markets like the **USA, Europe, India, and Japan** play a critical role in overseeing clinical trials, ensuring that the guidelines are implemented according to local laws and ethical expectations.

- In the **United States**, the **Food and Drug Administration (FDA)** is the primary regulatory body responsible for clinical trials. The FDA enforces strict adherence to **Good Clinical Practice (GCP)** guidelines, requiring that clinical trials undergo rigorous ethical review through **Institutional Review Boards (IRBs)**. The **Belmont Report** and the **Declaration of Helsinki** influence these guidelines, which emphasize **informed consent, safety, and data transparency**.
- In **Europe**, the **European Medicines Agency (EMA)** regulates clinical trials across **EU member states**. European guidelines place significant emphasis on **post-trial access to treatments**, ensuring that participants who benefit from experimental therapies have continued access once the trial ends. Ethical review committees and **data protection regulations**, such as the **General Data Protection Regulation (GDPR)**, are also key components of European standards, ensuring that personal data is handled responsibly.
- In **India**, the **Central Drugs Standard Control Organization (CDSCO)** oversees clinical trials, with ethical guidelines derived from the **Drugs and Cosmetics Act** and **ICH-GCP**. India has strengthened its regulations in recent years to ensure greater transparency and accountability in clinical research, particularly concerning **compensation for trial-related injuries** and the protection of **vulnerable populations**.
- In **Japan**, the **Pharmaceuticals and Medical Devices Agency (PMDA)** regulates clinical trials and adheres to GCP and the **Declaration of Helsinki**. Japan emphasizes **scientific validity** and **data transparency**, requiring trials to be scientifically justified before approval. The PMDA also works closely with the ICH to harmonize its guidelines with international standards.

Comparison of Ethical Aspects in Different Countries

1. **Informed Consent**

   The concept of **informed consent** is universally recognized across all regions, but its application can differ. In the **USA**, informed consent documents are typically lengthy and detailed, ensuring participants fully understand the risks and benefits of a trial. Similarly, in **Europe**, participants are provided comprehensive consent forms, with an emphasis on ensuring that vulnerable populations, such as **children** or **those with cognitive impairments**, are given extra protections.

In **India**, recent regulatory changes have strengthened informed consent procedures, ensuring that participants are informed in **regional languages**, and that **witnesses** are present during the process when participants have limited literacy skills. In **Japan**, informed consent is similarly rigorous, with a focus on ensuring that participants fully understand the scientific rationale behind the trial.

1. **Data Transparency**
   Data transparency is handled differently across regions. In **Europe**, the **EMA** mandates that all clinical trial data, including **negative results**, must be published and made publicly available. This transparency helps build public trust in clinical research and allows for **independent verification** of results. In the **USA**, the FDA also encourages data transparency, but there is less emphasis on the mandatory publication of all trial results, particularly for **negative findings**.

Japan follows global trends by requiring the publication of clinical trial data, though its guidelines are somewhat less stringent compared to the **EMA**. In **India**, recent reforms now require **clinical trial registries** to be maintained, making trial data more accessible to the public and ensuring **data integrity**.

3. **Post-Trial Obligations**
   One area where differences are evident is in the **post-trial obligations** of sponsors. In **Europe**, guidelines emphasize the need for **post-trial access** to treatments for participants who benefited from the experimental therapy during the trial. This is less commonly emphasized in the **USA**, where the focus is more on **compensation** for trial-related injuries rather than guaranteeing ongoing access to treatments after the trial ends.

India has adopted strict compensation laws to ensure that participants receive financial support in case of **adverse events** during a trial. This has led to a more participant-friendly approach, making trial sponsors more accountable for the outcomes of their studies. In **Japan**, post-trial obligations are addressed through the lens of **scientific and ethical responsibility**, ensuring that participants have access to care if needed after the study concludes.

Globalization of Clinical Trials and the Need for Harmonized Ethical Standards

The globalization of clinical trials has significantly increased the need for **harmonized ethical standards**. Today, over **60% of clinical trials** involve participants from multiple countries, highlighting the importance of ensuring that ethical guidelines are consistent across borders. The **International Conference on Harmonization (ICH)** plays a critical role in this process, working to create globally recognized standards through its **GCP** guidelines.

Harmonization is particularly important in **multinational trials**, where regulatory bodies from different regions must collaborate to ensure that participants are treated fairly and ethically. Without harmonized standards, there could be **discrepancies** in how trials are conducted, leading to potential exploitation of vulnerable populations in regions with weaker regulations. The **ICH-GCP** guidelines help bridge these gaps, ensuring that trials conducted in **India**, for example, meet the same ethical standards as those in **Europe** or **the USA**.

Data on International Clinical Trials

The trend toward globalization in clinical research has grown substantially over the past two decades. Data from **global health organizations** indicates that **over 60% of clinical trials** now involve **multiple countries**, and this number continues to rise as pharmaceutical companies seek to **diversify patient populations** and **accelerate drug development**. The increase in international trials has necessitated the harmonization of ethical standards, as varying guidelines could otherwise delay trial approvals and complicate **regulatory oversight**.

The ICH has worked to ensure that clinical trials conducted across borders adhere to consistent ethical principles, making it easier for **regulatory bodies** to approve trials while protecting **participant safety** and ensuring **data integrity**.

CHAPTER ELEVEN

Ethical Issues in Randomized Clinical Trials

Introduction

The landscape of clinical research is profoundly shaped by the principles of ethics, especially in randomized clinical trials (RCTs). These trials are considered the gold standard for evaluating the efficacy and safety of new treatments, but they also pose significant ethical challenges. As researchers strive to advance medical knowledge, they must navigate complex ethical terrain to ensure that their studies respect participants' rights and well-being.

Randomized Controlled Trials (RCTs) are a cornerstone of clinical research, designed to minimize biases and provide robust evidence on the efficacy of interventions. However, the inherent nature of these trials, which involves randomly assigning participants to different treatment groups, raises important ethical considerations. This chapter delves into these ethical issues, starting with the fundamental ethical principles underlying RCTs. We will explore the ethics of randomization itself, including how to balance scientific integrity with the obligation to protect participants from potential harm.

The role of **placebos** in clinical trials adds another layer of ethical complexity. While placebos are crucial for assessing the true effect of an intervention, their use must be carefully justified to avoid withholding effective treatments from participants. The chapter will examine the ethical implications of placebo use, including how to ensure that participants are not deprived of necessary treatments.

Balancing **scientific rigor** with **patient safety** is a central theme in RCTs. Researchers are tasked with designing trials that not only generate valid results but also safeguard the health and safety of participants. This section will discuss strategies for achieving this balance, including monitoring protocols and ensuring that trials are conducted with the highest ethical standards.

Finally, the chapter will address various **ethical dilemmas** that can arise during clinical trials, such as dealing with adverse events, informed consent issues, and the pressure to achieve positive results. By understanding these dilemmas and the ethical frameworks designed to address them, researchers can better navigate the complexities of conducting responsible and ethical clinical research.

Through a comprehensive exploration of these topics, this chapter aims to provide a detailed understanding of the ethical considerations that underpin randomized clinical trials, ensuring that advancements in medical research are achieved with the utmost respect for human dignity and welfare.

11.1 Ethics of Randomized Controlled Trials

Concept of Randomized Controlled Trials (RCTs)

Randomized Controlled Trials (RCTs) are widely regarded as the **gold standard** in clinical research for evaluating the **efficacy and safety** of medical interventions, including drugs, medical devices, or therapies. In an RCT, participants are **randomly assigned** to either the **treatment group**, which receives the experimental intervention, or the **control group**, which may receive a **placebo** or an **existing standard treatment**. The process of randomization is critical as it ensures that **bias** is minimized, allowing for **unbiased results** that can accurately reflect the intervention's true effects. This random assignment creates **equivalent groups**, ensuring that the differences in outcomes can be attributed solely to the intervention being tested, not to external factors.

RCTs are used in both **early-phase trials**, which explore safety and dosage, and **late-phase trials**, which determine the efficacy of interventions across larger populations. By comparing outcomes between the treatment and control groups, RCTs allow researchers to draw robust conclusions about the effectiveness of new interventions. This rigorous approach to research helps ensure that new treatments brought to market are both **safe** and **effective**.

Ethical Foundations of RCTs

The ethical principles underpinning RCTs are based on the core values of **respect for persons**, **beneficence**, and **justice**:

- **Respect for Persons:** This principle ensures that participants are treated as autonomous individuals capable of making informed decisions about their participation in a trial. It is reflected in the **informed consent** process, where participants are provided with all necessary information to make a voluntary decision. **Special protection** is given to individuals with diminished autonomy, such as children or those with cognitive impairments, ensuring they are not exploited in clinical research.
- **Beneficence:** The principle of **beneficence** requires that clinical trials are designed and conducted to **maximize benefits** while minimizing harm to participants. Before an RCT can begin, a thorough **risk-benefit analysis** is performed to ensure that the potential benefits to the participants or society outweigh any possible risks. Researchers have an ethical obligation to **protect participants from harm**, continuously monitoring for any adverse effects during the trial.
- **Justice:** The principle of **justice** ensures that the benefits and burdens of research are distributed fairly across society. In an RCT, participants are selected equitably, without **discrimination** or exploitation of vulnerable populations. The selection of participants must be based on **scientific reasoning**, ensuring that specific groups are not unfairly exposed to risks or denied access to the potential benefits of the treatment.

Role of Informed Consent in RCTs

Informed consent is a **fundamental ethical requirement** in all RCTs, ensuring that participants are fully aware of the study's **purpose, procedures, potential risks, and benefits** before agreeing to participate. This process respects the autonomy of individuals and ensures that participation is entirely **voluntary**. Participants must be provided with clear, understandable information and be given the opportunity to ask questions before signing the **informed consent form**. They also have the right to **withdraw from the study** at any time without penalty.

Informed consent protects participants by ensuring that they are **not misled** or coerced into participating in research. It also ensures that they understand any **potential risks**, including the possibility of being assigned to the **control group** where they may not receive the experimental treatment. Researchers are ethically obligated to ensure that participants fully comprehend the **randomization process** and its implications for their treatment.

Global Prevalence of RCTs and Their Impact on Drug Development

RCTs are used globally as the standard method for evaluating new medical interventions. According to recent estimates, more than **70% of all clinical trials** registered with regulatory authorities worldwide are RCTs, reflecting their **widespread use** and importance in clinical research. The impact of RCTs on **drug development** has been profound, leading to the approval of countless new therapies that have transformed patient care. For example, RCTs played a critical role in the **development of COVID-19 vaccines**, providing robust evidence for their **safety and efficacy** before widespread distribution.

Data from the **World Health Organization (WHO)** shows that RCTs are not only the preferred method in **high-income countries** like the USA and European nations, but they are also increasingly used in **low- and middle-income countries** to test interventions relevant to local health challenges, such as vaccines for infectious diseases. The global acceptance of RCTs underscores their reliability and importance in advancing medical science.

11.2 The Role of Placebo in Clinical Trials

Use of Placebos in Clinical Trials

In clinical trials, a **placebo** is an **inactive substance** or treatment designed to resemble the experimental intervention but without any therapeutic effect. **Placebo-controlled trials** are commonly used to assess the true efficacy of a new treatment by comparing outcomes in a group receiving the **active treatment** with those in a **placebo group**. The rationale behind using placebos is to eliminate **psychological or biased effects** on the participants, allowing researchers to determine whether the experimental treatment offers benefits beyond those that could be attributed to the **placebo effect**—the phenomenon where participants experience perceived or actual improvement solely because they believe they are receiving a treatment.

Placebo-controlled trials are particularly useful in early-phase studies, where the **efficacy** and **safety** of a new drug or intervention are still being evaluated. By using a placebo group, researchers can observe any **differences in outcomes** between the group receiving the active treatment and the group receiving the placebo, ensuring that any effects seen are due to the treatment itself rather than external factors.

Ethical Challenges of Using Placebos

While placebos are scientifically valuable, their use presents **ethical challenges**, particularly in situations where an **effective treatment** already exists. The **Declaration of Helsinki**, a key ethical guideline for clinical research, states that the use of placebos is only **ethically acceptable** in situations where no current proven treatment exists, or in cases where withholding treatment would not pose a significant risk to participants. This is to ensure that participants are not **denied effective care** in favor of a placebo, which could lead to **harm** or **unnecessary suffering.**

For example, in clinical trials for **life-threatening diseases** like cancer or HIV, using a placebo would be ethically problematic if an established standard of care is available. In these cases, trials must compare the new treatment to the **existing standard of care**, rather than using a placebo, to ensure that participants are not put at **undue risk** by receiving an inactive treatment. Ethical guidelines emphasize that the well-being of the participant must take precedence over the scientific goals of the trial.

Equipoise: Genuine Uncertainty in Trials

The ethical justification for using placebos in clinical trials is often based on the principle of **equipoise. Equipoise** exists when there is genuine uncertainty within the medical community about whether the new treatment being tested is **better, worse, or equivalent** to the standard treatment or placebo. In cases of equipoise, researchers are ethically justified in assigning participants to either the placebo or treatment group because there is no clear evidence that one option is superior to the other. This ensures that no participant is knowingly given **inferior care**.

When **equipoise** is lost, meaning that new evidence emerges suggesting that one treatment is significantly better than the other, the trial must be **modified or stopped** to ensure participants receive the best possible care. This often occurs during **interim analyses**, where ongoing trial data are reviewed to determine if continuing the placebo group is still ethically justified.

Examples of Placebo-Controlled Trials

One of the most famous placebo-controlled trials is the study of **penicillin for syphilis** in the **1940s**, which demonstrated the drug's profound effectiveness compared to a placebo. This trial laid the groundwork for using placebo controls to assess the **true efficacy** of new treatments. Another more recent example is the **COVID-19 vaccine trials**, where placebo groups were used to evaluate the effectiveness of various vaccines. In these studies, the placebo group played a crucial role in establishing the high efficacy rates of the vaccines.

However, placebo-controlled trials have also been the subject of ethical controversy. For instance, in studies conducted in developing countries to prevent **mother-to-child transmission of HIV**, placebos were used even though effective treatments were available in high-income countries. This sparked ethical debates about the **inequity** in access to proven treatments across different regions.

11.3 Balancing Scientific Rigor with Patient Safety

Tension Between Scientific Rigor and Patient Safety in Clinical Trials

One of the central challenges in designing and conducting clinical trials is achieving the right balance between **scientific rigor** and **patient safety**. **Scientific rigor** refers to the meticulous design and execution of trials to ensure that the results are **reliable, valid, and reproducible**. This includes **randomization**, **blinding**, and **adequate sample sizes** to minimize bias and produce data that can be confidently used to make medical decisions. However, the need for robust scientific outcomes must be carefully weighed against the need to protect the **safety and well-being of trial participants**.

Clinical trials, particularly those testing new treatments, inherently involve risks. Researchers must design trials that **minimize risks** to participants while still providing the opportunity to answer important scientific questions. For example, while larger sample sizes can increase the **statistical power** of a trial, they also mean exposing more people to the potential risks of an experimental treatment. In the early phases of trials, where **dose-finding** or **safety assessments** are conducted, there is a fine line between ensuring that the trial is **scientifically sound** and safeguarding participants from unnecessary harm.

Risk-Benefit Analysis in Clinical Trials

Before any clinical trial can begin, a thorough **risk-benefit analysis** is performed. This is a key ethical requirement in trial design, ensuring that the **potential benefits** of the research outweigh the risks to participants. The **Declaration of Helsinki** and **ICH-GCP guidelines** mandate that trials must only be conducted if there is a **favorable balance** between the risks posed to participants and the potential benefits, either to them directly or to society through scientific discovery.

This analysis takes into account several factors:

- The **nature and severity of the disease** being studied (e.g., trials for life-threatening conditions like cancer may justify higher risks).
- The **expected benefits** of the treatment, whether it's a **curative therapy** or simply an **improvement in quality of life**.

- The **availability of alternative treatments**—if an effective treatment already exists, the justification for exposing participants to risk in a trial is lower.

A well-conducted risk-benefit analysis ensures that participants are not **exposed to undue harm** and that the potential **scientific gains** justify the trial's conduct. It is an ongoing process, continually reassessed throughout the trial as new data emerge.

Role of Data Safety Monitoring Boards (DSMBs)

In ongoing clinical trials, **Data Safety Monitoring Boards (DSMBs)** play a critical role in ensuring **participant safety**. A DSMB is an independent group of experts—usually including clinicians, statisticians, and bioethicists—who monitor the trial's progress, paying close attention to **safety data** and emerging results. DSMBs are especially important in **long-term trials** or trials involving **high-risk interventions**, where participant safety must be monitored continuously.

The DSMB's main responsibilities include:

- **Reviewing safety data** at pre-specified intervals to identify any **adverse events** or unexpected risks.
- **Stopping the trial** early if it becomes clear that the treatment is **ineffective** or if significant risks emerge that outweigh any potential benefits.
- **Modifying trial protocols** if necessary to improve participant safety, such as by adjusting dosages or adding additional **monitoring measures**.

For example, in **COVID-19 vaccine trials**, DSMBs played a crucial role in ensuring the trials were conducted safely, pausing some trials when adverse events occurred and carefully evaluating whether it was safe to continue.

Impact of Rigorous Trial Designs on Medical Breakthroughs

Historically, rigorously designed clinical trials have led to some of the most important **medical breakthroughs**, while ensuring **patient safety**. For instance, the development of **antiretroviral therapies** for HIV involved numerous randomized controlled trials (RCTs) that balanced the need to test new drugs with ensuring the safety of patients suffering from a life-threatening disease. These trials provided **solid evidence** for the effectiveness of drug combinations that have since transformed HIV into a manageable chronic condition.

Similarly, **oncology trials** have advanced cancer treatments by rigorously testing new therapies through **phased trials** that prioritize patient safety while ensuring that the treatments offer a real **therapeutic advantage**. The **risk-benefit analyses** conducted in these trials are particularly important, as many cancer therapies involve significant side effects, requiring careful evaluation of whether the potential benefits of extending life or improving outcomes outweigh the risks.

11.4 Ethical Dilemmas in Clinical Trials

Introduction to Ethical Dilemmas in Clinical Trials

Ethical dilemmas in clinical trials arise when there are **conflicting interests** or **values** that make it difficult to determine the most ethically sound course of action. These dilemmas often involve balancing the **rights and well-being of participants** against the scientific goals of the research or the potential benefits to future patients. Ethical dilemmas are particularly complex because they require researchers, sponsors, and **ethics committees** to make decisions that may not have a clear or universally accepted solution. In such cases, there is no obvious "right" choice, and each option presents its own set of **ethical trade-offs**.

Ethical dilemmas can occur at various stages of a trial, from the **design phase** through to the **conduct and reporting of results**. Researchers must navigate these dilemmas carefully to ensure that the rights and safety of participants are upheld while also ensuring that valuable scientific knowledge is generated.

Common Ethical Dilemmas in Clinical Trials

1. **Continuing a Trial with Early Positive Results**
   One of the most common ethical dilemmas occurs when early trial results suggest a **significant benefit** for the treatment group. This raises the question: should the trial continue, or should it be stopped early so that all participants can access the beneficial treatment? On one hand, stopping the trial early would allow the control group to receive the potentially life-saving treatment sooner. On the other hand, continuing the trial could provide more robust data, ensuring that the early results are not misleading or based on a small sample size. Stopping early may result in **underpowered data**, but continuing may deny the control group an effective treatment.

An example of this occurred in trials for certain **oncology drugs**, where early data showed that the new treatment significantly improved survival rates. However, **ethics committees** were faced with the decision of whether to halt the trial and provide the treatment to all patients or continue for the sake of **scientific rigor** and long-term data collection.

1. **Trials Involving High-Risk Populations**
   Another common ethical dilemma is how to conduct clinical trials in **high-risk populations**, such as patients with life-threatening diseases or those in developing countries where access to medical care is limited. These populations may be more willing to participate in trials because they have no other treatment options, raising concerns about **exploitation**. Researchers must ensure that these participants are not **coerced** into trials and that they fully understand the **risks** involved.

For example, in trials conducted in **low-income countries**, ethical concerns have been raised about whether participants are adequately informed and whether they truly have **free choice** in their participation, especially when the trial offers medical care they would not otherwise have access to. This dilemma is particularly relevant in trials for **HIV/AIDS treatments**, where the patient population is often highly vulnerable and may feel compelled to participate due to a lack of other medical options.

Financial Conflicts of Interest in Clinical Trials

Ethical dilemmas also arise from **financial conflicts of interest**, where researchers or sponsors may have a vested interest in the trial's success. Such conflicts can undermine the **integrity of the research** and create biases in the **design, conduct**, or **reporting** of the trial. For example, a researcher who stands to gain financially from a successful trial outcome may unconsciously design the trial in a way that favors the treatment group or may downplay negative results.

To address this, ethical guidelines require **full transparency** and **disclosure of financial interests**. Researchers must declare any potential conflicts, and **Institutional Review Boards (IRBs)** or ethics committees are responsible for ensuring that these conflicts do not influence the trial. Measures such as **blinding** and **third-party data monitoring** can also help mitigate the effects of financial conflicts of interest.

An example of financial conflicts impacting research occurred in trials for certain **psychiatric medications**, where researchers with ties to pharmaceutical companies were found to have **underreported adverse events**. These ethical concerns led to increased scrutiny of financial ties in clinical research and the implementation of stricter guidelines around **conflict of interest disclosures**.

Real-World Examples of Ethical Dilemmas and Solutions

Several real-world clinical trials have highlighted the complexity of ethical dilemmas and the role of **ethics committees** in navigating these challenges. One such example is the **Tuskegee Syphilis Study**, which involved withholding treatment from African American men with syphilis to observe the disease's natural progression. This study violated the principle of **beneficence** and led to significant changes in how ethical dilemmas are handled, including the requirement for **informed consent** and the establishment of **IRBs** to review all clinical trials.

In contrast, trials for **COVID-19 vaccines** showed how ethical dilemmas can be managed effectively. DSMBs were involved throughout the trials, ensuring that when adverse events occurred, they were swiftly addressed, and participants were kept informed. **Ethics committees** played a vital role in ensuring that trials continued ethically even under **emergency conditions**, demonstrating how transparency, participant safety, and **scientific rigor** can be balanced.

CHAPTER TWELVE

Clinical Research in Special Populations

Introduction

Clinical research plays a pivotal role in advancing medical knowledge and developing new treatments. However, when research involves special populations, including children, pregnant women, the elderly, and other vulnerable groups, it presents unique ethical and practical challenges. These groups often have distinct physiological and psychological needs, making it crucial to tailor research approaches to protect their well-being while ensuring scientific validity.

This chapter explores the multifaceted issues associated with conducting clinical research in these special populations. We begin by examining **research in vulnerable populations**, focusing on children, pregnant women, and the elderly. Each of these groups has specific considerations that researchers must address to ensure their participation is both ethical and beneficial.

Ethical issues in pediatric research are particularly complex, as children are unable to provide informed consent themselves. This section will delve into the ethical frameworks and regulations designed to protect minors in clinical studies, ensuring that their participation is justified and that their rights and safety are upheld.

In **research involving geriatric populations**, the focus shifts to addressing the unique physiological changes and health conditions associated with aging. This section will explore how age-related factors influence drug absorption, metabolism, and efficacy, and how research can be designed to accommodate these factors while minimizing risks.

Safeguards for special populations are critical in ensuring that research is conducted ethically. This section will highlight the various protections in place, including ethical review processes and regulatory guidelines, to safeguard the rights and safety of participants in these vulnerable groups.

Through this chapter, we aim to provide a comprehensive overview of the ethical and practical considerations essential for conducting responsible and effective research involving special populations. By addressing these challenges, researchers can contribute to advancements in medical science while ensuring that the most vulnerable are treated with the utmost respect and care.

12.1 Research in Vulnerable Populations (Children, Pregnant Women, and Elderly)

Definition of Vulnerable Populations

Vulnerable populations are groups who may have **limited capacity** to provide **informed consent** or are at a higher risk of experiencing harm during clinical research due to their **physiological, psychological**, or **social conditions**. These include populations such as **children, pregnant women, and the elderly**. These groups are considered vulnerable because their **biological responses** to treatments may differ significantly from the general population, necessitating **special protections** and tailored research approaches.

- **Children** are vulnerable due to their **developing bodies** and **limited ability** to fully understand the risks and benefits of participating in research. They rely on **parents or guardians** to make decisions on their behalf, and ethical guidelines require that **child assent** is sought wherever possible.
- **Pregnant women** are vulnerable not only because of their own health but also because of the potential risks to the **developing fetus**. Clinical trials involving pregnant women must carefully weigh the **risks to the fetus** against the **potential benefits** to both the mother and child.
- The **elderly** population is vulnerable due to **age-related physiological changes** that can affect how their bodies metabolize drugs. They may also experience **cognitive decline**, which could impair their ability to provide fully informed consent. Additionally, the presence of **multiple comorbidities** in older individuals complicates clinical research, requiring careful monitoring and adjustments to standard treatment protocols.

These populations are **critical** in clinical research because their **medical needs** differ from those of younger, healthy adults. Understanding how drugs and treatments affect these groups is essential for **personalized medicine** and ensuring that therapies are safe and effective for everyone.

Unique Ethical Challenges in Research with Vulnerable Populations

1. **Informed Consent and Assent in Children**
   When conducting research involving children, **parental consent** is mandatory because children cannot legally consent to participate in clinical trials. However, wherever possible, researchers are also required to seek the **assent** of the child, meaning the child should be involved in the decision-making process if they are capable of understanding the trial. Ethical guidelines ensure that children are not coerced into participating, and that their **rights** and **welfare** are protected at all stages.
2. **Risk-Benefit Balance for Pregnant Women**
   Research involving **pregnant women** must navigate the difficult balance between the **risks to the fetus** and the **potential benefits** to both the mother and unborn child. For example, drug treatments that could benefit the mother might pose **teratogenic risks** to the developing fetus. Researchers must ensure that the **benefits outweigh the risks**, and extensive **preclinical testing** is often required before a drug can be tested in pregnant women. Additionally, **long-term monitoring** may be necessary to ensure that both the mother and child are not adversely affected.
3. **Drug Metabolism and Comorbidities in the Elderly**
   Elderly populations often experience **slower drug metabolism** due to age-related changes in their **liver and kidney function**. These physiological changes necessitate **dose adjustments** and close monitoring during clinical trials to avoid **adverse effects**. The presence of **multiple comorbidities** (e.g., heart disease, diabetes, arthritis) also complicates research involving older individuals, as these conditions can **interact with the experimental treatment**, affecting both **efficacy and safety**. Ethical guidelines require that elderly participants are **fully informed** about the potential risks and that trials are designed to **minimize harm**.

Examples of Treatment Impact on Vulnerable Populations

- In pediatric research, vaccines are often tested with careful attention to **age-specific dosing** and **immune response** variations. For example, children may require **different dosages** of vaccines due to their developing immune systems, and trials must account for this.
- For pregnant women, medications such as **thalidomide** and **isotretinoin** historically caused **severe birth defects** when prescribed without adequate testing, highlighting the importance of considering **teratogenic risks** in clinical trials involving this group.
- In elderly populations, drugs used to treat conditions such as **hypertension** or **diabetes** may have different effects due to **reduced organ function** or interactions with **existing medications**. For instance, the metabolism of **beta-blockers** is slower in older adults, requiring **dose adjustments** to avoid side effects such as **hypotension** or **bradycardia**.

12.2 Ethical Issues in Pediatric Research

Ethical Principles Guiding Pediatric Research

Pediatric research is guided by fundamental **ethical principles** aimed at protecting children as a **vulnerable population**. Children, unlike adults, lack the legal capacity to provide **informed consent** for participation in clinical trials. As a result, ethical guidelines mandate that **parental or guardian consent** must be obtained before enrolling a child in a study. In addition to parental consent, when a child is old enough to comprehend the nature of the research, **child assent** is also required. **Assent** involves explaining the study in language appropriate to the child's age and maturity, ensuring that they understand and agree to participate voluntarily, without coercion.

The ethical framework in pediatric research is built on the principles of:

- **Respect for Persons**: Ensuring that children's rights and autonomy are respected through **age-appropriate communication** and engagement in the decision-making process.
- **Beneficence**: Prioritizing the **well-being of the child**, ensuring that the study is designed to maximize benefits while minimizing harm.
- **Justice**: Ensuring that the risks and benefits of research are distributed fairly and that vulnerable populations, like children, are not exploited for the benefit of others.

Risk-Benefit Ratio in Pediatric Research

In pediatric research, a critical ethical consideration is the **risk-benefit ratio**. Trials must demonstrate that the **potential benefits** of the research outweigh the risks for the child participants. Children should only be exposed to **minimal risks** unless there is a compelling reason to believe that the research will provide **direct therapeutic benefits** to the child or generate knowledge that is important for improving pediatric care. The **minimal risk standard** is used to ensure that children are not unnecessarily exposed to harm. For example, a study might be classified as "minimal risk" if the likelihood and magnitude of harm are no greater than what a child would encounter in everyday life or during routine medical exams.

However, in cases where higher risks are involved, such as in **oncology trials**, researchers must provide a strong justification that the potential **therapeutic benefits** outweigh the risks. Ethics committees, **Institutional Review Boards (IRBs)**, and pediatric specialists rigorously evaluate the trial protocols to ensure that risks are minimized and benefits are maximized for the child participants.

Challenges in Determining Appropriate Dosing for Pediatric Populations

Determining the appropriate **dosing** for children poses a significant challenge in pediatric research. Children are not simply "small adults," and their **pharmacokinetics**—the way their bodies absorb, distribute, metabolize, and excrete drugs—differ substantially from adults. Drug responses in children are often **non-linear**, meaning that a child's weight or age cannot be used as a simple guide for dosing. Factors such as **organ development**, **growth**, and **metabolic rates** influence how children respond to medications.

For example, infants and toddlers may have immature **liver and kidney functions**, which can affect how quickly they metabolize certain drugs, leading to the need for **adjusted doses** to avoid toxicity. Conversely, adolescents may metabolize drugs more quickly than adults, necessitating higher doses to achieve the desired therapeutic effect. Because of these complexities, **pediatric dosing** is often determined through careful **pharmacokinetic studies**, where different age groups are studied to identify appropriate dosing regimens.

Examples of Ethically Conducted Pediatric Trials

One of the most successful examples of pediatric research conducted ethically is the development of vaccines for **childhood diseases**, such as the **measles, mumps, and rubella (MMR) vaccine**. These trials adhered to strict ethical standards, ensuring that risks to child participants were minimized while providing significant benefits in terms of preventing life-threatening diseases. Another example is research on **cystic fibrosis**, a rare genetic disorder that primarily affects children. Clinical trials in this area have been conducted with extensive parental involvement and monitoring to ensure that the children enrolled in the studies were protected and that the treatments developed had the potential to offer significant therapeutic benefits.

12.3 Research in Geriatric Populations

Growing Importance of Research in Geriatric Populations

The increasing **global population of elderly individuals** has made research in **geriatric populations** more critical than ever. As people live longer, the number of individuals aged **65 years and older** continues to rise, leading to a growing demand for medications and therapies that are specifically tailored to the **unique physiological conditions** of the elderly. The importance of studying the **age-related changes** in drug absorption, metabolism, and excretion cannot be overstated. With aging, the body's ability to process medications alters significantly, often leading to differences in drug **efficacy** and **safety** when compared to younger populations.

As individuals age, their **liver function** and **kidney function**—key organs involved in metabolizing and excreting drugs—tend to decline. This can result in **slower drug metabolism**, leading to **drug accumulation** and an increased risk of side effects. Additionally, changes in **gastric acidity** and **blood flow** can affect **drug absorption**, further complicating medication management in the elderly. Understanding these **pharmacokinetic** changes is crucial to developing **safe and effective treatments** for the elderly.

Challenges in Recruiting Elderly Participants for Clinical Trials

Despite the importance of geriatric research, there are significant challenges in **recruiting elderly participants** for clinical trials. One of the main challenges is the high prevalence of **multiple comorbidities** in elderly populations, meaning many older adults suffer from several chronic conditions, such as **hypertension**, **diabetes**, and **arthritis**, at the same time. This increases the complexity of clinical trials, as researchers must account for how these coexisting conditions interact with the experimental treatment and affect the trial's outcomes. Additionally, these comorbidities can introduce **confounding variables** that make it difficult to isolate the effects of the treatment being tested.

Another challenge is **polypharmacy**, or the use of multiple medications by a single individual, which is common among the elderly. Polypharmacy can lead to **drug-drug interactions** and complicate the interpretation of trial data. Researchers need to carefully monitor the **medication regimens** of elderly participants to ensure that these interactions do not skew the trial results or compromise the safety of the participants.

Recruiting elderly participants is also complicated by physical limitations, **mobility issues**, and **transportation barriers**, which may make it difficult for them to travel to clinical trial sites or participate in follow-up visits. These logistical issues can lead to **underrepresentation** of the elderly in clinical research, despite their growing presence in the patient population.

Ethical Concerns in Geriatric Research

Ethical concerns are paramount when conducting research in elderly populations, particularly in ensuring that participants fully understand the **risks and benefits** of participating in clinical trials. This can be especially challenging for elderly individuals with **cognitive impairments**, such as **dementia** or **Alzheimer's disease**, who may have difficulty comprehending complex information related to the study. In such cases, researchers must ensure that **legal guardians** or **family members** are involved in the consent process, and that the trial is designed to protect the **dignity and safety** of these participants.

Ethics committees and **Institutional Review Boards (IRBs)** must carefully evaluate the **informed consent process** to ensure that elderly participants are not coerced or unduly influenced to participate. Additionally, the **risk-benefit ratio** in geriatric trials must be closely examined, given that the elderly are more susceptible to **adverse effects** due to their age-related physiological changes. Researchers are ethically obligated to design trials that minimize these risks while offering potential benefits to participants.

Prevalence of Geriatric Research and Its Impact

Research focused on geriatric populations has seen significant growth, driven by the increasing demand for treatments targeting **age-related diseases** such as **Alzheimer's disease, osteoporosis**, and **cardiovascular conditions**. Data from clinical trial registries show that over the past decade, the number of trials specifically targeting the elderly has risen by more than **30%**, reflecting the growing recognition of the need for geriatric-focused research. For example, trials investigating new treatments for **dementia** or **fall prevention** in the elderly have been instrumental in improving the quality of life for aging populations.

12.4 Safeguards for Special Populations

Safeguards in Clinical Research for Special Populations

Special populations, such as **children, pregnant women, the elderly**, and those with **cognitive impairments**, require extra protections when participating in clinical research. To ensure their **safety and well-being**, a series of **safeguards** have been established. These include strict ethical review processes conducted by **Institutional Review Boards (IRBs)** or **Ethics Committees**, which are responsible for thoroughly evaluating the risks and benefits of studies involving vulnerable groups. IRBs are charged with ensuring that clinical trials are designed in a way that **minimizes harm** and that participants are **adequately informed** about the risks involved.

For trials involving special populations, additional safeguards are applied to protect against **exploitation**, ensure **informed consent**, and maintain the **scientific integrity** of the study. In cases where participants may have **limited decision-making capacity**, such as in pediatric or geriatric trials, ethical boards play a crucial role in ensuring that these individuals' rights and well-being are preserved throughout the research process.

International Guidelines Protecting Vulnerable Populations

Several **international guidelines** have been developed to protect vulnerable populations in clinical research. Among the most influential are the **International Conference on Harmonisation – Good Clinical Practice (ICH-GCP)** guidelines and the **Declaration of Helsinki**. These guidelines outline the ethical principles that must be adhered to when conducting research involving human subjects, with a particular focus on safeguarding **vulnerable groups**.

- The **ICH-GCP** guidelines emphasize the need for researchers to obtain **informed consent** from participants or their legal representatives, ensure that risks are minimized, and maintain transparency throughout the trial. For vulnerable populations, these guidelines mandate additional protections, such as the need for **special monitoring** and ethical reviews by qualified boards.

- The **Declaration of Helsinki** further strengthens these protections by stating that **the well-being of the research participant** must always take precedence over the interests of science and society. For vulnerable populations, the Declaration calls for the use of the **least risky methods** possible, and for clear justification whenever these groups are included in clinical trials.

These international guidelines are not only theoretical; they are applied in real-world settings, with **regulatory bodies** across the globe incorporating these principles into national laws and regulations to ensure ethical research practices.

Role of Data Safety Monitoring Boards (DSMBs)

In ongoing clinical trials, the role of **Data Safety Monitoring Boards (DSMBs)** is crucial to ensuring that **no undue harm** comes to participants, particularly those from vulnerable populations. DSMBs are independent groups of experts that continuously monitor the **safety data** during a clinical trial. Their role is to **review interim results** and assess whether the trial should continue as planned, be modified, or be stopped early if there are signs that participants are at risk.

DSMBs are especially important in trials involving **high-risk populations**, such as pregnant women or elderly individuals with multiple health conditions. For example, if the data show an **unexpected increase in adverse events** among a vulnerable group, the DSMB may recommend halting the trial to protect the participants. This oversight ensures that even if a trial was ethically approved at the start, ongoing risks are addressed in real time, further safeguarding participant welfare.

Real-World Examples of Safeguards Protecting Vulnerable Populations

Several **real-world clinical trials** illustrate how these safeguards have successfully protected vulnerable populations. One such example is clinical research in **maternal-fetal medicine**, where trials must carefully consider the **risk to both the mother and the unborn child**. For instance, in trials testing new treatments for **gestational diabetes** or **preeclampsia**, additional ethical reviews are required to ensure that the risks to the fetus are minimized while allowing the mother to potentially benefit from innovative therapies.

Similarly, in **pediatric oncology trials**, where children are treated for life-threatening cancers, IRBs and DSMBs play an active role in monitoring the trial's progress. The **Children's Oncology Group** is an example of a research network that conducts pediatric cancer trials under the oversight of ethical review boards and DSMBs, ensuring that child participants are not exposed to unnecessary risks and that parents are fully informed of the potential outcomes.

These examples demonstrate how safeguards, such as ethical reviews and ongoing safety monitoring, are applied in practice to protect those most vulnerable in clinical research.

CHAPTER THIRTEEN

Institutional Review Boards (IRBs) and Ethics Committees (ECs)

In clinical research, the protection of human participants is a foundational principle that upholds the integrity and ethical standards of scientific inquiry. Institutional Review Boards (IRBs) and Ethics Committees (ECs) are pivotal in this regard, serving as essential mechanisms to ensure that research is conducted with the highest regard for ethical principles and human rights.

These independent bodies are tasked with reviewing research proposals, ensuring that studies meet stringent ethical criteria, and safeguarding the welfare of participants throughout the research process. Their roles encompass a broad spectrum of responsibilities, from evaluating research protocols to monitoring ongoing safety and ensuring compliance with regulatory standards.

The composition of IRBs and ECs reflects a multidisciplinary approach, drawing on expertise from various fields to provide a comprehensive review of research practices. This diverse composition helps to ensure that all ethical aspects of a study are scrutinized from multiple perspectives.

As research progresses, the continuous oversight provided by IRBs and ECs is crucial. They are responsible for reviewing safety data, managing adverse events, and ensuring that any potential risks are addressed promptly. Their decisions can significantly impact the course of a study, influencing whether research continues, is modified, or is halted.

The thoroughness of reporting and documentation required by IRBs and ECs underscores the importance of transparency and accountability in clinical research. Accurate documentation not only supports the ethical conduct of research but also provides a critical record for future reference and review.

Understanding the role of IRBs and ECs is essential for appreciating how clinical research adheres to ethical standards and protects the rights and welfare of participants. This chapter delves into the structures, functions, and processes that define these vital oversight bodies, highlighting their critical contribution to ethical research practices.

13.1 Composition of IRBs and ECs

Institutional Review Boards (IRBs) and **Ethics Committees (ECs)** play a vital role in overseeing clinical trials to ensure they are conducted ethically and that participant safety is prioritized. The composition of these boards is critical to their function, as the members bring diverse perspectives and expertise that help in the comprehensive review of research protocols. Typically, IRBs and ECs are made up of a range of professionals, including **scientists**, **physicians**, **bioethicists**, **legal advisors**, and **community representatives**. This diversity ensures that clinical trials are assessed not only from a scientific and medical viewpoint but also through ethical, legal, and community lenses. Each of these members contributes unique expertise, which is essential for reviewing the various complex aspects of a trial.

The involvement of **scientists** and **physicians** is crucial in evaluating the **scientific validity** of the research and its potential risks and benefits. They assess whether the study design is sound, whether the interventions are likely to produce meaningful data, and whether participants are exposed to unnecessary risks. For example, a **physician** might evaluate the medical procedures proposed in the trial, ensuring that they align with standard clinical practices and do not introduce undue harm to participants. Similarly, a **biostatistician** might review the study's statistical methods to ensure that the trial is adequately powered to detect the expected outcomes, thus avoiding unnecessary exposure of participants to potentially harmful interventions without sufficient scientific justification.

In addition to scientific experts, the inclusion of **bioethicists** ensures that ethical principles are upheld throughout the review process. Bioethicists evaluate whether the trial respects the **autonomy** of participants, ensuring that **informed consent** processes are thorough and clear, and that vulnerable populations are not exploited. They also assess whether the potential benefits of the research justify any risks to participants. For instance, in a trial involving an experimental cancer treatment, a bioethicist would critically assess whether the risks of side effects are reasonable given the expected therapeutic outcomes.

Legal advisors play a crucial role in ensuring that the trial complies with **local laws** and **international regulations** governing clinical research. This includes assessing whether the trial meets the requirements for participant protection outlined in regulations such as the **Declaration of Helsinki** or **Good Clinical Practice (GCP) guidelines**. Legal experts ensure that the trial's legal framework is solid, protecting both the participants and the institution conducting the research.

The inclusion of **community representatives** or **lay members** is also a key aspect of the composition of IRBs and ECs. These individuals do not typically have a scientific or medical background but provide a **public perspective** on the ethical implications of the trial. Their presence ensures that the review process is not limited to technical experts but includes views that represent **society's interests**. Lay members can offer insights into how the trial might affect the community, particularly in terms of participant recruitment, consent processes, and how the risks and benefits of the research are communicated. They help bridge the gap between the scientific community and the general public, ensuring that the trial is evaluated with the **participant's rights** and the **public good** in mind.

Diversity in the **gender**, **ethnicity**, and **expertise** of IRB and EC members is essential to ensure a well-rounded review process. This diversity allows for a broader range of perspectives, which is particularly important in trials involving diverse participant populations. For example, in a trial involving reproductive health, having a gender-balanced IRB/EC ensures that the review process takes into account the perspectives of both male and female participants. Similarly, diversity in **ethnicity** helps in understanding cultural sensitivities, which is crucial in clinical trials that span multiple countries or regions with different **cultural norms** and **healthcare practices**.

The varied composition of IRBs and ECs ensures that all aspects of the trial—scientific, ethical, legal, and social—are thoroughly examined, resulting in a review process that protects participants while facilitating ethically sound and scientifically valid research.

13.2 Roles and Responsibilities

Institutional Review Boards (IRBs) and **Ethics Committees (ECs)** hold critical responsibilities in overseeing the ethical conduct of clinical trials. Their primary role is to ensure that all research involving human participants is conducted according to **ethical principles** and in compliance with **regulatory requirements**. These bodies are tasked with protecting the rights, safety, and well-being of participants by conducting a rigorous review of all aspects of the trial protocol before the study can commence. The objective is to ensure that the trial adheres to the highest standards of ethical conduct and that participants are not exposed to **undue risks**.

One of the key responsibilities of IRBs and ECs is the **initial review** of the trial protocol. This review involves a comprehensive assessment of the study's **scientific validity, methodology**, and ethical implications. IRBs and ECs examine whether the **design of the trial** is appropriate for answering the research questions and whether it adheres to ethical guidelines such as those laid out in the **Declaration of Helsinki** and **Good Clinical Practice (GCP)** standards. During this review, the committee evaluates all elements of the study, including the **recruitment process**, **informed consent procedures**, and **data collection methods**. It ensures that participants are not unnecessarily exposed to risks and that the research is designed to generate scientifically meaningful results that can justify any risks involved.

A key component of this review process is the **assessment of the risk-benefit ratio**. IRBs and ECs carefully balance the **potential risks** to participants, such as adverse events or the discomfort associated with medical procedures, against the **anticipated benefits** of the research. The benefits could be in the form of new knowledge that contributes to the field of medicine or potential direct benefits to the participants, such as access to innovative therapies. For example, in a trial testing a new treatment for **Alzheimer's disease**, the IRB/EC would assess the risks of drug-related side effects against the potential benefits of slowing cognitive decline in participants. If the risks are deemed too high in relation to the benefits, the IRB/EC may request **modifications to the trial design** to mitigate these risks or, in extreme cases, deny approval for the trial to proceed.

Another significant responsibility of IRBs and ECs is to ensure that the **informed consent process** is robust and ethically sound. Informed consent is a foundational element of ethical research, as it ensures that participants fully understand the nature of the trial, including the **potential**

risks, **benefits**, and **alternatives** before agreeing to take part. IRBs and ECs carefully review the **informed consent forms** (ICFs) to verify that the language is clear, transparent, and accessible to participants of all backgrounds and educational levels. This ensures that potential participants can make an **informed decision** without feeling pressured or misled. The informed consent process also includes providing participants with an opportunity to ask questions and withdraw from the study at any time without facing any negative consequences. For example, in a clinical trial involving a novel cancer treatment, the IRB/EC would ensure that the risks of potential side effects, such as **nausea** or **fatigue**, are clearly communicated to participants so that they can make an informed choice about their participation.

Beyond the initial review, IRBs and ECs have a **continuous role** in monitoring the conduct of the trial. They are responsible for overseeing any **amendments** to the trial protocol, such as changes in **dosage levels** or the addition of new study sites. Additionally, they review **safety reports**, including any **serious adverse events (SAEs)** that occur during the trial, to ensure that participant safety is consistently prioritized. If new risks emerge during the course of the study, the IRB/EC has the authority to require changes to the protocol or, if necessary, to halt the trial to prevent further harm to participants.

In conclusion, the roles and responsibilities of IRBs and ECs are comprehensive and extend from the **initial approval of trial protocols** to the ongoing **monitoring of participant safety**. Their work ensures that clinical trials are conducted ethically, that the **rights and welfare of participants** are protected, and that the research adheres to **international ethical standards**.

13.3 Review and Approval Process

The **review and approval process** conducted by **Institutional Review Boards (IRBs)** and **Ethics Committees (ECs)** is a critical step in ensuring that clinical trials are designed and implemented ethically. This process is designed to evaluate whether the trial adheres to **ethical standards**, protects participant safety, and complies with **regulatory requirements**. The review is thorough and involves multiple steps, from the submission of detailed documentation to final approval or requests for modifications. The entire process is structured to ensure that no aspect of the trial design compromises the rights and well-being of participants.

The first step in the review process is the **submission of the trial protocol** by the sponsor or investigator. The protocol is a comprehensive document that outlines the **objectives**, **methodology**, **design**, and **procedures** of the clinical trial. Along with the protocol, the investigator must submit additional supporting documents, including the **investigator's brochure**, which provides detailed information about the investigational product, such as its **pharmacological profile**, **safety data** from preclinical studies, and **previous clinical trial results** (if applicable). The submission package also includes **informed consent forms (ICFs)**, which are critical for ensuring that participants are fully informed about the trial, including its potential risks and benefits. Furthermore, a detailed **risk assessment** is typically provided, explaining the expected risks to participants and how these risks will be mitigated during the trial. Other documents, such as the **recruitment strategies**, **conflict of interest declarations**, and **data monitoring plans**, are also submitted for review.

Once the submission is complete, the protocol undergoes a **preliminary review** by specific members of the IRB or EC. These members are often experts in the trial's subject area, such as **physicians**, **biostatisticians**, or **ethicists**, who evaluate key aspects of the protocol within their area of expertise. For instance, a **biostatistician** may assess the **sample size calculation** and **statistical methods** to ensure that the trial is adequately powered to detect meaningful outcomes, while an **ethicist** may focus on the ethical considerations, such as the protection of vulnerable populations. These preliminary reviewers provide initial feedback, identifying any areas of concern or potential modifications needed to improve the trial's ethical or scientific integrity.

After the preliminary review, the protocol is presented in a **full board meeting**, where all IRB/EC members participate in the discussion. During this meeting, the reviewers share their findings, and the board collectively evaluates whether the trial is ethically justified. The discussion may focus on the **risk-benefit ratio**, ensuring that the potential benefits to participants or society outweigh the risks involved. The board also reviews the **informed consent process**, ensuring that participants will receive adequate information to make informed decisions about their participation. After a thorough discussion, the IRB/EC may grant **approval** for the trial to proceed, or they may request **modifications** to the protocol if they identify issues that need to be addressed. In cases where significant concerns are raised, the board may decide to **withhold approval** until all concerns are resolved.

The **timeline of reviews** can vary depending on the **complexity** of the clinical trial and the level of risk involved. For high-risk trials, such as those involving **new investigational drugs** or **vulnerable populations**, the review process may take longer due to the need for a more in-depth evaluation. Typically, the IRB/EC meets at regular intervals (e.g., monthly) to review protocols, and sponsors can expect an initial review to take several weeks to months, depending on the volume of submissions and the complexity of the study. However, for **lower-risk studies**, an **expedited review** process may be available. Expedited reviews are conducted for studies that pose minimal risk to participants, such as behavioral studies or **non-invasive** clinical trials, and allow for a faster review and approval process, often within a few weeks.

Throughout the review process, communication between the IRB/EC and the trial sponsor or investigator is crucial. If modifications are requested, the sponsor must submit an amended protocol that addresses the board's concerns, and the review process may involve multiple rounds of feedback before final approval is granted. Once approved, the trial can proceed, but the IRB/EC remains actively involved in **monitoring** the trial, ensuring continued compliance with ethical and regulatory standards.

13.4 Ongoing Safety Data Monitoring

Once a clinical trial is approved, the role of **Institutional Review Boards (IRBs)** and **Ethics Committees (ECs)** does not end. Their responsibilities extend to **ongoing safety data monitoring** throughout the entire duration of the trial. This continued oversight ensures that the trial remains compliant with **ethical standards** and that the safety of the participants is maintained at all stages of the research. The ongoing review is critical, as trials can introduce **new risks** over time, and emerging data may require adjustments to the original protocol.

One of the primary responsibilities of IRBs and ECs in ongoing safety monitoring is the regular review of **safety reports** submitted by the investigators. These reports include details of any **adverse events (AEs)** and **serious adverse events (SAEs)** that occur during the trial. **Adverse events** are any undesired effects experienced by participants, while **serious adverse events** are those that result in significant outcomes, such as hospitalization, disability, or even death. IRBs and ECs evaluate these reports to determine if the trial is posing **unacceptable risks** to participants. For instance, in a clinical trial testing a new drug, if a pattern of unexpected **SAEs** emerges, such as severe allergic reactions or organ toxicity, the IRB/EC will thoroughly investigate the data to assess the **risk-benefit balance**. This evaluation is essential to ensure that the risks do not outweigh the potential benefits of the research.

In addition to safety reports, IRBs and ECs require **periodic updates** from the investigators as the trial progresses. These updates often include **interim analyses**, which provide insights into the **ongoing risk-benefit ratio** based on the data collected up to that point. Interim analyses are particularly important in **long-term trials** or studies involving **high-risk populations**, as they allow for early identification of trends in participant responses to the intervention. For example, in a trial for a new **oncology treatment**, an interim analysis might reveal that the drug is providing significant therapeutic benefits, but at the same time, causing unanticipated side effects in a subset of participants. The IRB/EC will use this data to decide whether any **protocol amendments** are necessary to mitigate risks, such as lowering the drug dosage or implementing additional safety monitoring measures.

If safety concerns arise during the trial, the IRB/EC is empowered to take corrective action. This process may involve **amending the trial protocol**, such as adjusting the inclusion or exclusion criteria to limit the enrollment of high-risk participants or requiring additional **safety monitoring** measures to closely observe those already enrolled. For example, if the trial involves frequent **cardiac side effects**, the IRB/EC may require investigators to conduct more **frequent ECGs** or other cardiovascular assessments to monitor participant health. In extreme cases, where the risks to participants become too great, the IRB/EC may decide to **suspend or terminate** the trial entirely. For instance, in a scenario where a drug is linked to multiple life-threatening events, the IRB/EC may halt the study until a thorough investigation can determine the cause of these events and whether the trial can be modified to continue safely.

The **ongoing safety monitoring** conducted by IRBs and ECs is crucial for ensuring that clinical trials adhere to ethical principles throughout their duration. By reviewing safety data regularly and responding to new developments, IRBs and ECs help protect participants and ensure that trials remain aligned with **regulatory requirements** and **ethical guidelines**.

13.5 Reporting and Documentation

In the **Institutional Review Board (IRB)** and **Ethics Committee (EC)** process, **reporting and documentation** play a critical role in ensuring the transparency, accountability, and regulatory compliance of clinical trials. Proper and detailed documentation is not only a regulatory requirement but also serves as an essential safeguard in the ethical conduct of research. It provides a clear trail of the decisions, changes, and safety measures implemented during the trial, enabling both the regulatory bodies and the public to trust the integrity of the research.

One of the key aspects of documentation is the maintenance of **detailed minutes** from IRB/EC meetings. These minutes are a formal record of the discussions and decisions made during protocol reviews. Every meeting must include a thorough account of the **rationale** behind decisions to approve, modify, or reject clinical trial protocols. This level of detail ensures that there is a transparent and documented basis for every decision. For instance, if an IRB/EC decides to request modifications to a trial protocol due to concerns about participant safety, the minutes must clearly explain why these concerns were raised and what specific changes are required to address them. These records are essential for maintaining **institutional accountability** and for providing a clear reference point if questions or disputes arise later in the trial. Furthermore, detailed documentation is critical for audits or inspections by regulatory agencies, such as the **Food and Drug Administration (FDA)** or the **European Medicines Agency (EMA)**, which may require access to these records to verify that the trial followed proper ethical guidelines.

In addition to internal documentation, IRBs and ECs are responsible for **filing reports** to regulatory authorities, particularly when significant safety concerns or major trial modifications occur. These reports are necessary for ensuring that the trial remains in compliance with **local and international regulations**. For instance, if an **adverse event (AE)** or **serious adverse event (SAE)** occurs, the IRB/EC must report these incidents to the relevant regulatory bodies within a specified timeframe. The timely filing of these reports is crucial for ensuring that the regulatory agencies can monitor the safety of the trial in real-time and take any necessary action to protect participants. Similarly, when major **protocol amendments** are made—such as changes to dosing regimens or adjustments in the inclusion criteria—these must be properly documented and reported to ensure that the trial remains ethically sound and compliant with regulatory standards. Failure to properly file these reports can lead to penalties, the suspension of the trial, or even legal consequences.

The role of continuous documentation is vital for maintaining an accurate and comprehensive record of all trial-related activities, particularly in regard to **safety reports**, **participant consent forms**, and **trial modifications**. Throughout the duration of a clinical trial, the IRB/EC must document every safety report, including reports of minor and serious adverse events, to track the ongoing safety of the trial. Each **informed consent form** signed by participants must also be carefully documented to ensure that participants were properly informed about the risks and benefits of the trial before enrolling. If the trial undergoes any **modifications**, whether due to safety concerns or other factors, these changes must be meticulously recorded, with clear documentation of why the changes were necessary and how they impact the trial's risk-benefit ratio. This continuous documentation is essential for ensuring that there is a clear and transparent record of the trial from start to finish, protecting both the participants and the integrity of the research.

CHAPTER FOURTEEN

Data Safety Monitoring Boards (DSMBs)

Introduction

In the realm of clinical research, ensuring the safety of participants is paramount. Data Safety Monitoring Boards (DSMBs) play a crucial role in safeguarding participant well-being and maintaining the integrity of clinical trials. These independent committees are entrusted with the ongoing evaluation of safety data, providing a layer of oversight that is essential for the ethical conduct of research.

The primary function of DSMBs is to monitor the safety and efficacy of a trial in real time, ensuring that any potential risks are identified and addressed promptly. This oversight involves a rigorous review of data throughout the trial to detect any emerging safety concerns or unexpected outcomes that may impact participant welfare.

The role of DSMBs extends beyond mere monitoring; they are responsible for conducting interim data analyses to assess the ongoing risk-benefit balance of a study. By reviewing data at predefined intervals, DSMBs can make informed recommendations regarding the continuation, modification, or termination of a trial based on safety considerations.

One of the key responsibilities of DSMBs is to perform risk-benefit assessments. This involves evaluating whether the potential benefits of a trial outweigh the risks to participants, a process that is integral to making ethical decisions about the study's progression.

Understanding the role and functions of DSMBs is essential for appreciating how clinical trials are managed to protect participant safety while achieving scientific objectives. This chapter explores the various aspects of DSMBs, including their role in clinical trials, their approach to safety oversight, and their involvement in interim data analysis and risk-benefit assessments.

14.1 Role of DSMBs in Clinical Trials

In the context of clinical trials, **Data Safety Monitoring Boards (DSMBs)** play a critical role in ensuring the **safety** of participants and the **integrity** of the data collected. DSMBs are independent groups of experts tasked with reviewing safety data during the course of a clinical trial. Their primary function is to monitor the trial's progress, evaluate safety outcomes, and ensure that the trial can continue without compromising participant welfare. Unlike trial investigators or sponsors, who may have a vested interest in the trial's success, DSMBs operate with complete **independence**, ensuring that decisions are made without any conflicts of interest. This independence is key to maintaining trust in the trial's results and protecting participants.

DSMBs are composed of experts from various fields, typically including **clinicians**, **biostatisticians**, **ethics specialists**, and sometimes even **patient advocates**. This diversity of expertise allows the board to assess the trial data from multiple perspectives. For example, clinicians evaluate the medical aspects of safety, such as the occurrence of **adverse events (AEs)** and the trial's impact on patient health. Biostatisticians provide a critical analysis of the data, ensuring that the results are statistically valid and that any emerging trends are identified early. Ethics specialists ensure that the study is being conducted in a manner that upholds the rights and welfare of participants. The diverse composition of DSMBs ensures that all critical aspects of the trial are scrutinized, and no single viewpoint dominates the decision-making process.

Large-scale, long-term, or high-risk clinical trials are typically the focus of DSMB oversight, particularly those involving life-threatening conditions or novel treatments with unknown safety profiles. In such trials, the risks to participants may be greater, and the need for ongoing safety monitoring becomes paramount. Trials involving high-risk populations, such as patients with cancer or cardiovascular diseases, are often subject to frequent review by DSMBs to ensure that the benefits of the investigational treatment continue to outweigh the risks. For instance, in oncology trials where patients are treated with powerful experimental drugs, DSMBs closely monitor for severe side effects like **cytokine release syndrome** or **organ toxicity**, which may necessitate modifying the trial protocol or even halting the trial to protect participants.

One of the key principles behind the functioning of DSMBs is their **independence from sponsors and trial investigators**. The sponsor, typically a pharmaceutical company or research institution, finances and manages the trial, while investigators conduct the study. However, to ensure an **unbiased assessment** of participant safety, the DSMB operates separately from these entities. The DSMB is not influenced by the potential financial interests of the sponsor or the scientific goals of the investigators, which helps in maintaining the integrity of the trial. This structure is designed to ensure that decisions are made based purely on the data and safety outcomes, without external pressures. For example, if the DSMB finds that the risk of continuing the trial outweighs the potential benefits, it can recommend stopping the trial, even if it conflicts with the sponsor's interests.

DSMBs typically meet at **pre-specified intervals** to review the accumulating data. These meetings may occur every few months or after a certain number of participants have completed a stage of the trial. During these reviews, the DSMB examines the data for **adverse events**, evaluates the **risk-benefit ratio**, and decides whether the trial should proceed as planned, be modified, or be terminated. In some cases, the DSMB may recommend changes to the trial protocol, such as reducing the dosage of a drug to improve safety or modifying the inclusion criteria to limit the risk to certain populations. Their decisions are communicated to the sponsor and the regulatory authorities, who then take the necessary actions.

14.2 Safety Oversight During Trials

The role of **Data Safety Monitoring Boards (DSMBs)** in clinical trials extends far beyond the initial review and approval of the study design. DSMBs are tasked with providing **continuous safety oversight** throughout the entire duration of the trial to ensure that participants remain protected from any undue harm. Their responsibility is to monitor and assess safety data at **regular intervals**, keeping a close watch on emerging trends that may indicate a shift in the **risk-benefit ratio**. This ongoing surveillance is critical, particularly in trials involving high-risk treatments or vulnerable populations.

One of the primary functions of DSMBs is to regularly review all reported **adverse events (AEs)** and **serious adverse events (SAEs)**. Adverse events are any unwanted effects that participants experience during the trial, while serious adverse events may include life-threatening situations, hospitalizations, or permanent disabilities. DSMBs assess these events to determine whether they are related to the investigational product and whether they pose an **unacceptable risk** to the participants. For example, if a clinical trial for a new drug shows an unexpected increase in **severe liver toxicity** among participants, the DSMB would investigate the data to assess whether this side effect is linked to the drug and how widespread the problem is. If the DSMB finds that the risk outweighs the potential benefits, it may recommend immediate changes to the trial protocol.

DSMBs have the authority to **pause or terminate the trial** if they detect **safety concerns** that place participants at significant risk. This power is crucial because it allows DSMBs to act swiftly to prevent further harm. In some cases, DSMBs may recommend temporarily pausing a trial while additional data is gathered to clarify whether the observed risks are manageable or require more permanent action. For instance, if a sudden rise in **cardiac complications** is detected in a trial for a cardiovascular drug, the DSMB may halt the trial until the cause of these events is better understood. Similarly, if the DSMB concludes that the investigational product poses an immediate and serious danger to participants, it can terminate the trial altogether. This decision is made independently of the trial sponsor or investigators, ensuring that **participant safety** is always the top priority.

The DSMB is also responsible for reviewing any **protocol deviations or breaches** that could impact participant safety. Clinical trials are conducted according to **strict protocols** that define the study's procedures, dosing regimens, and eligibility criteria. If these protocols are violated, either unintentionally or due to external circumstances, it could introduce risks that were not initially accounted for. For example, if a clinical trial deviates from the approved dosing schedule and this deviation results in increased adverse effects, the DSMB must evaluate whether the protocol needs to be adjusted to minimize harm. In such cases, the DSMB may recommend **corrective actions**, such as altering the dosing regimen, increasing monitoring of participants, or revising the inclusion/exclusion criteria to prevent further issues. These recommendations are designed to **minimize risk** while allowing the trial to continue in a safer, more controlled manner.

The DSMB's role in ensuring safety extends from the trial's initiation all the way through to its completion. This means that DSMBs are not only responsible for addressing immediate safety concerns but also for ensuring that the trial's data remains reliable and ethically sound. For example, if the DSMB detects that a trial is significantly underreporting adverse events, they may intervene to ensure that proper **data collection** procedures are followed and that all safety data is fully captured and reported. Their continuous oversight is crucial to maintaining the integrity of the trial, as well as the trust of both the participants and the broader medical community.

14.3 Interim Data Analysis

The process of **interim data analysis** is a key responsibility of **Data Safety Monitoring Boards (DSMBs)** during clinical trials. These analyses occur at predefined intervals throughout the trial and serve the critical function of assessing **accumulating data** to ensure that the study is progressing safely and effectively. Interim analyses are particularly important in **long-term or high-risk trials**, where early signals of safety concerns or efficacy need to be identified and acted upon promptly. DSMBs use interim analyses to decide whether the trial can continue as planned, should be modified, or even stopped early in certain cases.

During interim data analysis, DSMBs carefully review the **accumulating data** to evaluate the trial's overall safety profile and its potential therapeutic benefits. The board scrutinizes the data to determine if any **adverse events (AEs)** or **serious adverse events (SAEs)** are emerging in a pattern that suggests increased risk to participants. For example, if a clinical trial for a new cancer therapy shows an increasing number of SAEs related to **organ toxicity**, the DSMB would assess whether this risk is acceptable or if modifications to the protocol are required. At the same time, DSMBs evaluate the **quality of the data**, ensuring that it is collected consistently and accurately across all trial sites. Poor data quality can lead to unreliable conclusions, so DSMBs often make recommendations to improve data collection if inconsistencies or gaps are identified.

In addition to safety, DSMBs assess whether the trial is showing clear signs of **efficacy**. Interim analyses allow DSMBs to monitor whether the investigational product is providing any clinical benefit to the participants. This is particularly important in cases where the product shows promising early results, as it may be possible to stop the trial early due to **clear efficacy**. If the DSMB determines that the product's effectiveness is already established based on the interim data, it may recommend stopping the trial to allow the investigational product to move to the next phase of development, reducing participant exposure to unnecessary risks and accelerating the delivery of the treatment to the broader population.

Predefined stopping rules are a critical part of the interim analysis process. These rules are set before the trial begins and outline the conditions under which the DSMB has the authority to stop the trial early. Stopping rules may include **safety thresholds**, where the trial would be terminated if a certain number of participants experience severe adverse effects, or **efficacy benchmarks**, where the trial would be halted if the investigational product demonstrates clear benefits early on. For example, in a trial investigating a new treatment for a **life-threatening condition**, the DSMB may establish a stopping rule that allows the trial to be terminated if the treatment shows a significant reduction in mortality rates after a specified number of participants have been treated. Conversely, if serious safety concerns arise, such as an unexpected **high rate of adverse reactions**, the DSMB may decide to stop the trial to protect the participants from further harm.

Maintaining **data confidentiality** during interim analyses is another essential aspect of the DSMB's role. It is crucial that the interim results remain **blinded** to trial investigators and sponsors to prevent **trial bias** or **influence on the final outcomes**. If investigators or sponsors were to gain access to the interim data, it could unintentionally affect how the trial is conducted, leading to biased decision-making or protocol changes that undermine the scientific integrity of the study. Therefore, DSMBs are careful to ensure that the interim data is reviewed independently, and only the necessary decisions regarding the continuation or modification of the trial are communicated to the trial team. This process ensures that the trial remains as **objective** as possible, and the final results reflect the true safety and efficacy of the investigational product.

14.4 Risk-Benefit Assessment by DSMBs

The **risk-benefit assessment** performed by **Data Safety Monitoring Boards (DSMBs)** is a continuous and dynamic process that lies at the heart of their responsibilities in a clinical trial. Throughout the study, DSMBs must carefully evaluate whether the **potential benefits** of the investigational product outweigh the **associated risks**. This ongoing assessment is critical to ensuring that participants are not exposed to **unacceptable levels of harm**, while also determining whether the product shows sufficient therapeutic promise to justify the continuation of the trial.

DSMBs balance the **risks**, such as the occurrence of **adverse events (AEs)** or **serious adverse events (SAEs)**, with the **benefits**, which could include **positive clinical outcomes** or **improvements in participant health**. For example, in a clinical trial testing a new drug for **chronic pain relief**, the DSMB would weigh the frequency and severity of side effects, such as gastrointestinal distress or headaches, against the reported improvements in pain management. If the participants experience significant relief from chronic pain with only mild side effects, the DSMB may conclude that the benefits outweigh the risks, allowing the trial to continue. However, if the drug leads to severe adverse effects like **liver toxicity** or **cardiovascular complications**, the DSMB would need to reassess whether the potential benefits are enough to justify these risks.

To make these assessments, DSMBs rely on both **qualitative** and **quantitative data**. Qualitative data includes **clinical observations** and participant-reported outcomes, while quantitative data is drawn from **statistical analysis** of trial results, such as the incidence rates of adverse events, **mortality rates**, or **disease progression metrics**. For example, a DSMB might analyze the statistical significance of improved **survival rates** in a cancer treatment trial, comparing it to the **frequency and severity** of side effects like **nausea**, **fatigue**, or more severe complications. If the survival rates show a marked improvement over existing treatments, the DSMB may determine that the benefits justify the continuation of the trial, even if some side effects are present. On the other hand, if the data shows only a minor improvement in survival coupled with frequent severe side effects, the DSMB might recommend **modifying the trial design** to reduce risks.

DSMBs also have the authority to recommend changes to the **trial design** based on their risk-benefit assessment. This could include **adjusting dosing regimens**, **modifying inclusion criteria**, or introducing **additional safety measures** to mitigate risks. For instance, if a DSMB notices that participants in the trial are experiencing **dose-dependent toxicities**, it may recommend lowering the dose to reduce the occurrence of adverse effects while still maintaining potential therapeutic efficacy. In another example, if a trial involves a vulnerable population such as **elderly patients** or those with **comorbid conditions**, the DSMB might suggest additional monitoring protocols to ensure their safety, such as more frequent health assessments or the use of **biomarkers** to detect early signs of harm. These adjustments are crucial in optimizing participant safety without compromising the scientific validity of the trial.

The DSMB's ability to **recommend stopping the trial** is one of its most significant responsibilities. If the risk-benefit analysis reveals that the risks are too great or the benefits too minimal, the DSMB can halt the study to protect the participants. In some cases, early signs of **clear efficacy** may also lead to the recommendation to stop the trial so that the investigational product can be made available to patients more quickly. For example, if a DSMB finds that a new treatment for **a rare genetic disorder** results in rapid, significant improvement for most participants with minimal side effects, it may recommend stopping the trial early to expedite the product's development and availability.

CHAPTER FIFTEEN

Responsibilities of Sponsors, CROs, and Investigators

In the framework of clinical research, the smooth execution of trials hinges on the clear delineation of responsibilities among key stakeholders, namely sponsors, Contract Research Organizations (CROs), and investigators. Each of these entities plays a critical role in ensuring that clinical studies are conducted rigorously, ethically, and in compliance with regulatory standards. The effective collaboration and accountability of these partics are essential for the integrity of the research process and the welfare of participants.

Sponsors, often pharmaceutical or biotech companies, bear the primary responsibility for initiating and managing clinical trials. They are charged with overseeing the design and funding of studies and ensuring that they comply with regulatory and ethical standards. Their commitment to maintaining the highest standards of scientific integrity and participant safety is fundamental to the success of clinical research.

Contract Research Organizations (CROs) provide specialized services to sponsors, handling various aspects of clinical trial management. Their role is crucial in implementing the trial protocol, managing data, and ensuring compliance with regulatory requirements. The relationship between sponsors and CROs is pivotal, as it influences the quality of the trial conduct and the reliability of the data collected.

Investigators, who carry out the trial at the site level, are directly responsible for the day-to-day conduct of the study. They ensure that the research is executed according to the protocol, uphold participant safety, and adhere to ethical standards. Their role encompasses obtaining informed consent, monitoring participant well-being, and maintaining the accuracy of data collection.

In this chapter, we explore the distinct yet interconnected responsibilities of sponsors, CROs, and investigators. Understanding these roles is essential for appreciating how they contribute to the ethical and scientific conduct of clinical trials. The effectiveness of clinical research depends significantly on the clear definition of these responsibilities and the collaborative efforts of all involved parties.

15.1 Roles and Responsibilities of Sponsors

In clinical research, sponsors play a pivotal role in the successful planning, execution, and completion of clinical trials. A sponsor is typically an individual, pharmaceutical company, or organization responsible for initiating, managing, and financing the clinical trial. The sponsor's responsibilities are multifaceted, starting from the conceptualization of the study to ensuring regulatory approval, adherence to ethical guidelines, and overseeing the trial's overall conduct. They are legally accountable for ensuring that the study complies with the appropriate regulatory frameworks, such as the International Council for Harmonisation of Technical Requirements for Pharmaceuticals for Human Use Good Clinical Practice (ICH-GCP), and that the rights, safety, and well-being of the participants are protected.

One of the primary responsibilities of sponsors is financial support for the clinical trial. This includes funding for trial design, recruitment, data collection, drug manufacturing, regulatory submissions, and post-study analysis. Financial commitment in clinical trials is significant; for instance, Phase I trials can cost approximately \$1.4 to \$6.6 million, while Phase III trials, being more extensive, may exceed \$20 to \$50 million. These figures underline the substantial investment sponsors must commit to ensuring the trials are conducted efficiently and ethically. Sponsors must also allocate resources for continuous monitoring of the study, which includes site visits, audits, and interim analysis to evaluate the safety and efficacy of the drug or intervention under investigation.

The responsibility for developing and approving the clinical trial protocol rests heavily on the sponsor. The protocol serves as the trial's blueprint, outlining the study's objectives, methodology, and data analysis plan. Sponsors must ensure that the protocol is scientifically sound and aligns with regulatory requirements. This includes making any necessary amendments to the protocol during the course of the study, as unforeseen issues or deviations from the initial plan may arise. These amendments must be approved by the ethics committee and submitted to regulatory authorities for review to ensure continued compliance with ethical standards and legal requirements.

Sponsors are also responsible for the selection and oversight of Contract Research Organizations (CROs) and clinical investigators. While CROs may be hired to manage the day-to-day operations of the trial, the sponsor retains ultimate responsibility for the trial's conduct. This includes ensuring that CROs adhere to the agreed-upon contracts, which outline specific roles in patient recruitment, trial management, and data handling. In cases where the sponsor delegates trial management tasks to a CRO, they must conduct regular audits and inspections to ensure that all activities are performed in compliance with regulatory standards, and that the data generated is accurate and reliable. Furthermore, sponsors must maintain open communication with CROs and investigators, ensuring that any adverse events or serious adverse events are promptly reported and managed according to the protocol and regulatory requirements.

The sponsor's involvement extends to regulatory submissions and ensuring that all trial documentation, including investigational new drug applications (INDs), clinical study reports (CSRs), and safety reports, are completed and submitted in a timely manner. They must interact with regulatory bodies such as the FDA, EMA, and national health authorities to obtain approval before the trial can commence. The submission process can be complex and time-consuming, with the sponsor needing to navigate various regulations depending on the jurisdiction in which the trial is conducted. Failure to meet regulatory deadlines can result in significant delays in the trial and potential financial losses. Sponsors must also submit ongoing safety updates to these regulatory bodies, which include any adverse events or changes in the trial's risk-benefit profile.

Another critical responsibility of sponsors is ensuring patient safety and monitoring adverse events throughout the trial. Sponsors must establish a comprehensive risk management plan that outlines procedures for identifying, assessing, and managing risks to participants. This includes setting up data monitoring committees (DMCs) to review interim data and advise whether the trial should continue, be modified, or stopped. In the case of serious adverse events, sponsors are required to report these incidents to regulatory authorities within 24 hours, ensuring transparency and prompt action to protect participant welfare.

In addition to financial and operational responsibilities, sponsors have a legal and ethical obligation to ensure the integrity of the clinical trial data. They must implement rigorous data monitoring systems to ensure the accuracy and completeness of all data collected. This includes establishing procedures for data verification and conducting regular audits to ensure compliance with the trial protocol. Any deviations from the protocol or non-compliance with regulatory standards must be addressed immediately through corrective and preventive actions (CAPA).

The sponsor's role does not end with the conclusion of the clinical trial. Post-trial obligations include the analysis and publication of study results, submission of final reports to regulatory authorities, and, in some cases, providing post-trial access to the investigational product for participants who may benefit from continued use. Additionally, sponsors are responsible for maintaining trial records for a specified period after the trial's completion, as required by regulatory authorities. These records are crucial for future audits, inspections, or legal proceedings, ensuring that the study's conduct and results can be thoroughly reviewed if necessary.

and Ethical Obligations of Contract Research Organizations (CROs)

Contract Research Organizations (CROs) play a crucial role in the management and execution of clinical trials, often handling many of the operational responsibilities on behalf of the sponsor. The collaboration between sponsors and CROs allows for the smooth progression of clinical trials, particularly when the sponsor lacks the resources or expertise to manage all trial-related activities. However, with these responsibilities come significant legal and ethical obligations that CROs must adhere to. CROs are legally bound to follow international, national, and local regulations, as well as the ethical guidelines established by various regulatory bodies like the FDA, EMA, and ICH-GCP (International Council for Harmonisation of Technical Requirements for Pharmaceuticals for Human Use - Good Clinical Practice).

One of the primary legal obligations of a CRO is to comply with the contracts established between the sponsor and the CRO. These contracts typically outline the scope of the CRO's responsibilities, which can range from patient recruitment and clinical trial monitoring to data management and regulatory submissions. Any deviation from these contractual obligations can result in legal liabilities, financial penalties, or loss of business for the CRO. Therefore, CROs must establish robust systems to ensure that they deliver on all aspects of their contract, while simultaneously adhering to the ethical principles governing clinical trials. For instance, failure to meet data integrity standards, or delays in submitting required documents, can lead to delays in trial approvals, compromising the sponsor's ability to proceed with drug development.

Ethical conduct is paramount in clinical trials, and CROs are responsible for ensuring that all trial activities are conducted in accordance with ethical guidelines, particularly those outlined in ICH-GCP. These guidelines emphasize the importance of ensuring patient welfare and the integrity of clinical trial data. CROs must ensure that informed consent is properly obtained from all participants, which involves providing participants with clear, understandable information about the potential risks, benefits, and procedures of the trial. The ethical obligation to protect participants' rights and safety requires CROs to closely monitor the trial's progress and immediately report any adverse events to the sponsor and regulatory authorities. Failure to meet these obligations can lead to serious ethical violations, and in some cases, legal actions.

In the area of data management, CROs must ensure that all data collected during a clinical trial is accurate, complete, and securely stored. The integrity of clinical trial data is critical for ensuring that the trial's findings are valid and reliable. CROs must implement data monitoring and quality control processes to prevent errors or fraudulent data from being entered into the trial database. According to industry standards, nearly **10-15% of clinical trial data** is typically subject to source data verification (SDV) to ensure its accuracy. This process involves comparing data recorded in the trial's database to the original source documents, such as medical records or laboratory results, to verify that the information is correct. CROs must ensure that their data management systems comply with regulatory requirements, such as **21 CFR Part 11** in the United States, which governs the use of electronic records and electronic signatures in clinical trials.

Another critical responsibility of CROs is ensuring compliance with regulatory requirements for reporting safety data. CROs are often tasked with preparing and submitting regulatory documents such as **Investigational New Drug (IND)** applications, **New Drug Applications (NDAs)**, and **Clinical Study Reports (CSRs)**. These submissions must be prepared in accordance with strict regulatory guidelines, and any errors or omissions can delay the approval process, costing sponsors both time and money. For example, the average time for an NDA review by the **FDA** can range from **6 to 10 months**, and any delays in submission or responses can significantly extend this timeline. Furthermore, CROs must ensure that any serious adverse events (SAEs) or other safety concerns are promptly reported to the appropriate regulatory bodies and ethics committees. CROs must submit safety reports within the required timeframes, such as **24 hours** for serious and unexpected adverse events, to ensure that regulatory authorities are informed of any potential risks to participants.

CROs are also ethically obligated to maintain transparency in their operations and to avoid any conflicts of interest that could compromise the integrity of the trial. For example, CROs should not have a financial interest in the outcome of the trial that could influence their conduct. Ensuring transparency involves clear communication with both the sponsor and regulatory authorities, providing regular updates on the trial's progress, and reporting any deviations from the trial protocol. CROs must also ensure that their staff members are trained in the ethical conduct of clinical trials and are aware of their responsibilities in maintaining the highest standards of ethical behavior.

Finally, CROs must establish systems for handling protocol deviations, non-compliance, and other challenges that may arise during the course of the trial. This involves conducting regular audits and implementing **Corrective and Preventive Actions (CAPA)** to address any issues that could compromise the trial's integrity. Non-compliance with regulatory requirements can result in penalties, including fines or the suspension of the trial. For example, CROs operating in the European Union are subject to the **EU Clinical Trials Regulation** (Regulation (EU) No 536/2014), which outlines specific requirements for trial conduct and reporting. Failure to comply with these regulations can result in significant penalties, including the revocation of trial approvals.

15.3 Investigator Responsibilities in Conducting Clinical Trials

The role of the investigator, particularly the Principal Investigator (PI), in clinical trials is central to ensuring that the study is conducted with the highest standards of scientific and ethical rigor. Investigators are responsible for the day-to-day management of the clinical trial at their site, ensuring compliance with the trial protocol, safeguarding the welfare of participants, and ensuring the integrity of the data collected. The responsibilities of the investigator are comprehensive, encompassing various aspects of patient care, data management, regulatory compliance, and collaboration with other stakeholders such as sponsors, Contract Research Organizations (CROs), and regulatory authorities.

At the core of an investigator's responsibility is the protection of the rights, safety, and well-being of participants. This begins with obtaining

informed consent from all individuals who volunteer to participate in the clinical trial. The process of obtaining informed consent must be done with utmost care, ensuring that participants fully understand the potential risks, benefits, and procedures involved in the study. The investigator is responsible for presenting this information in a clear and understandable manner, addressing any questions or concerns participants may have. Informed consent is not a one-time event but an ongoing process, and the investigator must continue to provide relevant information to participants throughout the trial, particularly if new risks or findings emerge.

The investigator is also tasked with ensuring that the clinical trial is conducted according to the approved protocol. The trial protocol serves as the official guide for the study, outlining the objectives, design, methodology, and statistical considerations. Investigators must strictly adhere to the protocol, as deviations can compromise the validity of the trial's findings and may pose risks to participants. However, if unforeseen circumstances arise that necessitate a change in the protocol, the investigator must seek approval from the **Institutional Review Board (IRB)** or **Ethics Committee (EC)** before implementing any changes. Failure to do so can result in regulatory penalties and, more importantly, harm to participants.

In addition to protocol adherence, investigators are responsible for maintaining accurate and complete documentation throughout the trial. This includes maintaining **Case Report Forms (CRFs)**, which are used to capture data from each participant in the trial. The accuracy and completeness of CRFs are critical for the integrity of the trial's data. Investigators must ensure that all data entered into the CRFs is accurate and corresponds with the source documents, such as medical records, laboratory results, and participant questionnaires. Regulatory bodies such as the **FDA** and **EMA** require investigators to maintain these records for a certain period after the trial's completion to allow for future audits or inspections. Typically, these records must be kept for at least **two years** following the approval of a drug in the market, or longer if specified by local regulations.

Monitoring patient safety is another critical responsibility of investigators. Throughout the clinical trial, investigators must closely monitor participants for any **adverse events (AEs)**, particularly **serious adverse events (SAEs)**. An SAE is defined as any untoward medical occurrence that results in death, is life-threatening, requires hospitalization, or causes persistent or significant disability. When an SAE occurs, the investigator must immediately report it to the sponsor, IRB, and regulatory authorities, often within **24 hours**. The investigator must assess the relationship between the investigational product and the SAE to determine whether the event is likely related to the drug or other interventions in the trial. This assessment is crucial for determining whether the trial should continue, be modified, or be terminated to protect participant safety.

Investigators also play a key role in patient recruitment and ensuring that participants meet the **inclusion and exclusion criteria** outlined in the trial protocol. Proper selection of participants is essential for the validity of the trial's results, as enrolling participants who do not meet the criteria can introduce confounding variables that compromise the study's findings. Investigators must implement robust screening processes to ensure that only eligible participants are enrolled in the study. Furthermore, investigators must ensure that the trial population is diverse and representative, as regulatory bodies increasingly emphasize the importance of **diversity in clinical trials** to ensure that the results are generalizable to the broader population.

In addition to their scientific and medical responsibilities, investigators must ensure that the trial is conducted in compliance with all applicable regulatory and ethical guidelines, such as **ICH-GCP**. This includes submitting regular progress reports to the IRB and regulatory authorities, including updates on participant recruitment, adverse events, and any protocol deviations. Investigators are also required to ensure that the trial site is prepared for audits or inspections by regulatory bodies. These inspections may occur at any time during or after the trial, and investigators must ensure that all trial-related documents are readily accessible and that the trial is conducted in accordance with the protocol and regulatory requirements.

Collaboration with sponsors and CROs is another essential aspect of an investigator's role. Investigators must maintain open communication with the sponsor and CROs to ensure that any issues that arise during the trial are addressed promptly. This includes reporting any deviations from the protocol, adverse events, or other challenges that may impact the trial's progress. Investigators are also responsible for ensuring that the investigational product is stored and administered correctly, following the sponsor's instructions and maintaining proper records of drug accountability. Any discrepancies in the handling of the investigational product can lead to issues with data integrity and regulatory compliance.

The integrity of the clinical trial data is heavily dependent on the investigator's attention to detail and commitment to accuracy. Any errors or inconsistencies in the data can compromise the study's findings and result in regulatory delays or the rejection of the study's conclusions. Investigators must ensure that data collection is consistent with the protocol and that any deviations or errors are corrected promptly. In cases where a **data monitoring committee (DMC)** is involved, the investigator may be required to submit interim data to the DMC for review. The DMC is responsible for evaluating the data and making recommendations on whether the trial should continue, be modified, or stopped based on the findings.

15.4 Ensuring Compliance with Ethical Guidelines

Ensuring compliance with ethical guidelines is one of the most critical responsibilities in the conduct of clinical trials. Ethical compliance safeguards the rights, safety, and dignity of participants while also ensuring the integrity of the data generated during the study. All stakeholders, including sponsors, Contract Research Organizations (CROs), and investigators, must strictly adhere to ethical standards outlined by regulatory authorities, institutional review boards (IRBs), and international bodies such as the International Council for Harmonisation of Technical Requirements for Pharmaceuticals for Human Use - Good Clinical Practice (ICH-GCP).

Central to the ethical conduct of clinical trials is the protection of participants' rights. This begins with the informed consent process, a cornerstone of ethical compliance in research. Informed consent must be obtained from every participant before they are enrolled in the trial, ensuring that they are fully aware of the potential risks, benefits, and procedures involved. The process must be carried out in a way that allows participants to make a voluntary and informed decision, free from any coercion or undue influence. Investigators are responsible for ensuring that the informed consent form (ICF) is written in clear, simple language that the participant can easily understand. In some cases, trials involve vulnerable populations, such as children, the elderly, or individuals with cognitive impairments. In these cases, additional safeguards must be implemented to ensure their protection, such as obtaining consent from a legally authorized representative or providing extra explanations and support during the consent process.

The role of Institutional Review Boards (IRBs) and Ethics Committees (ECs) is essential in ensuring ethical compliance throughout the clinical trial. These bodies are responsible for reviewing and approving the trial protocol before it can commence, ensuring that the study is designed with participant safety in mind and that it complies with ethical standards. The IRB/EC evaluates the scientific validity of the trial, the risk-benefit ratio for participants, and the adequacy of the informed consent process. Regular review meetings are also conducted to monitor the trial's progress and assess whether any amendments to the protocol are necessary to address emerging ethical concerns or adverse events. The trial cannot proceed without IRB/EC approval, and ongoing monitoring is mandatory to ensure that all changes are documented and approved.

Another key aspect of ethical compliance is the reporting and handling of adverse events, especially serious adverse events (SAEs). Investigators and sponsors must have systems in place to monitor and report these events promptly to the IRB, sponsor, and regulatory authorities. The reporting timelines are often very strict; for instance, SAEs must typically be reported within **24 hours** of occurrence. The timely reporting of adverse events ensures that necessary actions can be taken to minimize harm to participants, such as halting the trial, adjusting the dosage, or implementing additional safety measures. Investigators are also responsible for documenting all adverse events accurately, as this data plays a crucial role in assessing the safety of the investigational product.

Ethical guidelines also emphasize the importance of transparency in clinical trials. All stakeholders must ensure that trial data is collected, analyzed, and reported honestly and without manipulation. Fabrication or falsification of data is a serious ethical violation that can lead to significant legal and regulatory consequences. Investigators must ensure that the data recorded in the case report forms (CRFs) reflects the true outcomes of the trial and that any deviations or errors are addressed promptly through corrective and preventive actions (CAPA). Audits and inspections by regulatory authorities are often conducted to verify compliance with ethical standards, and any discrepancies or non-compliance can result in trial suspension, fines, or even legal action.

Protocol adherence is another critical aspect of ensuring ethical compliance. Investigators must ensure that the trial is conducted in strict accordance with the approved protocol. Deviations from the protocol, whether intentional or accidental, can compromise the scientific validity of the trial and pose risks to participants. In cases where protocol deviations are necessary, such as changes in dosage or adjustments due to unforeseen safety concerns, investigators must seek approval from the IRB/EC before implementing these changes. Failure to obtain approval for protocol amendments can result in the trial being halted and may jeopardize the validity of the data already collected.

Compliance with Good Clinical Practice (GCP) guidelines is mandatory for all clinical trials, ensuring that trials are conducted ethically and scientifically. GCP outlines the roles and responsibilities of all parties involved in the trial, including sponsors, investigators, and CROs. It also provides detailed instructions on the conduct of the trial, from planning and protocol development to data analysis and reporting. Adherence to GCP is not only an ethical obligation but also a legal requirement in many countries. Failure to comply with GCP guidelines can lead to significant legal consequences, including fines, sanctions, or even trial termination.

Data integrity is a crucial element of ethical compliance, as the results of the trial are used to make decisions about the safety and efficacy of new treatments. Investigators must ensure that all data is collected and recorded accurately, and that any errors or discrepancies are addressed promptly. Data monitoring committees (DMCs) are often established to review interim data and ensure that the trial is progressing according to plan. These committees play a vital role in protecting participant safety by recommending trial modifications or termination if safety concerns arise. Investigators are responsible for providing accurate and timely data to the DMC and for implementing any recommendations made by the committee.

Finally, the ethical treatment of participants after the trial is completed is an often overlooked but important responsibility. Once the trial is concluded, investigators must ensure that participants are provided with appropriate follow-up care, especially if the investigational product has caused any adverse effects. In some cases, participants may benefit from continued access to the investigational product after the trial, particularly if it has shown significant therapeutic potential. Investigators and sponsors must work together to develop post-trial access plans, ensuring that participants are not abandoned after the trial's conclusion.

CHAPTER SIXTEEN

Informed Consent in Clinical Research

In clinical research, informed consent stands as a fundamental ethical and legal requirement, ensuring that participants voluntarily agree to participate in a study with full awareness of its scope, risks, and benefits. This chapter delves into the principles and practices surrounding informed consent, a crucial process that upholds the autonomy and rights of research participants.

Informed consent is not merely a formality but a dynamic and ongoing process that begins with clear and comprehensive communication between the research team and the potential participants. This chapter examines the essential components of informed consent, emphasizing the need for transparency and clarity in presenting information. Each component plays a role in ensuring that participants are well-informed and able to make decisions that align with their values and understanding.

The patient information sheet and the informed consent form are critical documents in this process. These documents must convey detailed information about the study in a manner that is accessible and understandable to participants. They serve as key tools in documenting the participant's understanding and willingness to participate in the research.

The informed consent process itself is a crucial aspect of clinical trials, involving not just the initial agreement but also continuous dialogue and re-evaluation throughout the study. Researchers must ensure that participants fully comprehend the information provided and that their consent is freely given without coercion or undue influence.

Documentation and ethical safeguards are integral to maintaining the integrity of the informed consent process. Accurate documentation provides evidence of the consent process and helps in upholding ethical standards in research. Safeguards ensure that participants' rights are protected and that the consent process is conducted in accordance with regulatory and ethical guidelines.

This chapter provides a comprehensive overview of the informed consent process, highlighting the importance of each component and the need for meticulous attention to ethical standards. Understanding these elements is essential for conducting research that respects participant autonomy and maintains the highest ethical standards.

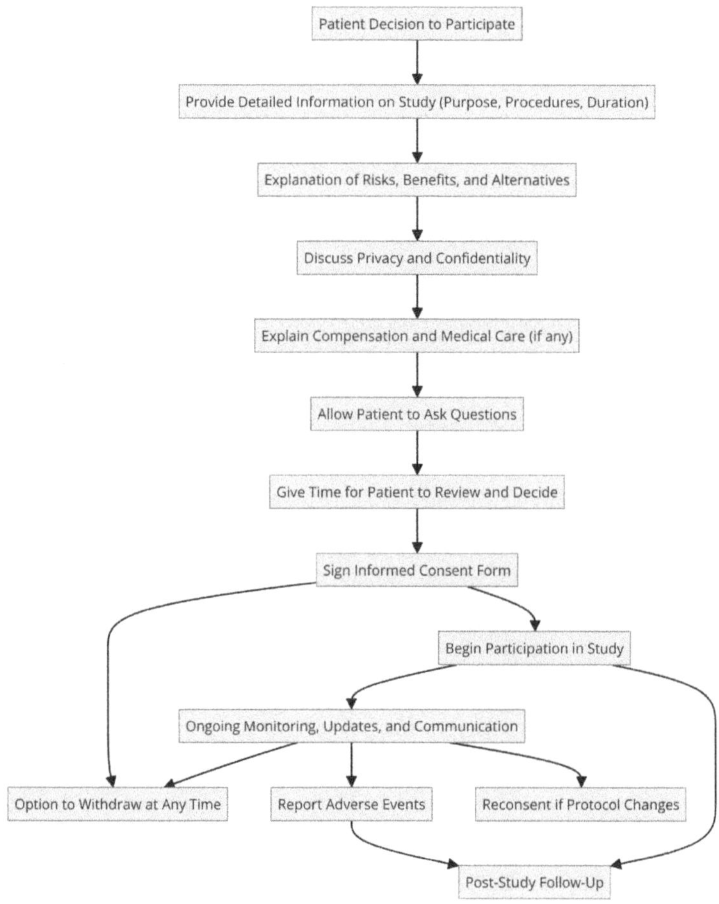

Flowchart illustrating the Informed Consent Process

16.1 Components of Informed Consent

Informed consent is a fundamental aspect of clinical research, acting as both a legal and ethical safeguard for participants. The principle of informed consent ensures that individuals are fully aware of what participation in a clinical trial involves, enabling them to make an educated decision about whether to take part. In clinical research, participants are often exposed to investigational products or procedures that may carry risks, and informed consent ensures they understand these risks along with the potential benefits. Informed consent is not merely a formality but a key process in protecting participants' autonomy, ensuring that they enter into the study voluntarily and with full knowledge of the study's purpose, procedures, and potential outcomes.

The key components of informed consent include several vital elements that help provide participants with a clear understanding of the clinical trial. First, the study must be clearly described, including its purpose, objectives, and the rationale for why it is being conducted. This helps participants understand the larger context of the research and what contribution their involvement will make to medical knowledge. The potential risks and benefits must also be clearly communicated. Risks can include side effects, discomfort, or potential harm, while benefits might range from direct health improvements for the participant to the advancement of medical science. Participants must be aware that not all studies provide direct therapeutic benefits, and in some cases, the risks may outweigh any potential benefits. Additionally, the consent process should include a discussion of alternative treatments that might be available outside of the study. Participants should know they are free to pursue other treatment options, which may offer similar or better outcomes without the risks associated with an experimental intervention.

The procedures involved in the study, such as medical tests, blood draws, or follow-up visits, must also be explained in detail. Participants need to know what is expected of them, the time commitment involved, and any potential discomfort they might experience. One of the most crucial elements of informed consent is the participant's right to withdraw from the study at any time. Participants should understand that their decision to withdraw will not affect the standard of care they receive or their relationship with their healthcare providers. Confidentiality agreements must also be clearly outlined, assuring participants that their personal and medical information will be protected and used only in accordance with ethical guidelines and regulatory requirements.

Regulatory guidelines such as those outlined in **ICH-GCP (International Council for Harmonisation - Good Clinical Practice)** provide a framework for informed consent in clinical trials. According to ICH-GCP, informed consent must cover all key elements, including the trial's purpose, risks, benefits, and procedures. It must be presented in a manner that is understandable to the participant. Regulatory agencies such as the **FDA** and **EMA** monitor adherence to these guidelines, often conducting inspections and audits to ensure compliance. Non-compliance with informed consent regulations can lead to severe legal consequences, including fines, trial suspension, or even trial termination. Data from regulatory audits show that **20-30% of trial deficiencies** are related to inadequate informed consent documentation or processes, underlining the importance of following these guidelines strictly.

Informed consent must be tailored to specific populations to ensure that all participants, regardless of their background, can understand and consent to the study. This is particularly important when dealing with vulnerable populations such as children, pregnant women, or individuals with cognitive impairments. For example, in pediatric research, the consent process involves obtaining **assent** from the child, where appropriate, and **consent** from the parent or legal guardian. Special consideration must be given to the language and presentation of the information to ensure it is accessible to both the child and the guardian. Similarly, for pregnant women, the risks to both the mother and fetus must be clearly explained, as well as the potential impact of participation on the pregnancy. Vulnerable populations require additional protections to ensure that their participation is voluntary and that they are not subject to undue influence or coercion. Real-world examples from trials involving these groups show that tailoring the informed consent process can significantly improve understanding and reduce the risk of ethical violations. For instance, trials in **India** and **Sub-Saharan Africa** involving pregnant women have shown that carefully designed consent materials that consider cultural and educational backgrounds greatly increase participant comprehension.

16.2 Patient Information Sheet and Informed Consent Form

The **Patient Information Sheet (PIS)** plays a critical role in the informed consent process by providing participants with comprehensive and detailed information about the clinical trial. The purpose of the PIS is to serve as an educational tool that helps participants fully understand the trial before they decide to participate. It goes beyond the basic explanation provided in the informed consent form (ICF) by elaborating on the study's purpose, design, and potential impact on participants. The PIS ensures that participants have access to all the necessary information in a clear and concise format, empowering them to make an informed decision. The primary difference between the PIS and the ICF lies in their functions: while the PIS is intended to educate and inform, the ICF is the legal document that records the participant's voluntary agreement to take part in the study. The PIS is often presented to the participant first, allowing them to review the trial details at their own pace, ask questions, and clarify any concerns before signing the ICF.

A well-structured **Patient Information Sheet** should include several essential elements to provide participants with a thorough understanding of the trial. These elements typically include the **background of the study**, explaining why the research is being conducted and its potential contribution to medical knowledge. The **purpose of the research** should be clearly outlined, indicating the study's objectives and how the investigational product or intervention is expected to work. The PIS should also include information on the **duration** of the trial, giving participants an idea of how long they will be involved, and the **number of participants** expected to take part in the study, which can help them understand the scale of the research. Additionally, the PIS should provide a **description of the procedures** involved in the trial, such as medical tests, blood draws, or visits to the clinic. Participants should also be made aware of any **potential risks** they may encounter, such as side effects or discomfort, as well as the **expected benefits**, whether direct (to the participant) or indirect (to future patients or scientific advancement). An example of a well-structured PIS can be seen in trials for vaccines, where the PIS outlines not only the standard risks of vaccination but also the broader public health benefits. In one real-world case, a PIS used during a COVID-19 vaccine trial included clear and accessible explanations of both immediate side effects and long-term monitoring plans, which helped improve participant understanding and trust in the trial.

The **Informed Consent Form (ICF)**, on the other hand, is a legal document that records the participant's decision to take part in the clinical trial. Unlike the PIS, which serves to inform, the ICF is a binding agreement that must meet specific regulatory requirements to ensure it is compliant with international guidelines such as **ICH-GCP**. The ICF must include several mandatory fields, starting with the **date** the consent was given and the **signature** of the participant to confirm their voluntary participation. In many cases, a **witness** signature is also required, particularly in situations where the participant may have limited literacy or the trial involves vulnerable populations. The ICF must also include **version control** to ensure that the most current version of the document is being used, particularly when amendments are made to the trial protocol. Data from regulatory audits often reveal that incomplete or improperly filled ICFs are among the most common causes of compliance issues. For example, a **2019 audit by the FDA** found that nearly **30% of inspected clinical trial sites** had deficiencies related to the informed consent process, often because key information such as the date of consent or witness signatures were missing.

Both the PIS and the ICF must adhere to strict **language and readability standards** to ensure that all participants, regardless of their education level or background, can fully understand the content. International guidelines recommend that the language used in these documents should not exceed an **8th-grade reading level**, ensuring accessibility for a wide range of participants. This is particularly important in regions with low literacy rates, where complex medical jargon may prevent participants from comprehending the risks and procedures involved. For instance, in some rural parts of India, where literacy rates are below **75%**, studies have shown that simplifying the language used in consent forms has led to improved comprehension and participation rates. When the language is too complex, participants may feel confused or hesitant to join the trial, which can undermine both the ethical and scientific validity of the study. Therefore, it is crucial to balance the need for thorough information with the requirement that the documents remain accessible and easy to understand.

In conclusion, the **Patient Information Sheet** and **Informed Consent Form** are integral to the informed consent process, each serving distinct but complementary roles. The PIS provides participants with detailed information about the clinical trial in an educational format, while the ICF is the formal agreement to participate, meeting specific regulatory standards. Both documents must be written in simple, clear language to ensure that participants can make informed, voluntary decisions, particularly in regions with low literacy or vulnerable populations. By adhering to these guidelines, clinical trials can uphold the ethical standards required for participant protection and data integrity.

16.3 The Informed Consent Process

The informed consent process is an interactive and ongoing engagement between the investigator or trial staff and the participant, ensuring that participants fully understand the clinical trial at every stage. Informed consent is not a single event; rather, it is a continuous process of communication, clarification, and affirmation. At the heart of this process is the commitment to participant autonomy, ensuring that individuals have the opportunity to ask questions, seek further information, and reconsider their involvement as new information becomes available. The role of the investigator or trial staff is crucial in facilitating this dialogue, as they are responsible for explaining the study's details, procedures, and risks in a manner that is easily understandable. This ongoing communication helps to build trust between the participants and the research team, reducing potential misunderstandings and ensuring that participants are comfortable with their decision to participate.

The timing and location of the informed consent process are also critical factors in ensuring that participants are given ample opportunity to make informed decisions. Informed consent must be obtained before any trial-related procedures are conducted, and participants should never feel rushed or pressured to sign the consent form. Ideally, the consent process should take place in a setting that allows for privacy and uninterrupted discussions, giving participants time to consider the information provided and consult with family members or trusted individuals if necessary. Providing adequate time is especially important in studies involving complex procedures or high-risk interventions, where participants need to thoroughly understand the implications of their involvement. Regulatory bodies like the **FDA** and **EMA** emphasize the importance of obtaining consent in a setting that encourages open communication and thoughtful decision-making, ensuring that the participant's consent is fully informed and voluntary.

Documenting the participant's understanding is a key responsibility of the investigator. It is not enough to simply present the information and obtain a signature; the investigator must confirm that the participant genuinely understands the trial's risks, benefits, and procedures. This can be done through follow-up questions, discussions, or even quizzes designed to test comprehension. For example, in some studies, participants are asked to explain key aspects of the trial in their own words to demonstrate their understanding. Data from clinical trials show that failure to confirm participant understanding can lead to ethical breaches and adverse outcomes. In one study, it was found that **25% of participants** in a high-risk drug trial did not fully understand the potential side effects they might experience, leading to confusion and distress when these effects occurred. Such situations underscore the importance of ensuring comprehension, as participants cannot make truly informed decisions without a clear understanding of the study.

Voluntariness is another cornerstone of the informed consent process, and participants must be made aware that their participation is entirely voluntary. Regulatory guidelines, including those set forth by **ICH-GCP**, mandate that participants have the right to withdraw from the study at any time without penalty. This right must be clearly communicated during the initial consent process and throughout the trial, ensuring that participants feel empowered to make decisions about their involvement. Investigators are responsible for documenting any withdrawals and ensuring that participants understand they are not obligated to stay in the study. This is especially important in long-term studies, where participants may experience changes in their health or personal circumstances that influence their ability or desire to continue.

Re-consent is a critical part of the informed consent process, particularly in situations where there are significant changes to the trial protocol or new risks are identified. If the study duration extends beyond the original timeframe, or if additional data emerge that may affect participant safety, investigators must revisit the consent process and inform participants of these updates. Re-consent involves providing participants with updated information and obtaining their consent again, ensuring they are fully aware of any new developments that may impact their decision to continue. For example, in studies where unexpected side effects are identified during the trial, investigators must immediately inform participants and allow them to reassess their involvement. Re-consent is also required if there are substantial changes to the trial procedures or if the inclusion of new data significantly alters the risk-benefit ratio of the study.

In conclusion, the informed consent process is an interactive, ongoing, and dynamic part of clinical research, aimed at protecting participant autonomy and ensuring their safety. By emphasizing continuous communication, confirming participant understanding, respecting voluntariness, and implementing re-consent when necessary, investigators can maintain ethical standards throughout the trial. These measures are essential in ensuring that clinical trials are conducted with the highest degree of respect for participants' rights and well-being.

16.4 Documentation and Ethical Safeguards

Maintaining proper documentation of informed consent is a critical aspect of ensuring compliance with ethical standards in clinical research. Each participant's signed informed consent form must be securely stored and easily retrievable for regulatory inspections and audits. These records must include not only the participant's signature but also the date of consent, as well as any updates or amendments to the consent process over the course of the trial. Proper documentation helps create a clear audit trail, demonstrating that participants were fully informed before agreeing to participate and that their consent was obtained in accordance with regulatory requirements. Failure to maintain adequate documentation can lead to serious consequences, including trial suspensions or legal penalties. For example, in a 2018 FDA audit, several trials were flagged for non-compliance due to incomplete or missing informed consent records, resulting in the suspension of two ongoing studies. Such cases highlight the importance of meticulous record-keeping as part of the ethical obligations of investigators and sponsors.

The role of the **Institutional Review Board (IRB)** or **Ethics Committee** is central to overseeing the informed consent process. These bodies are responsible for reviewing the consent documents, ensuring they meet ethical standards, and confirming that they are presented in a manner that is understandable to participants. The IRB/EC evaluates whether the language used is clear, whether risks are adequately described, and whether participants are fully informed of their rights, including the right to withdraw at any time. In addition to the initial review, the IRB/EC also provides ongoing oversight throughout the trial. Investigators are required to submit periodic updates to the IRB, especially if there are changes in the consent process or new risks emerge that may affect participants. For example, if the trial protocol is amended or new data about adverse events become available, the IRB must review and approve updated consent forms to ensure continued ethical compliance. This ensures that participants are kept fully informed at all stages of the trial and that their rights are protected.

Handling participant complaints or concerns regarding the informed consent process is another important responsibility of investigators. Clear channels of communication must be established so that participants can voice their concerns or report misunderstandings related to the trial. It is essential that participants feel comfortable raising issues without fear of repercussions, and that their concerns are addressed promptly and transparently. Investigators must ensure that any issues related to misrepresentation, lack of clarity, or misunderstanding in the informed consent process are resolved quickly to prevent ethical breaches. Providing participants with contact information for both the trial team and the IRB/EC is a common practice to facilitate communication. In some cases, unresolved complaints can lead to regulatory reviews or audits, especially if there is evidence that participants were not adequately informed or felt pressured to consent. Addressing these concerns early helps maintain trust between participants and researchers and upholds the ethical integrity of the trial.

Ethical compliance with the informed consent process is subject to regular monitoring and audits by regulatory agencies, such as the **FDA** and the **European Medicines Agency (EMA)**. These audits often focus on ensuring that informed consent documentation is complete, accurate, and up-to-date. Agencies typically check for key elements, such as whether the consent form includes all required information (e.g., description of risks, benefits, and procedures), whether it is signed and dated, and whether there is clear evidence that participants were given sufficient time to consider their decision. In many audits, **informed consent forms** are among the most scrutinized documents. A 2020 EMA report indicated that **25% of clinical trial audit findings** were related to deficiencies in informed consent documentation, including missing signatures, incomplete information about risks, and failure to update consent forms when the trial protocol was amended. These audits help ensure that clinical trials meet the ethical standards required to protect participants and uphold the integrity of the research process. Non-compliance can lead to penalties, including trial delays, fines, or termination.

CHAPTER SEVENTEEN

Clinical Research Regulations in India

In India, the landscape of clinical research is shaped by a complex framework of regulations designed to ensure the safety, efficacy, and ethical conduct of studies. This chapter provides a detailed examination of the regulatory environment governing clinical research in India, focusing on key regulations and oversight mechanisms that guide the conduct of clinical trials.

The regulatory framework is primarily outlined in Schedule Y of the Drugs and Cosmetics Act. This comprehensive guideline establishes the requirements for conducting clinical trials, including the process for obtaining regulatory approval, the responsibilities of trial sponsors, and the ethical standards that must be upheld. Understanding Schedule Y is crucial for navigating the regulatory landscape and ensuring compliance with national standards.

The regulatory approval process for clinical trials in India involves multiple steps, each designed to ensure that research is conducted ethically and that participants' rights are protected. This process includes the submission of detailed protocols, obtaining approvals from ethics committees, and fulfilling the requirements set forth by regulatory authorities. Familiarity with these steps is essential for researchers and sponsors to efficiently and effectively navigate the regulatory pathways.

In addition to drug trials, the guidance for medical devices in India outlines specific regulatory requirements for the development and approval of medical devices. This section addresses the distinct regulatory processes for medical devices, including the submission of clinical data, safety evaluations, and compliance with standards set by the regulatory authorities.

The Central Drugs Standard Control Organization (CDSCO) plays a pivotal role in the oversight and regulation of clinical research in India. The CDSCO is responsible for the implementation of regulatory guidelines, review of clinical trial applications, and enforcement of compliance with the Drugs and Cosmetics Act. Understanding the role of the CDSCO is crucial for researchers, sponsors, and other stakeholders involved in clinical research.

This chapter provides a thorough overview of the regulatory framework governing clinical research in India, offering insights into the key regulations, approval processes, and oversight mechanisms. By understanding these elements, stakeholders can ensure that their research practices align with regulatory requirements and uphold the highest standards of ethical conduct.

17.1 Overview of Schedule Y of the Drugs and Cosmetics Act

Schedule Y of India's **Drugs and Cosmetics Act** is a crucial regulatory framework governing clinical trials for new drugs, biologicals, and medical devices in India. Its primary purpose is to ensure that clinical trials are conducted in a manner that prioritizes participant safety and adheres to ethical standards. Clinical trials are essential for determining the safety and efficacy of new therapeutic interventions, and Schedule Y outlines the requirements for conducting these trials in compliance with both national and international guidelines. The introduction of Schedule Y was a significant step in aligning India's clinical research regulations with global standards, ensuring that clinical trials conducted in India are accepted and recognized internationally. Its provisions focus on safeguarding the rights, safety, and well-being of participants, while also ensuring that trial results are scientifically valid and ethically obtained.

One of the key provisions of Schedule Y is the requirement for clinical trial approval by the **Central Drugs Standard Control Organization (CDSCO)** before the commencement of any study. The sponsor of the trial must submit detailed documentation, including the trial protocol, investigator qualifications, and participant consent forms, for review. This documentation must demonstrate that the trial has been designed with participant safety in mind and that all potential risks and benefits have been carefully considered. Schedule Y also outlines the responsibilities of investigators, requiring them to adhere to **Good Clinical Practice (GCP)** guidelines, which are integrated into the framework of Schedule Y. Investigators must ensure that trials are conducted in accordance with the approved protocol and that any adverse events are promptly reported to regulatory authorities. The emphasis on adverse event reporting ensures that participant safety is continuously monitored, and any unexpected side effects are addressed in a timely manner. The reporting of **serious adverse events (SAEs)** within **24 hours** is mandatory, reflecting the priority placed on participant protection. Furthermore, Schedule Y includes provisions for the ethical review of clinical trials by **Institutional Review Boards (IRBs)** or **Ethics Committees (ECs)**, which play a critical role in overseeing the informed consent process and ensuring that the trial meets ethical standards.

Schedule Y categorizes clinical trials into **four phases**, each with specific requirements and objectives. **Phase I** trials, also known as first-in-human studies, involve a small number of participants and focus on evaluating the safety and pharmacokinetics of the drug. These trials typically take **6–12 months** to complete and involve around **20–100 participants**. **Phase II** trials expand the participant pool to around **100–300 individuals** and assess the drug's efficacy in treating the targeted condition, alongside continued safety monitoring. These trials usually last **1–2 years**. **Phase III** trials are large-scale studies that include **1,000–3,000 participants** and are designed to confirm the drug's efficacy and monitor for rare or long-term side effects. These trials are critical for the drug's approval and can take up to **3–5 years** to complete. **Phase IV**, or post-marketing studies, occur after the drug has been approved and is available to the public. These trials provide additional data on long-term safety and effectiveness. Schedule Y emphasizes participant safety at every phase, requiring continuous monitoring and periodic safety updates to ensure that the risk-benefit profile remains favorable as the trial progresses. Data from regulatory reviews show that trials adhering to Schedule Y's requirements for each phase result in more robust safety and efficacy data, leading to smoother approval processes both in India and abroad.

Since its introduction, Schedule Y has undergone several amendments to keep pace with advancements in clinical research and to align with evolving international standards. One of the most significant amendments was made in **2005**, when Schedule Y was revised to more closely align with the **International Council for Harmonisation of Technical Requirements for Pharmaceuticals for Human Use (ICH)** guidelines, particularly in relation to GCP. This amendment made it mandatory for all clinical trials in India to adhere to internationally recognized standards, facilitating the acceptance of Indian clinical trial data by global regulatory agencies such as the **U.S. FDA** and **EMA**. Another notable amendment was the introduction of stricter requirements for **ethics committee registration** and oversight, which enhanced the protection of participants in clinical trials. Real-world examples of successful clinical trials conducted under Schedule Y demonstrate the framework's effectiveness. For instance, several global pharmaceutical companies have conducted large-scale trials in India that complied with Schedule Y, leading to the global approval of drugs for conditions such as **diabetes** and **cancer**. These trials were praised for their rigorous adherence to safety standards and ethical oversight, which ensured the timely approval of the drugs both in India and internationally.

17.2 Regulatory Approval Process for Clinical Trials in India

The process of obtaining approval to conduct a clinical trial in India involves several regulatory steps that are designed to ensure participant safety, ethical compliance, and scientific integrity. The sponsor, typically a pharmaceutical company or research institution, is required to submit a comprehensive application to the **Central Drugs Standard Control Organization (CDSCO)**, which is the primary regulatory body overseeing clinical trials in India. The application begins with the submission of **Form 44**, which is the official request for permission to conduct a clinical trial. This form must be accompanied by extensive documentation that outlines every aspect of the proposed study. Key documents include the **trial protocol**, which details the study design, methodology, and endpoints; the **investigator brochures**, which provide information on the investigational product, including preclinical and clinical data; and the **informed consent forms**, which explain the trial procedures, risks, and benefits to participants. In addition to these documents, sponsors must also submit information on the qualifications of the investigators, site facilities, and a risk assessment of the trial. These detailed submissions ensure that the CDSCO has all necessary information to evaluate the scientific and ethical soundness of the proposed trial before granting approval.

Once the application is submitted, the next critical step is the **Ethics Committee (EC) review**. Ethics Committees play a pivotal role in the regulatory approval process by reviewing the clinical trial from an ethical standpoint, ensuring that participant rights are protected and that the trial complies with the principles of **Good Clinical Practice (GCP)**. These committees are composed of experts from various fields, including medicine, law, and ethics, as well as laypersons who represent the interests of the public. The EC's primary focus is on the **informed consent process**, ensuring that participants are provided with clear, comprehensive information about the study and that their consent is obtained voluntarily without coercion. The committee also evaluates **patient safety** measures, such as the procedures for monitoring adverse events, and the **confidentiality** of participant data. Typically, the EC review process takes between **30 to 60 days**, though this can vary depending on the complexity of the trial and the committee's workload. During this time, the EC may request revisions to the trial documents or additional clarifications from the sponsor before granting approval.

Following the Ethics Committee's review, the **Drug Controller General of India (DCGI)**, operating under the CDSCO, is responsible for granting the final approval for the clinical trial. The DCGI evaluates the trial based on the data provided in the application, as well as the recommendations from the Ethics Committee. The approval process at this stage typically takes between **60 to 90 days**, although it may take longer if the trial involves complex investigational products, such as biologicals or novel therapies. Several factors can expedite the approval process, including the trial being for drugs that address urgent public health needs or involve products with significant prior data from global clinical trials. Conversely, delays may occur if the trial raises significant safety concerns or if additional documentation is required. The DCGI may also impose conditions on the trial approval, such as the requirement to submit interim safety reports or to limit participant enrollment until more data on the drug's safety is available.

Once the trial receives final approval, the sponsor is required to follow stringent **post-approval monitoring** protocols to ensure ongoing compliance with **Schedule Y**. This includes submitting **periodic safety updates** to the CDSCO, which report on the progress of the trial and any emerging safety data. These updates are typically required every **six months**, although the frequency may increase if there are concerns about the safety profile of the investigational product. The CDSCO also conducts **inspections** of clinical trial sites to ensure that the trial is being conducted in accordance with the approved protocol and GCP guidelines. During these inspections, the CDSCO reviews the trial's documentation, participant records, and investigational product handling procedures. Any deviations from the protocol or instances of non-compliance are documented and must be corrected by the sponsor or investigator. Additionally, sponsors are required to report **serious adverse events (SAEs)** within **24 hours** of occurrence. These reports must be submitted to the CDSCO, the DCGI, and the Ethics Committee to ensure that prompt action is taken if the investigational product poses unforeseen risks to participants. In some cases, the occurrence of SAEs may lead to the suspension or modification of the trial until further safety assessments can be conducted.

17.3 Medical Device Guidance in India

India's medical device regulations are governed by the **Medical Device Rules, 2017**, which were implemented to streamline the regulation of medical devices and align with global standards. Unlike pharmaceuticals, which involve drug trials primarily to assess efficacy and safety, medical device trials must also account for the mechanical and functional aspects of the devices. The Medical Device Rules categorize devices into four classes—**Class A, B, C, and D**—based on their risk levels. **Class A** devices are considered low-risk, such as surgical gloves, while **Class D** devices are high-risk, including pacemakers and heart valves. This classification determines the level of regulatory scrutiny required, with higher-risk devices needing more extensive evaluation. The regulation of medical devices is complex due to the diversity of devices, which range from simple tools like bandages to sophisticated technologies such as MRI scanners. These devices must undergo stringent testing to ensure they meet safety and performance standards, considering their potential impact on patient health.

For clinical trials of medical devices, the approval process follows a structured pathway defined by the Medical Device Rules. Sponsors must submit an application through **Form MD-14** to the **Central Drugs Standard Control Organization (CDSCO)**, seeking permission to conduct the trial. The documentation required for submission is comprehensive and includes the clinical investigation plan, preclinical data, details about the device's design and manufacturing, and information on the investigators involved. In addition, sponsors must adhere to the **Good Clinical Practice for Medical Devices (GCPMD)** guidelines, which ensure that trials are conducted ethically and scientifically. These guidelines emphasize the need for well-designed protocols, rigorous participant monitoring, and accurate data collection to ensure the trial's outcomes are valid. Following approval, medical device trials in India proceed similarly to drug trials, with safety and efficacy being the primary focus, although the functional and mechanical aspects of the device are also critically assessed. The duration of approval for medical device trials can vary, but it typically takes **6 to 9**

months for higher-risk devices (Class C and D) due to the need for more detailed evaluations.

One of the unique aspects of medical device trials in India is the emphasis on **post-market surveillance** and **real-world data collection**. Even after a medical device has been approved for use, manufacturers are required to monitor its performance in the market to identify any long-term safety issues or device failures. Post-market surveillance involves continuous monitoring of adverse events and user feedback, ensuring that any unforeseen complications are addressed promptly. This is particularly important for devices that interact directly with critical body functions, such as heart stents or artificial joints. In addition, medical device trials often involve collecting **real-world evidence (RWE)** to assess how the device performs in a broader population outside the controlled environment of a clinical trial. This has become increasingly important in India, where diverse population groups present unique challenges for medical device performance. Between **2018 and 2022**, over **500 medical devices** were approved under the Medical Device Rules, reflecting a growing focus on ensuring that devices meet high safety and quality standards. Notably, trials involving advanced medical technologies, such as robotic surgical systems and artificial intelligence-powered diagnostic tools, have gained prominence, showing the evolving landscape of medical device research in the country.

Despite significant advancements, there are challenges in the approval and regulation of medical devices in India. One of the main challenges is the **delay in approval timelines**, especially for high-risk devices, which can sometimes take longer than expected due to the complexity of the evaluations required. Inconsistent enforcement of guidelines is another issue, as not all regulatory bodies have the same capacity or resources to ensure that medical device trials are conducted uniformly across different regions. Additionally, there is often a lack of clarity in the classification of devices, particularly for novel or hybrid technologies that do not fit neatly into the existing categories. These challenges create hurdles for manufacturers trying to bring innovative devices to market in a timely manner. However, there are also significant opportunities to improve the regulatory framework. Streamlining the approval process by adopting **electronic submissions** and creating a centralized database for medical device trials could reduce delays and improve transparency. Furthermore, enhancing **regulatory capacity** through better training and more resources for inspectors and reviewers would help ensure that devices are evaluated consistently and efficiently. With these improvements, India has the potential to become a leading hub for medical device innovation and research.

17.4 Role of Central Drugs Standard Control Organization (CDSCO)

The **Central Drugs Standard Control Organization (CDSCO)** serves as the national regulatory authority in India responsible for overseeing clinical trials, drug approvals, and medical device regulation. Operating under the **Ministry of Health and Family Welfare**, CDSCO ensures that pharmaceuticals, medical devices, and clinical research activities conducted in India meet established safety, efficacy, and quality standards. As the primary body governing the country's drug and device regulation, CDSCO plays a critical role in protecting public health by ensuring that all therapeutic products entering the market are backed by rigorous scientific data and comply with ethical standards. Over the years, CDSCO has expanded its regulatory purview, incorporating evolving international guidelines and best practices to strengthen its oversight of India's growing pharmaceutical and medical device industries. With India becoming a key player in global clinical research, CDSCO's role in harmonizing domestic regulations with global standards is increasingly important, ensuring that clinical trial data generated in India is accepted worldwide.

One of CDSCO's primary responsibilities is the **evaluation of clinical trial applications**. Before any clinical trial can be conducted in India, the sponsor must submit a detailed application to CDSCO, which includes the trial protocol, investigator qualifications, and ethical approvals from Institutional Review Boards (IRBs). CDSCO evaluates these applications to ensure that the proposed trial design meets the scientific and ethical requirements outlined in **Schedule Y** of the **Drugs and Cosmetics Act**. In addition to trial approvals, CDSCO is responsible for **granting marketing approvals** for new drugs and medical devices. This process involves a thorough review of clinical trial data to confirm that the investigational product is safe and effective for its intended use. CDSCO also monitors **adverse events** that occur during trials, ensuring that any unexpected risks are promptly addressed to protect participants. Moreover, CDSCO conducts **inspections of clinical trial sites** to ensure that trials are being conducted according to **Good Clinical Practice (GCP)** guidelines. These inspections involve reviewing participant records, monitoring protocols, and investigational product handling practices to verify compliance with regulatory standards. On average, CDSCO approves between **350 to 400 clinical trials per year**, reflecting the country's significant involvement in global clinical research. CDSCO's role in conducting site inspections and enforcing safety reporting requirements helps maintain the integrity of clinical trials conducted in India.

In terms of **drug approvals**, CDSCO evaluates the safety and efficacy of new drugs before they are approved for marketing in India. This evaluation is based on the comprehensive review of **clinical study reports** generated from preclinical and clinical trials, which provide detailed information on the drug's pharmacodynamics, pharmacokinetics, and therapeutic benefits. The organization's expert committees assess whether the data supports the product's intended use and ensures that the risk-benefit profile is favorable. For new drug applications (NDAs), CDSCO requires data from **Phase I to Phase III clinical trials**, which must demonstrate that the drug is safe for human use and effective in treating the targeted condition. Additionally, CDSCO ensures that these trials meet both **Indian** and **international standards** before granting approval. This alignment with global standards is particularly important as India becomes a hub for global drug development, with many multinational companies conducting trials in the country. CDSCO's stringent review process is designed to protect public health by ensuring that drugs meet rigorous safety criteria before reaching the market.

International collaboration is another key aspect of CDSCO's regulatory efforts. In recent years, CDSCO has worked closely with international regulatory agencies such as the **World Health Organization (WHO)** and the **U.S. Food and Drug Administration (FDA)** to harmonize India's clinical trial regulations with global best practices. This collaboration helps ensure that Indian clinical trial data is recognized globally, allowing drugs and medical devices developed in India to be marketed internationally. CDSCO is also actively involved in the **International Council for Harmonisation (ICH)**, particularly in promoting adherence to **ICH-GCP** guidelines, which provide a unified standard for the ethical and scientific quality of clinical trials. By aligning with the ICH-GCP guidelines, CDSCO ensures that clinical trials conducted in India are accepted by regulatory authorities in other countries, thereby facilitating the global approval of Indian-manufactured drugs. One example of CDSCO's successful collaboration with international agencies is its participation in WHO's **prequalification program**, which has helped several Indian pharmaceutical companies gain international recognition for their products. Through these partnerships, CDSCO continues to enhance its regulatory framework, ensuring that India's clinical research and drug approval processes are both globally competitive and locally robust.

CHAPTER EIGHTEEN

Clinical Research Regulations in the USA

Introduction

The regulatory framework for clinical research in the United States is pivotal in ensuring the safety, efficacy, and ethical conduct of medical trials. The Food and Drug Administration (FDA) oversees this landscape, establishing guidelines that govern the approval of new drugs, the conduct of clinical trials, and the use of data in regulatory submissions. Understanding these regulations is essential for researchers, sponsors, and stakeholders involved in clinical research, as they set the standards for compliance and ethical practices in the development of new therapies.

This chapter focuses on key regulatory mechanisms, starting with an overview of the **New Drug Application (NDA)** process. The NDA 505(b)(1) pathway outlines the requirements for submitting applications for new drugs, emphasizing the data needed to demonstrate safety and effectiveness. This section will provide insights into the rigorous evaluation process that new drug applications undergo before receiving FDA approval.

Following this, we will explore **NDA 505(b)(2)** applications, which allow for submissions based on existing data. This pathway provides flexibility for drug developers by enabling them to leverage previously conducted studies and published literature, facilitating the approval process for drugs that may not fit neatly into traditional NDA requirements.

The chapter will also address **Abbreviated New Drug Applications (ANDA 505(j))**, which are critical for the approval of generic medications. This section will detail how generic drugs can be brought to market through a streamlined process that relies on the safety and efficacy data of reference products, promoting competition and accessibility in the pharmaceutical market.

Another important aspect covered in this chapter is the FDA's guidance for industry regarding the **acceptance of foreign clinical studies**. This guidance outlines the criteria under which data from international trials can be accepted for regulatory submissions in the U.S., thereby expanding the scope of clinical research and collaboration.

Lastly, we will examine **Good Clinical Practice (GCP)** regulations in the USA, which establish the ethical and scientific quality standards for designing, conducting, and reporting clinical trials. Understanding GCP is essential for ensuring that clinical research is conducted with integrity and respect for participants.

Through this chapter, readers will gain a comprehensive understanding of the regulatory framework governing clinical research in the USA, highlighting the pathways for drug approval and the standards that ensure participant safety and ethical conduct in research.

18.1 Overview of NDA 505(b)(1) – New Drug Application

The **New Drug Application (NDA)** process under **Section 505(b)(1)** of the **Federal Food, Drug, and Cosmetic Act** is the principal regulatory pathway for gaining approval to market new drugs in the United States. It is the most comprehensive and rigorous route, requiring innovator companies to submit complete clinical and preclinical data that they have generated through their own research. The goal of the NDA process is to ensure that any new drug introduced to the market is safe, effective, and produced under high-quality standards. For innovator companies developing new molecular entities (NMEs) or biologics, the NDA represents the final step in a lengthy and expensive research and development journey, culminating in a formal request for the **U.S. Food and Drug Administration (FDA)** to evaluate and approve their drug for commercial use. This pathway is designed for original drug products that have not been previously approved by the FDA, making it distinct from other pathways that rely on existing data or abbreviated approvals.

To gain approval under the 505(b)(1) pathway, the sponsor must submit an extensive array of data that demonstrates the safety, efficacy, and quality of the drug. This includes results from **preclinical studies**, which are conducted in the laboratory and in animal models to assess the potential toxicity and biological activity of the drug. These studies are essential for identifying any early safety concerns before the drug is tested in humans. Once the preclinical phase is successfully completed, the drug enters the clinical trial phase, which is divided into **three stages: Phase I, Phase II,** and **Phase III**. **Phase I clinical trials** are typically small studies involving **20 to 100 participants** and focus on evaluating the drug's safety, dosage range, and pharmacokinetics. **Phase II trials** involve larger participant groups, often between **100 and 300 individuals**, and aim to assess the drug's efficacy and further evaluate its safety. Finally, **Phase III trials** are large-scale studies involving **1,000 to 3,000 participants** that seek to confirm the drug's efficacy, monitor side effects, and compare it to existing treatments. These trials are the most critical for gaining FDA approval, as they provide the robust clinical evidence needed to support the drug's safety and effectiveness. However, it is well-documented that drug development is a high-risk venture, with only about **10%** of drugs that enter clinical trials ultimately progressing to the NDA stage. The remaining **90%** fail at various points in the clinical trial process, often due to safety concerns or a lack of demonstrated efficacy.

In addition to clinical trial data, the NDA submission must include comprehensive information on the drug's **chemistry, manufacturing, and controls (CMC)**. This section details the methods used to manufacture the drug, the controls in place to ensure its quality, and the drug's stability over time. The NDA also includes **toxicology studies**, which provide further insights into the drug's safety profile, particularly with long-term use. These studies are crucial for understanding the potential risks associated with the drug, including any carcinogenic, reproductive, or developmental effects. The level of detail required in these sections reflects the FDA's commitment to ensuring that only drugs with a favorable risk-benefit profile are approved for use in the general population.

Once the NDA is submitted, the **FDA's Center for Drug Evaluation and Research (CDER)** is responsible for reviewing the application. The FDA's review process is highly structured and involves multiple stages, including a preliminary review to ensure that the NDA is complete and contains all necessary data. Once the application is accepted for filing, the FDA begins its formal review, which typically takes between **10 to 12 months** for standard applications, though this timeline can be shortened for drugs that address **unmet medical needs** or are designated for **priority review**. During the review process, CDER evaluates the clinical trial data to assess the drug's efficacy and safety profile, while the **Office of New Drugs (OND)** conducts a thorough analysis of the CMC and toxicology data. The FDA also reviews the proposed labeling for the drug, ensuring that it accurately reflects the drug's uses, dosages, and potential risks. At the end of the review, if the FDA concludes that the drug is safe and effective for its intended use, it will issue an approval letter allowing the sponsor to market the drug. Conversely, if the FDA identifies any deficiencies or concerns, it may issue a **Complete Response Letter (CRL)**, outlining the issues that must be addressed before the drug can be approved.

18.2 NDA 505(b)(2) – Applications Based on Existing Data

The **NDA 505(b)(2)** pathway provides a regulatory mechanism that allows sponsors to gain approval for new drugs by relying on existing clinical data, such as published studies, research conducted by other sponsors, or data from previously approved drugs. This is in contrast to the more traditional **NDA 505(b)(1)** process, which requires sponsors to generate all necessary clinical trial data themselves. NDA 505(b)(2) is typically used for drugs that involve **reformulations**, **new combinations of existing drugs**, **new dosages**, or **different routes of administration** of previously approved drugs. It allows companies to bypass the lengthy and expensive process of conducting full-scale clinical trials for every new drug formulation, as long as they can demonstrate that the new version is safe and effective based on existing data. For example, a company developing an extended-release version of an already approved drug may use the **505(b)(2) pathway**, supplementing their application with published studies on the immediate-release formulation. This pathway not only facilitates innovation in drug delivery methods but also helps bring improved therapies to the market faster.

One of the key aspects of NDA 505(b)(2) is the ability to utilize **third-party data** alongside data generated from new clinical trials. This includes **published literature**, **data from previous NDAs**, or even **data from drug studies not originally intended for regulatory submission**. The 505(b)(2) applicant must show that the data they rely on is relevant to their product and that any gaps in the data are addressed through additional **bridging studies**. These bridging studies are typically smaller and more focused than full-scale clinical trials and are designed to connect the existing data with the specific new product. For instance, if a sponsor wants to market a **nasal spray version** of an oral drug, they may use pre-existing clinical data from studies on the oral formulation but will need to conduct bridging studies to demonstrate the bioequivalence or clinical efficacy of the nasal spray. This approach has been successfully used in real-world examples, such as the development of new **inhalable insulin** formulations based on earlier data from injectable insulin studies. By leveraging third-party data, the

505(b)(2) pathway reduces the burden on sponsors while still maintaining rigorous standards for safety and efficacy.

One of the major advantages of the **505(b)(2)** application process is its **shorter review timeline** compared to traditional NDAs under 505(b)(1). Since much of the data required for approval is already available and does not need to be newly generated, the **FDA's Center for Drug Evaluation and Research (CDER)** can complete its review more quickly. In most cases, 505(b)(2) applications are reviewed within **6 to 10 months**, depending on the drug's therapeutic significance and whether it qualifies for **priority review**. This accelerated timeline allows sponsors to bring modified versions of approved drugs to the market faster, benefiting both the companies and patients who need access to these improved formulations. Additionally, the reduced cost of development under the 505(b)(2) pathway makes it an attractive option for smaller pharmaceutical companies or for products targeting niche markets. For example, **injectable biologics** that are reformulated into **self-administrable forms** have gained faster market entry through this pathway, providing patients with more convenient alternatives. The **505(b)(2)** pathway, by utilizing existing data and focusing on innovation in drug delivery or formulation, plays a crucial role in advancing pharmaceutical development while ensuring that safety and efficacy standards are upheld.

18.3 ANDA 505(j) – Abbreviated New Drug Applications for Generics

The **Abbreviated New Drug Application (ANDA)** under **Section 505(j)** of the **Federal Food, Drug, and Cosmetic Act** provides a streamlined approval process for **generic drugs**, allowing manufacturers to bring lower-cost alternatives to market without conducting new clinical trials. Generic drugs are bioequivalent versions of brand-name drugs, and the ANDA pathway enables manufacturers to demonstrate that their product is **therapeutically equivalent** to the **Reference Listed Drug (RLD)**. This means that the generic must have the same active ingredient, strength, dosage form, and route of administration as the RLD, but it can differ in characteristics such as **inactive ingredients**. The **FDA's Office of Generic Drugs (OGD)** evaluates ANDA submissions primarily by assessing **bioequivalence**, which ensures that the generic drug delivers the same amount of active ingredient into the bloodstream in the same timeframe as the RLD. Because generics do not require new safety and efficacy studies, the approval process is faster and less costly, making it possible for companies to produce affordable medications that meet the FDA's strict quality standards.

Bioequivalence studies are the cornerstone of the ANDA process. To demonstrate bioequivalence, generic drug manufacturers conduct studies comparing the rate and extent of absorption of their product with that of the RLD. These studies typically involve a **two-way crossover design** in which a small group of healthy volunteers receives both the generic and the reference drug under controlled conditions. The FDA requires that the generic drug's pharmacokinetic parameters—such as **maximum concentration (Cmax)** and **area under the curve (AUC)**—fall within **80% to 125%** of those of the RLD. This range ensures that the generic provides the same therapeutic effect and safety profile as the brand-name drug. Bioequivalence studies do not need to replicate the large-scale clinical trials conducted for the original drug, significantly reducing development costs. The impact of ANDA approvals is substantial; in the United States, **90% of all prescriptions** are filled with generic drugs, thanks to the ANDA process. This has led to savings of over **$300 billion annually** for consumers and the healthcare system, making medications more accessible and affordable for millions of patients. Generic drugs are particularly important in treating chronic conditions like hypertension, diabetes, and mental health disorders, where long-term use of brand-name drugs can become prohibitively expensive for patients.

The typical timeline for **ANDA review** ranges from **8 to 10 months**, although it can vary depending on the complexity of the application and the FDA's workload. Once the ANDA is submitted, the **FDA's Office of Generic Drugs** reviews the bioequivalence data, manufacturing controls, and labeling to ensure that the generic product meets all regulatory standards. However, certain challenges can delay the approval process. One of the most common issues is **patent litigation**. Many brand-name drug manufacturers hold multiple patents on different aspects of their products, including formulations, methods of use, or delivery systems. Generic manufacturers must navigate these patents and may face lawsuits from the original patent holders if they attempt to market a generic version before the patent's expiration. Another challenge is **market exclusivity** granted to the first generic applicant, which can delay the entry of additional generics for a certain period, typically **180 days**. During this exclusivity period, the first-to-file generic manufacturer has a competitive advantage, but it also delays broader competition. Despite these challenges, the ANDA process remains a critical pathway for bringing cost-effective drugs to market, ensuring that patients have access to safe, effective, and affordable medications. The FDA continues to refine the process, improving efficiency and addressing challenges to further promote the availability of generics.

18.4 FDA Guidance for Industry: Acceptance of Foreign Clinical Studies

The **FDA's guidelines** on accepting clinical data from studies conducted outside the U.S. are outlined under **21 CFR 312.120**, allowing data from foreign trials to be used in support of **New Drug Applications (NDAs)** and **Abbreviated New Drug Applications (ANDAs)**. This provision recognizes the increasingly global nature of clinical research, where many pharmaceutical companies conduct trials in countries outside the U.S. to leverage cost efficiencies, diverse patient populations, and faster recruitment rates. However, for the FDA to accept these data, the foreign trials must adhere to the same **Good Clinical Practice (GCP)** standards required for U.S.-based studies. These GCP standards ensure that clinical trials are designed, conducted, and reported in an ethical manner that protects the rights and well-being of participants, while also maintaining the integrity and reliability of the data. Compliance with GCP is essential for ensuring that the results from foreign trials are as rigorous and trustworthy as those from domestic studies. Sponsors must provide the FDA with a detailed explanation of how the foreign study was conducted and demonstrate that the study was equivalent in terms of scientific and ethical standards to those conducted in the U.S.

To ensure the **acceptance of foreign clinical data**, the FDA has established specific requirements that sponsors must meet. First, the **study design** must be comparable to what is required for U.S. trials, including the selection of appropriate control groups and the use of endpoints that reflect clinically meaningful outcomes. The **patient population** in the foreign trial should also resemble the population intended to use the drug in the U.S., ensuring that the data are relevant and applicable to the American market. For instance, if the foreign trial involves patients with a specific genetic or ethnic background that is not well-represented in the U.S., the FDA may question the generalizability of the results. Additionally, the trial's **endpoints**—whether they measure efficacy, safety, or another relevant clinical outcome—must be comparable to those typically used in U.S. trials. Furthermore, the FDA requires documentation of the **study protocol**, **investigator qualifications**, and **informed consent process**, all of which must comply with GCP guidelines. The FDA may also conduct **audits of**

foreign trial sites to verify data integrity and ensure compliance with regulatory requirements. These audits are critical in maintaining the credibility of foreign clinical data, as they allow the FDA to assess whether the trial was conducted in a manner that meets U.S. standards. Data from these audits have shown that the majority of foreign trials meet FDA standards, though certain regions may face challenges in maintaining consistent GCP adherence.

Conducting clinical trials in countries such as **India** or **Brazil** offers both opportunities and challenges for sponsors. One of the primary advantages is the **cost savings**, as conducting trials in these countries is often significantly less expensive than in the U.S. Additionally, these countries have **diverse patient populations**, which allows sponsors to study the drug's effects across different genetic, cultural, and environmental backgrounds, potentially making the data more robust. Fast recruitment rates are another advantage, as populations in countries like India tend to be large and have less access to certain treatments, leading to higher interest in participating in clinical trials. However, there are also notable challenges. **Language barriers** and **cultural differences** can complicate the informed consent process and patient communication, increasing the risk of misunderstandings. Ensuring that trial participants fully understand the potential risks and benefits of participation is essential for compliance with GCP. Moreover, maintaining **GCP compliance** in foreign trials can be difficult due to varying levels of regulatory infrastructure and oversight in different countries. Sponsors must invest in rigorous training for investigators and site staff to ensure that the trial is conducted according to international standards. In some cases, **FDA inspections** of foreign trial sites have identified gaps in documentation, protocol adherence, or ethical safeguards, leading to delays in the acceptance of the data. Despite these challenges, the opportunity to reduce costs and access diverse patient populations makes foreign clinical trials an attractive option for many sponsors, provided they can navigate the regulatory and operational complexities.

18.5 Good Clinical Practice (GCP) in the USA

In the United States, clinical trials are conducted in accordance with **Good Clinical Practice (GCP)** guidelines, which are derived from the **International Council for Harmonisation (ICH)** standards. The **ICH-GCP** guidelines provide a framework for ensuring that clinical trials are conducted ethically and scientifically, with a focus on protecting participant rights and maintaining data integrity. These guidelines cover every aspect of a clinical trial, from the initial **trial design** and **patient recruitment** to **data collection** and **reporting of results**. GCP standards also ensure that clinical trials are conducted in compliance with regulatory requirements, such as those enforced by the **U.S. Food and Drug Administration (FDA)**. In addition to ensuring the safety and well-being of trial participants, adherence to GCP is critical for the reliability and accuracy of clinical trial data, which forms the basis for regulatory decisions on the approval of new drugs and medical devices. By following ICH-GCP guidelines, sponsors and investigators can ensure that their trials meet both ethical and scientific benchmarks, while also facilitating international acceptance of the trial data.

Compliance with GCP is the shared responsibility of several key stakeholders, including **sponsors**, **investigators**, and **Institutional Review Boards (IRBs)**. Sponsors, typically pharmaceutical companies or research institutions, are responsible for ensuring that the trial is designed according to GCP standards and that the trial sites have the resources and expertise to conduct the study appropriately. Sponsors must also monitor the trial to ensure that the data collected are accurate and that any **adverse events** are promptly reported to the FDA. **Investigators**, who conduct the trial at the clinical sites, are responsible for obtaining **informed consent** from participants, adhering to the trial protocol, and ensuring participant safety throughout the study. They are also required to maintain detailed records of all trial activities, which may be audited by the FDA to verify compliance with GCP. **IRBs**, which are independent ethics committees, play a critical role in overseeing the ethical aspects of the trial. They are responsible for reviewing the trial protocol, informed consent forms, and other trial documents to ensure that the rights and welfare of participants are protected. The **FDA's Office of Good Clinical Practice (OGCP)** is tasked with overseeing compliance with GCP across all clinical trials conducted in the U.S. This office conducts **inspections and audits** of clinical trial sites to ensure that trials are being conducted according to GCP standards and that participants' rights are safeguarded. Data from these inspections help identify areas where compliance may be lacking, allowing the FDA to intervene when necessary.

Despite the stringent guidelines in place, **GCP violations** can and do occur in clinical trials. Common violations include **inadequate informed consent**, where participants are not properly informed about the risks, benefits, or procedures involved in the trial, leading to ethical breaches.

Another frequent violation is the **failure to report adverse events** or serious adverse events (SAEs) within the required timelines, which can jeopardize participant safety and affect the integrity of the trial. For example, failure to report SAEs within the FDA's **24-hour reporting window** for life-threatening events can lead to significant delays in the trial or even regulatory penalties. Additional violations include **protocol deviations**, such as enrolling participants who do not meet the inclusion criteria or failing to follow the prescribed treatment regimen. **FDA audits** of clinical trial sites have revealed that approximately **15%** of inspected sites fail to fully comply with GCP guidelines, with issues ranging from poor record-keeping to lack of adequate oversight by the investigator. These violations can result in **trial delays**, the need for corrective actions, or, in severe cases, the **suspension** of the trial. For sponsors, these delays can have significant financial and operational impacts, while for participants, they can undermine the trust in the clinical research process.

CHAPTER NINETEEN

Clinical Research Regulations in the EU

In the European Union, clinical research is guided by a detailed set of regulations that aim to ensure both safety and effectiveness in the development of new medical products. The regulatory system in the EU is designed to protect public health while promoting innovation and collaboration among member states. This framework is crucial for maintaining high standards in clinical trials and ensuring that all studies adhere to ethical principles.

The EU's approach to clinical research is comprehensive and involves various directives, regulations, and guidelines. These regulations cover all aspects of clinical trials, including their design, execution, and monitoring. The goal is to ensure that trials are conducted with the utmost regard for participants' rights and safety.

For those involved in clinical research—whether they are researchers, sponsors, or regulatory professionals—understanding the EU's regulatory environment is essential. It provides a structured and harmonized process for conducting trials, which helps in managing the complexities of clinical research and contributes to the advancement of medical science within an ethical framework. This chapter will explore the key regulations and guidelines that shape clinical research in the EU, reflecting the region's commitment to both scientific rigor and the protection of human subjects.

19.1 European Medicines Agency (EMA) Regulations

The **European Medicines Agency (EMA)** plays a central role in the regulation of medicinal products across the European Union, ensuring that drugs and therapies introduced to the market meet the highest standards of safety, efficacy, and quality. Established in 1995, the EMA is responsible for coordinating the evaluation and supervision of medicinal products for both human and veterinary use, acting as a central authority that ensures uniformity across all EU member states. Its overarching goal is to protect public health by ensuring that the medicines available in the EU are thoroughly evaluated and monitored throughout their lifecycle. Through a centralized process, the EMA provides a streamlined mechanism for pharmaceutical companies to submit a single application for drug approval, which, if granted, becomes valid in all EU countries. This process not only facilitates market access for companies but also ensures that patients across the EU have equal access to high-quality medicines.

The **approval process** managed by the EMA is known as the **centralized procedure**, which is mandatory for certain categories of medicines, including those for rare diseases, biotechnology products, and innovative therapies. The process begins with a **pre-submission phase**, during which pharmaceutical companies engage with the EMA to discuss the requirements and provide preliminary data on the medicinal product. This interaction helps to streamline the submission by ensuring that all necessary documentation is in place before the formal application. Once the application is submitted, it undergoes a rigorous **scientific evaluation** by the **Committee for Medicinal Products for Human Use (CHMP)**, which is composed of experts from various EU member states. The CHMP conducts a thorough review of the drug's safety, efficacy, and quality based on clinical trial data, manufacturing processes, and other relevant information. The evaluation process typically takes **210 days**, although this may vary depending on the complexity of the application and the need for additional data. If the CHMP issues a positive opinion, the EMA then forwards the recommendation to the **European Commission**, which grants the final **marketing authorization** that allows the medicine to be sold throughout the EU. Throughout this process, the EMA works closely with **national regulatory authorities** to ensure that any country-specific requirements are met and that the product is monitored post-approval.

A key component of the EMA's regulatory structure is the **Committee for Medicinal Products for Human Use (CHMP)**, which plays a pivotal role in evaluating all new drug applications submitted through the centralized procedure. The CHMP is made up of representatives from each EU member state, as well as experts in various scientific and medical fields, who collaborate to assess the scientific merits of each application. The CHMP meets regularly to review applications, discuss clinical data, and provide recommendations on whether a drug should be approved for use. According to recent data, the CHMP reviews approximately **100 to 120 applications** annually, with an average approval rate of **80%**. One of the notable recent approvals includes a groundbreaking gene therapy for **spinal muscular atrophy**, which was reviewed and approved through the EMA's centralized procedure. The CHMP's work ensures that only medicines with a favorable **risk-benefit profile** reach the market, safeguarding public health while promoting pharmaceutical innovation.

19.2 EudraLex Guidelines for Clinical Trials in the EU

EudraLex is the comprehensive collection of rules and regulations that govern medicinal products across the European Union. It serves as the legal framework for ensuring that all aspects of drug development, approval, and monitoring are conducted according to established safety, quality, and efficacy standards. Of particular importance is **Volume 10** of EudraLex, which specifically addresses the **conduct of clinical trials**. This volume lays out the obligations of **sponsors** and **investigators**, providing detailed guidance on how clinical trials should be designed, conducted, and reported to ensure that participant safety and data integrity are maintained. Volume 10 is central to the regulation of clinical trials in the EU, covering everything from **good clinical practice (GCP)** requirements to the submission of trial applications and safety reporting procedures. The overarching goal of these guidelines is to promote transparency and consistency in clinical research while protecting the rights and well-being of participants involved in trials.

One of the key regulatory advancements within EudraLex is the **Clinical Trials Regulation (EU) No 536/2014**, which came into full application in **2022**. This regulation was introduced to harmonize and streamline the approval process for clinical trials conducted across multiple EU member states, replacing the earlier **Clinical Trials Directive**. One of the major improvements under this regulation is the requirement for a **centralized application process** via the **Clinical Trials Information System (CTIS)**, which allows sponsors to submit a single trial application for approval in multiple countries simultaneously. This has significantly reduced the administrative burden on sponsors and helped to expedite the start of multinational trials. The regulation also places a strong emphasis on **transparency**, requiring sponsors to make certain trial-related information publicly available, such as trial protocols and summary results. Additionally, the regulation mandates **robust safety reporting** mechanisms, ensuring that any **adverse events** or **serious adverse reactions** encountered during a trial are promptly reported to the regulatory authorities and addressed. By introducing these measures, **EU No 536/2014** has created a more efficient and transparent environment for conducting clinical trials, while also ensuring that the safety and rights of trial participants are safeguarded.

Ethical oversight is another critical component of the EudraLex guidelines for clinical trials, with **Ethics Committees** playing a key role in ensuring that trials meet ethical standards. Before a clinical trial can commence, the trial protocol must be reviewed and approved by an Ethics Committee in each participating member state. These committees are responsible for evaluating the ethical aspects of the trial, such as the **informed consent process, participant recruitment**, and the overall risk-benefit profile of the study. The Ethics Committees ensure that trials are designed in a way that protects the rights, safety, and dignity of participants, particularly those from vulnerable populations. The introduction of **EU No 536/2014** has further strengthened the role of Ethics Committees by ensuring that their review is integrated into the centralized trial approval process, reducing the duplication of effort and enabling faster approval timelines. Recent data indicate that the streamlined application process has led to a **30% reduction** in the time required to obtain trial approval across multiple member states. This has facilitated faster trial initiation, particularly for large-scale **multinational studies**, making the EU a more attractive environment for clinical research. The integration of ethical oversight within this regulatory framework ensures that clinical trials not only meet scientific standards but also adhere to the highest ethical principles.

19.3 Volume 9A – Pharmacovigilance for Medicinal Products for Human Use

Volume 9A of the **EudraLex** guidelines forms the foundation of the **pharmacovigilance framework** within the European Union. It outlines the requirements for monitoring the safety of medicinal products once they are authorized and available on the market. Pharmacovigilance involves the continuous assessment of the safety profile of a medicine, and it is critical in identifying, evaluating, and preventing adverse drug reactions (ADRs). The guidelines specify the obligations of both **sponsors** and **marketing authorization holders** (MAHs) to systematically monitor the safety of their products. MAHs must implement robust pharmacovigilance systems that ensure any emerging safety concerns are identified early and reported to regulatory authorities. This includes collecting data on ADRs, analyzing trends, and making necessary adjustments to product labeling or usage recommendations to enhance patient safety. The ultimate aim of Volume 9A is to protect public health by ensuring that medicines remain safe and effective throughout their lifecycle, and by enabling quick action if safety concerns arise.

A key component of the pharmacovigilance framework outlined in Volume 9A is the requirement for **safety reporting. Adverse drug reactions (ADRs)** must be reported promptly by MAHs, ensuring that regulators are kept informed of any safety issues that may arise after a product is launched. One of the primary tools for ensuring this is the submission of **Periodic Safety Update Reports (PSURs)**, which provide an ongoing assessment of the risk-benefit balance of a medicinal product. PSURs must be submitted at regular intervals and include all relevant safety data, including ADRs, collected during the reporting period. Another crucial document is the **Risk Management Plan (RMP)**, which outlines how risks associated with the medicinal product will be monitored and minimized. The RMP is a proactive document submitted as part of the initial marketing application and updated throughout the product's lifecycle. Data shows that the introduction of systematic ADR reporting and the use of PSURs and RMPs have significantly enhanced **transparency** and consumer safety. For instance, the **European Medicines Agency (EMA)** reported that in **2020**, more than **1.5 million ADRs** were collected across the EU, contributing to a more comprehensive understanding of drug safety profiles. This increase in transparency has allowed for better-informed regulatory decisions and more effective communication with healthcare professionals and patients.

The **European Medicines Agency (EMA)** plays a central role in coordinating pharmacovigilance activities across the EU, with the **Pharmacovigilance Risk Assessment Committee (PRAC)** taking the lead in overseeing the safety of medicinal products. PRAC is responsible for evaluating data on ADRs, assessing the risk-benefit balance of medicines, and recommending regulatory actions if safety concerns arise. The committee is composed of pharmacovigilance experts from EU member states, as well as patient and healthcare professional representatives, ensuring a well-rounded approach to safety evaluation. PRAC works closely with national regulatory agencies to ensure that safety signals are promptly identified and acted upon. For example, if PRAC determines that a medicine presents a serious safety risk, it may recommend changes to the **safety labeling** or restrictions on the product's use. In some cases, PRAC may even recommend the **withdrawal of a medicine** from the market if the risks outweigh the benefits. A notable example of pharmacovigilance in action is the withdrawal of certain **COX-2 inhibitors**, a class of anti-inflammatory drugs, after post-market safety data revealed an increased risk of cardiovascular events. This proactive safety monitoring framework ensures that the benefits of medicinal products continue to outweigh the risks and that swift action is taken when necessary to protect public health.

19.4 ISO 14155 – Clinical Investigation of Medical Devices

ISO 14155 is the internationally recognized standard for conducting **clinical investigations** on **medical devices** within the **European Union**. It aligns closely with **Good Clinical Practice (GCP)** guidelines, ensuring that the **safety** and **performance** of medical devices are carefully evaluated during clinical trials. ISO 14155 focuses on upholding ethical and scientific standards, much like in pharmaceutical trials. This standard is designed to provide a framework for planning, conducting, recording, and reporting clinical investigations of medical devices, ensuring that patient safety and data integrity are maintained throughout the study. It is essential in Europe for ensuring that medical devices, particularly high-risk ones, are thoroughly evaluated before they reach the market. Compliance with ISO 14155 is not only critical for regulatory approval but also necessary for maintaining public trust in the safety and effectiveness of medical devices.

There are several **key components** of **ISO 14155** that sponsors and investigators must adhere to. These include **study design**, which must be carefully constructed to test the safety and performance of the device in real-world settings. The standard also requires detailed **risk management**, meaning that potential risks to participants must be identified, assessed, and mitigated throughout the trial. **Ethical considerations** are also a core element, with ISO 14155 requiring that all investigations be conducted in a manner that respects the rights, safety, and well-being of participants. This includes obtaining informed consent and ensuring that the trial undergoes review and approval by an independent **ethics committee**. Another critical aspect is the need for **post-market follow-up**, where the performance of the device is monitored after it has been approved and introduced into the market. This follow-up ensures that any long-term risks or complications are identified and managed appropriately. Like pharmaceutical trials, medical device trials under ISO 14155 must meet stringent scientific and ethical standards, guaranteeing that the device performs safely and effectively before it can be widely used.

Sponsors conducting medical device trials in Europe often face several **challenges**. One key challenge is ensuring compliance with both **ISO 14155** and the **EU Medical Device Regulation (MDR)**, which came into full effect in 2021. The MDR imposes additional regulatory requirements on medical devices, particularly those in higher risk categories, which means that sponsors must ensure that their trials meet all the necessary regulatory standards. This can create additional complexity, especially when conducting multinational trials across different regulatory environments within the EU. Another challenge is ensuring that data collected during the trials is robust and can withstand regulatory scrutiny. Many medical devices, especially those that are innovative or based on new technologies, require sophisticated clinical trials to demonstrate their safety and performance. Despite these challenges, there have been numerous successful applications of ISO 14155 in Europe. For instance, clinical investigations for **implantable cardiac devices** and **advanced diagnostic tools** have been conducted under this standard, leading to regulatory approval and successful market introduction. These examples demonstrate that adherence to ISO 14155 can help bring innovative and life-saving medical devices to market while ensuring the highest levels of safety and effectiveness.

CHAPTER TWENTY

GCP Guidelines and Global Regulations

In the realm of clinical research, adhering to Good Clinical Practice (GCP) guidelines is essential for ensuring the ethical conduct of trials and the reliability of their results. GCP provides a framework for designing, conducting, recording, and reporting trials that involves human subjects. Its guidelines are intended to ensure that research is conducted with the highest standards of scientific integrity and respect for participants' rights and welfare.

Globally, different countries and regions have developed their own sets of regulations and guidelines based on GCP principles. These regulations are designed to standardize practices and ensure that clinical trials meet both local and international ethical and scientific standards. Understanding these guidelines is crucial for researchers and sponsors who operate in multiple jurisdictions, as it helps them navigate the complexities of conducting international trials.

This chapter delves into the core principles of GCP and explores how these principles are applied across different regulatory frameworks around the world. By examining the similarities and differences between global regulations, this chapter aims to provide a comprehensive overview of how GCP guidelines influence clinical research practices globally.

20.1 ICH GCP E6: Good Clinical Practice Guidelines

The **ICH GCP E6** guidelines are recognized globally as the gold standard for conducting **clinical trials**. These guidelines were developed by the **International Council for Harmonisation (ICH)** to ensure that clinical trials are conducted ethically, with a strong emphasis on **participant safety** and **data reliability**. The main purpose of these guidelines is to protect the rights, well-being, and confidentiality of trial participants while ensuring that the data generated from these trials are credible and reliable enough to support regulatory decisions. ICH GCP E6 is designed to be a comprehensive framework that guides the conduct of trials across different stages, from **protocol design** and **trial management** to **data recording** and **reporting**. By adhering to these guidelines, researchers, sponsors, and regulators can ensure that clinical trials meet both **scientific** and **ethical standards**, enabling the development of new therapies and medicines that are safe for public use. The guidelines emphasize **Good Clinical Practice (GCP)**, which means that all trials must be conducted according to a standardized set of principles that ensure the **quality** and **integrity** of the data.

One of the key aspects of the **ICH GCP E6 guidelines** is that they provide detailed instructions on the roles and responsibilities of all stakeholders involved in a clinical trial. This includes **sponsors**, **investigators**, and **Institutional Review Boards (IRBs)**. For example, sponsors are responsible for ensuring that trials are designed in a scientifically sound manner, with adequate resources to conduct the study and proper systems in place to monitor the trial. Investigators, on the other hand, are responsible for protecting the rights and safety of participants by ensuring **informed consent** is obtained and maintaining accurate trial records. **IRBs** play a crucial role in reviewing the trial protocol to ensure that it meets ethical standards and that the risks to participants are minimized. The guidelines also emphasize the importance of **monitoring** throughout the trial to ensure compliance with the protocol and GCP standards. Sponsors must implement effective monitoring plans, while investigators are required to report **adverse events** and **protocol deviations** to the appropriate authorities. This framework ensures that all parties involved are held accountable for the ethical and scientific conduct of the trial, ultimately safeguarding the health and safety of participants.

Another critical component of **ICH GCP E6** is the emphasis on **data integrity**. The guidelines require that all data collected during a clinical trial must be recorded, handled, and stored in a manner that allows for accurate reporting, interpretation, and verification. This includes maintaining a comprehensive **audit trail** that documents all changes made to trial data. Ensuring data integrity is essential for the validity of the study results, as any discrepancies or errors in the data could compromise the **credibility** of the trial outcomes. Additionally, the guidelines mandate the use of **standard operating procedures (SOPs)** to ensure consistency in data collection and management. SOPs help prevent errors and ensure that trials are conducted in a systematic and reproducible manner. By maintaining high standards for data integrity, ICH GCP E6 ensures that clinical trials produce reliable and reproducible results that can be used to support **regulatory submissions** and ultimately lead to the approval of new therapies.

The global impact of the **ICH GCP E6** guidelines has been significant, as their adoption has enabled greater **harmonization** in clinical research across multiple regions. Regulatory authorities in over **100 countries**, including the **U.S. Food and Drug Administration (FDA)**, **European Medicines Agency (EMA)**, and **Japan's Pharmaceuticals and Medical Devices Agency (PMDA)**, have integrated ICH GCP standards into their own regulations. This harmonization has facilitated the **acceptance of clinical trial data** across international borders, enabling sponsors to conduct global clinical trials and submit data to regulatory agencies in different countries. This global acceptance of ICH GCP standards has been particularly important for **multinational clinical trials**, where data generated in one country can be used to support drug approval in another. For example, global trials involving **oncology** and **cardiovascular** treatments have benefited from the streamlined regulatory processes made possible by adherence to ICH GCP. This harmonization not only accelerates the **drug approval process** but also reduces the need for duplicative trials, saving time and resources. Ultimately, the widespread adoption of ICH GCP E6 has led to more efficient drug development processes, ensuring that patients around the world have access to safe and effective treatments more quickly.

20.2 Indian GCP Guidelines

The **Indian GCP guidelines** serve as the national framework for conducting clinical trials in India, designed to regulate and ensure the ethical and scientific integrity of clinical research within the country. Developed in alignment with international standards such as **ICH GCP**, these guidelines were introduced to address the growing number of clinical trials in India, driven by the country's expanding pharmaceutical sector and its role as a global hub for clinical research. The Indian GCP guidelines aim to ensure that all clinical trials conducted in India adhere to the same ethical principles and scientific rigor as trials conducted elsewhere in the world. This is particularly important given India's diverse population, which offers unique opportunities for medical research, but also raises ethical concerns around participant rights and safety. By implementing these guidelines,

India seeks to maintain high standards for trial conduct, enhance data reliability, and protect the rights of trial participants, while also facilitating the growth of its clinical research industry.

The **Indian GCP guidelines** outline several **specific requirements** that must be followed by sponsors, investigators, and ethics committees to ensure that clinical trials are conducted ethically and scientifically. One of the primary requirements is obtaining **trial approvals** from regulatory bodies such as the **Central Drugs Standard Control Organization (CDSCO)** and from **Institutional Ethics Committees (IECs)**. These approvals are mandatory before any clinical trial can commence and ensure that the trial protocol meets ethical standards. The guidelines also emphasize the importance of **safety reporting**, requiring investigators to report all **adverse events (AEs)** and **serious adverse events (SAEs)** to the appropriate authorities, including the ethics committee and CDSCO, within specified timelines. This ensures that any risks to participants are identified and addressed in a timely manner. Additionally, the guidelines mandate that **informed consent** be obtained from all participants, with clear explanations of the trial's purpose, procedures, risks, and benefits. This consent must be given voluntarily and documented appropriately, ensuring that participants are fully aware of their rights. Ethical conduct is emphasized at every stage of the trial, from design and recruitment to data collection and reporting, ensuring that trials are not only scientifically sound but also respect the dignity and rights of participants.

While the Indian GCP guidelines have helped establish a robust framework for clinical trials, there are still several **challenges** in ensuring full compliance. One of the primary challenges is **infrastructure limitations**, particularly in rural areas where clinical trials may lack the resources and facilities required to meet GCP standards. **Regulatory bottlenecks** also present a challenge, as delays in approval processes and inconsistencies in enforcement can slow down the initiation and progress of clinical trials. However, there have been significant efforts to improve compliance with Indian GCP guidelines. India has made strides in GCP **training** for clinical trial personnel, ensuring that investigators, study coordinators, and ethics committee members are well-versed in GCP principles and can conduct trials according to the highest standards. Additionally, the **CDSCO** has worked to strengthen **regulatory enforcement**, increasing the frequency of **site inspections** and ensuring that non-compliance is addressed promptly. These improvements are aimed at making India a more attractive destination for clinical trials while maintaining the highest standards of participant safety and data integrity. Despite the challenges, India's commitment to strengthening its GCP framework is evident, and ongoing efforts to enhance infrastructure, training, and regulatory oversight are expected to further improve the quality and credibility of clinical trials conducted in the country.

20.3 ICMR Ethical Guidelines for Biomedical Research

The **Indian Council of Medical Research (ICMR)** plays a pivotal role in establishing ethical guidelines for **biomedical research** in India. These guidelines are critical for ensuring that clinical and biomedical research is conducted in a manner that respects the **rights and dignity** of participants, particularly in a country as diverse as India, where vulnerable populations are often involved in research. The ICMR guidelines serve as a comprehensive framework for both researchers and ethics committees, ensuring that research is conducted ethically while balancing scientific progress with participant safety. Introduced to regulate the ethical aspects of research, these guidelines are aligned with global ethical standards and provide a foundation for research integrity in India. They are especially important in trials involving **vulnerable populations**, such as children, pregnant women, and economically disadvantaged individuals, who may be more susceptible to exploitation or harm. The ICMR guidelines ensure that such groups are afforded extra protection, requiring additional layers of review and safeguards to minimize risk.

The **ICMR guidelines** are built on several key **ethical principles** that must be adhered to in all biomedical research. One of the foundational principles is **respect for participants**, ensuring that individuals are fully informed about the nature of the research and give their **informed consent** before participating. This principle is particularly important in a country like India, where educational, social, and linguistic barriers may affect the understanding of trial information. Researchers are required to communicate clearly and in a culturally sensitive manner to ensure that participants understand their rights and the risks and benefits of the trial. The guidelines also emphasize a thorough **risk-benefit assessment**, ensuring that the potential benefits of the research outweigh any risks to participants. This assessment is a mandatory part of the ethical review process and is conducted by **Institutional Ethics Committees (IECs)**. For trials involving **vulnerable populations**, such as children or pregnant women, the ICMR guidelines require additional protections. Researchers must justify the inclusion of these groups and demonstrate that their participation is essential for the scientific objectives of the study. Moreover, the guidelines mandate that research involving such groups be conducted with **minimal risk** and that their involvement is accompanied by heightened **ethical scrutiny**. Before commencing any biomedical research, researchers are required to obtain **ethical clearance** from an IEC, which reviews the trial protocol to ensure that the ethical principles outlined in the ICMR guidelines are upheld.

The **ICMR** also plays a key role in overseeing the application of these guidelines through the work of **Institutional Ethics Committees (IECs)**. IECs are responsible for reviewing all research protocols and ensuring that they meet the ethical standards set forth by the ICMR. This oversight includes a thorough review of the **informed consent process**, ensuring that participants are not only informed but also understand the nature of the research and their rights. The **ICMR guidelines** are applied rigorously, and compliance is closely monitored to ensure that ethical standards are maintained throughout the research process. In addition to protocol review, IECs are tasked with **monitoring the ongoing progress** of research projects, ensuring that any **adverse events** or deviations from the approved protocol are reported and addressed. The ICMR's oversight has been particularly critical in large-scale research projects conducted in India, such as vaccine trials and studies on communicable diseases. These projects, often involving thousands of participants across multiple sites, require a robust ethical framework to ensure that participant safety is prioritized and that the research is conducted with integrity. The application of ICMR guidelines in these large-scale trials has not only helped safeguard the rights of participants but also contributed to **ethical integrity** in Indian biomedical research. By fostering a culture of ethical conduct, the ICMR guidelines continue to play a crucial role in advancing scientific research in India while ensuring that the welfare of participants remains the top priority.

20.4 CDSCO Guidelines for Clinical Trials

The **Central Drugs Standard Control Organization (CDSCO)** is India's national regulatory body, tasked with overseeing the approval and regulation of clinical trials and ensuring the safe and ethical conduct of biomedical research in the country. Operating under the **Ministry of Health and Family Welfare**, CDSCO is responsible for enforcing the **Drugs and Cosmetics Act, 1940**, and ensuring that all clinical trials comply with **Schedule Y** of the Act. Schedule Y outlines the requirements for conducting clinical trials in India, focusing on ensuring participant safety, data integrity, and the ethical conduct of trials. CDSCO's primary goal is to regulate clinical trials efficiently while balancing the need for innovation with the protection of public health. This regulatory framework helps to streamline the approval process for new drugs while ensuring that trials are conducted with the highest ethical and scientific standards. By maintaining oversight over all clinical trials conducted in India, CDSCO plays a crucial role in promoting **transparency** and **accountability** in clinical research.

The **CDSCO guidelines** for clinical trials provide a detailed roadmap for sponsors and investigators to follow. One of the key requirements for conducting a clinical trial is obtaining **approval from CDSCO** before the study begins. Sponsors must submit an application, including **Form 44**, which is the official document requesting approval for a new drug trial. This submission must also include the trial protocol, investigator brochures, informed consent forms, and ethics committee approvals. The **Drug Controller General of India (DCGI)**, who heads CDSCO, is responsible for reviewing the application and making decisions regarding trial approval. This review process typically involves an assessment of thc **safety**, **efficacy**, and **scientific merit** of the trial. The DCGI ensures that the proposed trial complies with **Good Clinical Practice (GCP)** guidelines and that the rights and safety of participants are adequately protected. In addition to the initial approval, CDSCO places significant emphasis on the **timely reporting of adverse events (AEs)** and **serious adverse events (SAEs)**. Investigators are required to report all SAEs to the DCGI and ethics committees within a defined timeframe, typically **24 hours** for life-threatening events. This system helps ensure that any risks to participants are identified and mitigated quickly, protecting participant welfare throughout the trial.

CDSCO also plays an active role in **monitoring and inspecting clinical trial sites** to ensure that the studies are conducted according to the approved protocol and meet ethical standards. Site inspections are conducted both during the trial and after approval, with a focus on verifying that **informed consent** has been obtained, **trial data** is being accurately recorded, and **adverse events** are being reported promptly. CDSCO conducts both announced and unannounced inspections to ensure **compliance** with GCP guidelines and Schedule Y requirements. The organization is responsible for **post-approval monitoring**, ensuring that once a drug or treatment is approved for the market, it continues to meet safety standards. Regular **audits** and **inspections** help ensure ongoing compliance with regulatory requirements. According to recent data, CDSCO reviews and approves approximately **350 to 400 clinical trials** annually, highlighting its significant role in regulating research activities in India. These inspections and post-approval checks are vital for maintaining the **integrity** of clinical research and ensuring that participant safety remains a priority throughout the lifecycle of a clinical trial. Through its stringent oversight and regulatory framework, CDSCO has established itself as a key player in the global clinical research landscape, ensuring that India remains a hub for safe and ethical clinical trials.

CHAPTER TWENTY-ONE

Global Harmonization Task Force (GHTF) and Study Group 5

In the field of medical device regulation, global consistency and collaboration are vital to ensure the safety and efficacy of products across international markets. The Global Harmonization Task Force (GHTF) was established to address these needs by developing and promoting harmonized standards and guidelines for medical device regulation. Its efforts aimed to simplify and standardize regulatory practices, thereby facilitating the international trade of medical devices while ensuring high standards of patient safety.

Study Group 5, a key component of the GHTF, focused on the development and implementation of guidelines concerning the clinical evaluation of medical devices. The group's work was instrumental in providing a consistent framework for evaluating clinical evidence, which is essential for both regulatory approval and clinical use of devices. Study Group 5's guidelines have helped shape regulatory practices worldwide, promoting more effective and efficient assessment of medical devices.

This chapter explores the role of the GHTF and Study Group 5 in advancing global harmonization in medical device regulation. It examines the contributions of these bodies to standardizing regulatory processes, improving the quality of clinical evaluations, and fostering international cooperation. Through a detailed discussion of their guidelines and impacts, this chapter highlights the significance of these efforts in achieving global regulatory alignment and ensuring the safety and effectiveness of medical devices.

21.1 Overview of the Global Harmonization Task Force

The **Global Harmonization Task Force (GHTF)** was established in **1992** with the primary goal of harmonizing medical device regulations across different regions. It was founded by the regulatory authorities of five major regions: the **European Union (EU)**, the **United States**, **Japan**, **Canada**, and **Australia**. The creation of GHTF marked a significant step towards creating a more unified global framework for regulating medical devices, which, at the time, were subject to varying regulatory standards across countries. These disparities made it challenging for manufacturers to navigate the approval processes in different regions and often led to delays in bringing safe and innovative devices to market. By establishing GHTF, these founding regions sought to align regulatory requirements, making the process of medical device approval more streamlined and consistent worldwide. The task force brought together **regulators**, **manufacturers**, and **industry experts** to work collaboratively on developing guidelines that would serve as a common standard for medical device regulation.

The **objectives of GHTF** were centered around reducing regulatory barriers, streamlining approval processes, and improving **patient safety**. One of the key goals was to create uniform standards for **medical device classification**, **quality management systems**, and **post-market surveillance**. These standards aimed to reduce the complexity and redundancy in regulatory submissions by allowing manufacturers to submit a single dossier that could be accepted by regulatory bodies in multiple regions. GHTF guidelines also focused on ensuring that devices met stringent safety and efficacy standards before reaching the market, thus improving patient outcomes. The task force's efforts led to a significant reduction in the time taken to approve new medical devices. Data shows that the adoption of GHTF recommendations by participating regions resulted in a **20-30% decrease** in the time required for regulatory approvals. Additionally, GHTF's guidelines were adopted or adapted by many countries beyond its founding members, further expanding its impact. By 2010, more than **50 countries** had implemented GHTF standards, reflecting the global acceptance of its harmonization efforts. This widespread adoption facilitated international trade in medical devices, allowing manufacturers to more easily enter new markets and ensuring that patients worldwide had faster access to new medical technologies.

In **2011**, the GHTF was succeeded by the **International Medical Device Regulators Forum (IMDRF)**, which continues the mission of global harmonization for medical device regulations. The IMDRF was established to build upon the foundational work of GHTF and expand its scope to address emerging challenges in medical device regulation. While GHTF laid the groundwork for harmonizing regulations across key regions, IMDRF has broadened its focus to include **global convergence** in areas such as software as a medical device (SaMD), artificial intelligence in healthcare, and more advanced post-market surveillance mechanisms. The IMDRF also works to enhance collaboration between regulators in **developed and developing countries**, ensuring that all regions benefit from harmonized standards and improved patient safety. The transition from GHTF to IMDRF reflects the evolution of global medical device regulation, where the focus has shifted from harmonization to creating a regulatory environment that supports innovation while maintaining high safety standards.

21.2 GHTF Study Group 5 Guidance

GHTF had several study groups, each focusing on different aspects of medical device regulation:

- **Study Group 1**: focused on pre-market approval and regulatory submissions for medical devices.
- **Study Group 2**: concentrated on post-market surveillance and vigilance systems (adverse event reporting).
- **Study Group 3**: worked on quality systems for medical devices.
- **Study Group 4**: addressed auditing practices for regulatory compliance.
- **Study Group 5**: focused on clinical safety, specifically **post-market surveillance** and adverse event reporting.

Study Group 5 of the **Global Harmonization Task Force (GHTF)** was formed to address the critical area of **post-market surveillance** and **adverse event reporting** for medical devices. As medical devices are used in real-world settings after approval, it is essential to have systems in place that monitor their performance and detect any safety concerns that may arise during use. Study Group 5 was tasked with developing standardized guidelines to ensure that adverse events, device malfunctions, and other safety issues were consistently reported across different countries. The group's efforts focused on creating a global framework for post-market vigilance that would allow manufacturers and regulators to track the safety and performance of medical devices more effectively. By harmonizing the approach to safety reporting, Study Group 5 aimed to reduce inconsistencies between regions, making it easier for regulators to identify and address potential safety risks. The development of these guidelines has played a vital role in improving global patient safety by ensuring that all countries follow the same procedures for monitoring medical device safety once the devices are in use.

One of the key contributions of **Study Group 5** is the development of guidance on **adverse event reporting**. The group established clear procedures for manufacturers to follow when reporting **adverse events**, particularly those involving **serious injury** or **death**. This guidance ensures that all incidents related to medical device malfunctions or safety issues are promptly reported to the appropriate regulatory authorities. The guidelines recommend specific timelines for reporting, such as requiring manufacturers to report events involving death or serious injury within **10 days** of becoming aware of the incident. For less severe events, the reporting timeline may be extended, but the emphasis remains on timely and accurate reporting to ensure that safety risks are identified as quickly as possible. Study Group 5 also provided recommendations on the types of information that should be included in adverse event reports, such as details about the device involved, the nature of the incident, and any actions taken to address the issue. These recommendations have helped manufacturers establish **post-market vigilance systems** that allow for systematic tracking of adverse events, ensuring that potential safety concerns are addressed before they escalate.

The global impact of **Study Group 5's guidance** on post-market surveillance has been profound. By creating a standardized approach to **adverse event reporting**, the group has enabled more consistent and reliable monitoring of medical devices across different regulatory systems. This harmonization has led to quicker responses to safety concerns, as regulators in different countries can now rely on a uniform reporting mechanism to identify potential issues. Real-world examples highlight the effectiveness of this approach. For instance, the harmonized reporting guidelines were instrumental in the rapid detection of safety concerns related to certain **implantable cardiac devices**, which experienced malfunctions in multiple countries. Because of the standardized reporting framework, regulators were able to quickly gather data on the incidents, leading to **device recalls** and safety updates that prevented further harm to patients. Similarly, issues with **metal-on-metal hip implants** were identified through harmonized post-market surveillance, allowing for prompt regulatory action to address the risks associated with these devices.

21.3 Safety and Efficacy in Clinical Trials

The **Global Harmonization Task Force (GHTF)** and **Study Group 5** have made significant contributions to enhancing the **safety and efficacy** of medical devices through the development of **standardized protocols** for clinical trials. These protocols provide a consistent framework for ensuring that medical devices are rigorously tested for both safety and effectiveness before they are approved for use. Safety is continuously monitored throughout the clinical trial process, particularly for devices that pose a **high risk** to patients, such as implantable devices or devices used in critical medical procedures. GHTF guidelines require that safety assessments are integrated into every phase of the trial, from initial **feasibility studies** to large-scale **pivotal trials.** Continuous monitoring of adverse events and device performance allows for timely interventions if any safety concerns arise. This proactive approach helps prevent serious incidents and ensures that high-risk devices meet the highest safety standards before they reach the market.

One of the key areas emphasized by **GHTF** is **risk management** in clinical trials. The GHTF guidelines mandate that all potential risks associated with a medical device are identified, thoroughly assessed, and minimized during the trial process. This **risk management** approach ensures that clinical trials are designed to carefully weigh the **risks and benefits** of the device, especially when it is being tested on vulnerable populations or in critical medical applications. A comprehensive **risk-benefit analysis** is a central component of trial design, where the potential therapeutic benefits of the device are compared to the likelihood and severity of risks it may pose to patients. The guidelines encourage manufacturers to establish **risk mitigation strategies**, such as designing robust trial protocols, ensuring thorough investigator training, and closely monitoring participants for any adverse events. An example where this has been crucial is the development of **implantable defibrillators**, which are lifesaving but carry a risk of malfunction. By following GHTF's rigorous risk management protocols, manufacturers have been able to demonstrate that the benefits of these devices far outweigh the risks, leading to their successful approval and widespread use.

Regulatory consistency is another significant achievement of GHTF's harmonization efforts. By aligning **safety standards** across countries, GHTF has made it easier for clinical trial data generated in one region to be accepted by regulatory authorities in other regions. This harmonization has reduced the need for duplicative trials and has streamlined the global medical device approval process. Manufacturers can now conduct a single set of trials that meet international safety standards, allowing them to submit the data to regulatory agencies in multiple countries with confidence that the data will be accepted. Data from GHTF's harmonization efforts show that this approach has significantly reduced the time to market for medical devices. For instance, the time required for the global approval of **cardiac stents** was reduced by approximately **30%** due to the acceptance of harmonized trial data across key regulatory regions. This consistency not only accelerates the approval process but also ensures that patients around the world have faster access to **innovative medical technologies** while maintaining high safety standards. By promoting global regulatory consistency, GHTF has played a crucial role in advancing both the safety and efficacy of medical devices in clinical trials and beyond.

21.4 Global Standards for Clinical Research

The **Global Harmonization Task Force (GHTF)** has played a pivotal role in the development of **global standards** for medical device clinical research, establishing standardized protocols for conducting trials, monitoring, and reporting data. By creating a unified framework for medical device trials, GHTF has facilitated consistent and rigorous evaluation of devices across different regions, ensuring that safety and efficacy are prioritized throughout the process. One of the key contributions of GHTF has been the establishment of **standardized clinical trial protocols** that outline the requirements for study design, participant selection, data collection, and ethical considerations. These protocols ensure that trials are conducted in a scientifically valid manner, allowing for reliable data generation that supports regulatory decision-making. Additionally, GHTF developed detailed **monitoring requirements** to ensure that trials are continuously supervised, particularly for high-risk devices, to detect and address any safety concerns in real-time. The organization also set standards for **data reporting**, requiring manufacturers to present trial results in a clear, consistent format that can be easily reviewed by regulatory bodies in multiple regions.

The **harmonization of global standards** has brought numerous benefits to both manufacturers and patients. By adhering to unified global standards, medical device manufacturers are able to achieve **faster regulatory approvals** for their products, as they no longer need to conduct separate trials or navigate varying regulatory requirements in different countries. This streamlining of the approval process has significantly reduced **costs** for manufacturers, as duplicative testing and documentation efforts are minimized. For example, the cost of conducting a clinical trial across multiple regions can be reduced by up to **20-30%** when harmonized standards are followed, allowing manufacturers to bring their products to market more efficiently. Moreover, harmonized standards have improved **patient access** to innovative medical technologies by speeding up the time it takes for devices to be approved and made available globally. Patients now have quicker access to life-saving devices, as manufacturers can submit a single set of trial data to regulatory agencies in multiple regions, knowing that the data will meet the necessary standards for approval.

Several **case studies** highlight the impact of harmonized global standards in improving the efficiency and safety of medical device development. For example, the approval process for **implantable cardiac devices**, such as pacemakers and defibrillators, has been greatly accelerated due to the acceptance of harmonized trial data across the **European Union**, **United States**, and **Japan**. By following the GHTF-developed global standards, manufacturers were able to demonstrate the safety and efficacy of these devices through a single set of trials, leading to faster approvals and widespread availability of the devices. Similarly, the development and approval of **orthopedic implants**, such as hip and knee replacements, have benefited from global standards that ensure consistent testing of materials, device performance, and patient outcomes. These case studies illustrate how **global standards** have improved both the **efficiency** of the approval process and the **safety** of medical devices, as harmonized guidelines ensure that all devices are held to the same high standards, regardless of the region in which they are tested or marketed. Through its contributions to global standardization, GHTF has made significant strides in advancing medical device development and ensuring that patients worldwide benefit from the latest medical innovations.

CHAPTER TWENTY-TWO

ICH Efficacy Guidelines

The International Council for Harmonisation of Technical Requirements for Pharmaceuticals for Human Use (ICH) plays a pivotal role in the global pharmaceutical landscape by establishing guidelines that ensure the safety, quality, and efficacy of medicines. Among its various guidelines, the ICH Efficacy Guidelines are essential for providing a framework for the design and conduct of clinical trials aimed at assessing the effectiveness of new pharmaceutical products. These guidelines serve as a foundation for harmonizing the regulatory requirements across different regions, facilitating smoother drug development and approval processes.

The ICH Efficacy Guidelines encompass several key areas, including the planning, implementation, and analysis of clinical trials. They outline best practices for trial design, the selection of appropriate endpoints, and the interpretation of clinical data. By promoting consistency in clinical trial methodologies, the guidelines help to ensure that the results are reliable and can be effectively compared across different studies.

One significant aspect of the ICH Efficacy Guidelines is their emphasis on patient-centered outcomes and the importance of considering the patient's perspective in clinical research. This focus not only enhances the relevance of clinical trials but also supports the development of treatments that address real-world patient needs. Additionally, the guidelines provide guidance on statistical considerations, ensuring that trials are adequately powered to detect meaningful treatment effects.

As global collaboration in pharmaceutical development continues to grow, the ICH Efficacy Guidelines are vital in promoting regulatory alignment and facilitating the timely availability of new therapies to patients. This chapter will delve into the key components of the ICH Efficacy Guidelines, exploring their significance in clinical research and their impact on the drug development process. By understanding these guidelines, stakeholders can better navigate the complexities of clinical trials and contribute to the advancement of safe and effective medications

22.1 ICH E4 – Dose Response Information to Support Drug Registration

The **ICH E4 guideline** provides a structured framework for generating and evaluating **dose-response data** during the drug development process. Dose-response studies are essential in determining the optimal dosage of a drug, ensuring that it is administered at levels that maximize **efficacy** while minimizing **adverse effects**. The guideline addresses the importance of studying how different doses of a drug impact both its **therapeutic effect** and its **safety profile**, which is crucial for regulatory approval. Dose-response data are used to establish the minimum amount of the drug that produces the desired therapeutic effect (**minimum effective dose**) and the highest dose that patients can tolerate without experiencing unacceptable side effects (**maximum tolerated dose**). This information is critical for developing the **labeling** and **dosage recommendations** that physicians use when prescribing the drug. ICH E4 plays a key role in guiding sponsors through the process of collecting and analyzing dose-response data to ensure that the final dosage regimen approved for use is both safe and effective for the intended patient population.

Several factors influence the design and interpretation of **dose-response studies**. One of the key considerations is **patient variability**, which refers to differences in how individuals respond to the same drug due to factors such as age, weight, genetics, and the presence of **comorbidities**. These variations can significantly affect both the **pharmacokinetics** (how the body absorbs, distributes, metabolizes, and excretes the drug) and the **pharmacodynamics** (how the drug interacts with its target to produce a therapeutic effect). For example, elderly patients may require lower doses due to reduced renal or liver function, while patients with faster metabolic rates may need higher doses to achieve the same therapeutic effect. ICH E4 emphasizes the need for dose-response studies to account for such variability by including diverse populations in clinical trials. Another critical aspect of dose-response studies is the need to establish the **minimum effective dose**—the lowest dose that provides the desired effect without unnecessary exposure to the drug. On the other hand, the **maximum tolerated dose** must be defined to prevent patients from experiencing **dose-limiting toxicities**. The ICH E4 guideline ensures that clinical trials are designed to explore a wide range of doses, allowing for a comprehensive understanding of the drug's therapeutic window.

The application of ICH E4's recommendations is a vital component of the **drug approval process**. Regulatory agencies such as the **U.S. Food and Drug Administration (FDA)**, the **European Medicines Agency (EMA)**, and Japan's **Pharmaceuticals and Medical Devices Agency (PMDA)** rely on dose-response data to evaluate whether the proposed dose regimen is appropriate for the target population. These agencies assess the data to determine if the **benefit-risk ratio** of the drug justifies its approval. One prominent example of the importance of dose-response information in drug registration is the development of **oncology drugs**, where establishing the optimal dose is critical due to the narrow therapeutic window of many cancer therapies. In the case of **immunotherapy drugs**, dose-response studies have been used to identify the lowest dose that effectively stimulates the immune system to attack cancer cells while minimizing the risk of **immune-related adverse events**. By following the structured framework provided by ICH E4, sponsors are able to generate robust dose-response data that satisfy regulatory requirements and support the approval of new therapies. This ensures that patients receive treatments that are not only effective but also safe when used at the recommended doses.

22.2 ICH E7 – Studies in Geriatric Populations

The **ICH E7 guideline** is specifically focused on ensuring that clinical trials are conducted in **geriatric populations**, which refers to patients aged **65 and above**. This guideline was developed in recognition of the fact that older adults often respond differently to medications compared to younger populations due to age-related physiological changes. As the global population ages, the proportion of elderly patients taking medications increases, making it essential to test new therapies in this demographic. ICH E7 emphasizes that clinical trials must evaluate both the **safety** and **efficacy** of drugs in older adults, ensuring that the therapies being developed are suitable for use in this group. Without adequate representation of elderly patients in clinical trials, there is a risk that new treatments may not be as safe or effective when used in this population. By following the ICH E7 guideline, sponsors can generate data that supports the safe use of medications in older patients, allowing for more informed regulatory decisions and better outcomes for elderly patients.

Conducting clinical trials in geriatric populations requires special considerations due to the **pharmacokinetic** and **pharmacodynamic** differences that emerge with aging. As patients grow older, various physiological changes occur that can affect how drugs are absorbed, distributed, metabolized, and excreted from the body. For example, elderly patients often experience **reduced renal function**, which can lead to slower clearance of drugs that are eliminated through the kidneys, increasing the risk of drug accumulation and toxicity. Additionally, liver metabolism may be impaired in older adults, affecting how drugs are processed and potentially leading to **higher drug concentrations** in the bloodstream. The **pharmacodynamics** of drugs, or how they interact with the body, can also be altered in geriatric patients. Older adults are often more **susceptible to adverse drug reactions (ADRs)** due to increased sensitivity to medications and a higher likelihood of **drug-drug interactions** from polypharmacy. ICH E7 stresses the need for trials to carefully monitor for these age-related changes and to adjust dosing regimens accordingly. This ensures that the drug is not only effective but also safe when used in older populations who may be more vulnerable to side effects.

Designing clinical trials for geriatric populations under the **ICH E7** guideline requires a thoughtful approach that accounts for the unique challenges of studying older adults. One of the primary requirements is the **appropriate selection of patients**, ensuring that elderly individuals from a wide range of ages and health conditions are included. This is important because the elderly population is highly diverse, with some patients being relatively healthy while others may have multiple chronic diseases (**comorbidities**). The presence of comorbidities can influence how a drug behaves in the body, making it essential to include older patients with conditions such as diabetes, hypertension, or cardiovascular disease in clinical trials. Additionally, ICH E7 recommends **longer follow-up periods** to monitor for **delayed adverse events**, as elderly patients may experience side effects that take longer to manifest. For example, certain drugs may cause **cognitive decline** or affect mobility, but these effects may not be immediately apparent during short-term studies. A longer follow-up allows for a more comprehensive assessment of the drug's safety in elderly patients.

Several drugs have been specifically tested in geriatric populations, with data generated from these trials leading to important insights into treatment strategies for older adults. For instance, **anticoagulants** used to prevent strokes in older patients with **atrial fibrillation** have undergone extensive testing in geriatric populations. These studies revealed that elderly patients are at higher risk of bleeding complications, leading to the development of

age-adjusted dosing regimens to minimize this risk. Another example is the testing of **antipsychotic medications** in elderly patients with dementia. These trials uncovered an increased risk of cardiovascular events and death in older adults, prompting regulatory agencies to issue **black box warnings** and limiting the use of these drugs in this population. By conducting trials that adhere to ICH E7 guidelines, sponsors can ensure that their drugs are optimized for use in older adults, improving safety and efficacy while addressing the unique needs of this growing patient group.

22.3 ICH E8 – General Considerations in Clinical Trials

The **ICH E8 guideline** provides a fundamental framework for conducting clinical trials, ensuring that they are designed and executed in a way that is **scientifically valid, ethically sound**, and capable of addressing important clinical questions. This guideline serves as the foundation for all clinical trials, setting forth general principles that apply across different types of studies, from early-phase exploratory trials to large-scale confirmatory trials. The primary goal of ICH E8 is to ensure that clinical trials generate reliable data that can be used to evaluate the **safety** and **efficacy** of new therapies, while protecting the rights and well-being of trial participants. It emphasizes that trials must be conducted in accordance with **Good Clinical Practice (GCP)**, ensuring that the study design, execution, and reporting adhere to the highest standards of scientific integrity. The principles outlined in ICH E8 guide sponsors, investigators, and regulators in the development and evaluation of clinical trial protocols, helping to ensure that trials meet both **regulatory** and **ethical** requirements.

One of the key aspects of the **ICH E8 guideline** is its focus on the **core elements of clinical trial design**, which are critical for ensuring that a trial addresses its scientific objectives effectively. The first step in designing a trial is to clearly define the **trial objectives**, which outline the purpose of the study and the specific clinical questions it aims to answer. These objectives guide every aspect of the trial, from patient selection to data analysis. For example, a trial may aim to determine the **efficacy** of a new drug in reducing the symptoms of a disease, or it may focus on evaluating the **safety profile** of the drug in a particular patient population. Once the objectives are established, the next key component is selecting the appropriate **patient population** for the study. This involves defining **inclusion and exclusion criteria** to ensure that the trial enrolls patients who are representative of the population that will use the drug once it is approved. Proper patient selection helps ensure that the trial results are generalizable to real-world clinical practice. Another critical element of trial design is determining the **endpoints**, which are the specific outcomes that will be measured to evaluate the success of the treatment. Endpoints must be **clinically meaningful** and directly related to the trial objectives, such as improvements in disease symptoms, overall survival, or quality of life. In addition to these elements, **ICH E8** emphasizes the importance of developing a well-structured protocol that minimizes **bias** and **variability**. A carefully designed protocol ensures that the trial is conducted in a consistent and reproducible manner, reducing the potential for confounding factors that could distort the results.

A major focus of **ICH E8** is ensuring the **quality and integrity of data** generated during clinical trials. High-quality data are essential for drawing reliable conclusions about a drug's safety and efficacy. One of the key challenges in clinical trials is **minimizing missing data**, which can compromise the **validity** of the trial results and lead to **biased conclusions**. ICH E8 encourages sponsors to implement robust data collection methods and to design trials that minimize the likelihood of missing data. This may involve strategies such as ensuring regular follow-up visits and providing support for patients to remain in the study. The guideline also highlights the importance of **accurate reporting** of outcomes, ensuring that all trial results are documented transparently and consistently. Poor trial design or inadequate data quality can have significant consequences. For example, trials with **inconsistent data collection** or poorly defined endpoints may lead to inconclusive or misleading results, delaying the approval of potentially beneficial therapies. One prominent example of the impact of poor data quality is the case of several trials for **Alzheimer's disease therapies**, where high rates of missing data and inconsistent outcome measures led to **failed regulatory submissions**. These failures highlight the importance of following ICH E8's recommendations to ensure that clinical trials produce **robust, reliable data** that can support regulatory decision-making and ultimately improve patient care.

22.4 ICH E10 – Choice of Control Groups

The **ICH E10 guideline** provides a framework for selecting the appropriate **control group** in clinical trials, a decision that plays a critical role in the design of the study and significantly influences how trial results are interpreted. The choice of control group impacts the **validity** of comparisons between the experimental treatment and existing therapies or no treatment at all. By establishing clear guidelines for selecting control groups, ICH E10 ensures that trials are designed to yield meaningful, scientifically sound data that support the **efficacy** and **safety** of new treatments. The guideline emphasizes that the control group must be chosen carefully based on the **clinical context**, disease being studied, and **ethical considerations**, particularly when the trial involves vulnerable populations or serious medical conditions. Properly selecting the control group helps avoid **bias** and ensures that the trial's outcomes are both reliable and relevant for regulatory submissions and clinical practice.

ICH E10 outlines several types of **control groups** that can be used in clinical trials, each with its own advantages and appropriate use cases. **Placebo controls** are commonly used when there is no standard treatment available or when the existing treatments have not proven to be effective. Placebo-controlled trials are typically used in conditions where the effects of the placebo can be well understood, but their use raises **ethical concerns** in serious or life-threatening conditions where withholding effective treatment could harm patients. In such cases, **active treatment controls**, where the new treatment is compared against a **standard therapy**, may be more appropriate. Active treatment controls allow researchers to assess whether the new treatment provides additional benefits over the existing standard of care. Another type of control group described in ICH E10 is the **historical control**, where the results of the current trial are compared to data from past studies or clinical records. This approach is often used in rare diseases or conditions where conducting a new randomized trial with a control group may not be feasible. However, historical controls are subject to more variability, as the data may have been collected under different conditions, making it less reliable than other types of control groups.

The **choice of control group** has a profound impact on the **statistical power** and **clinical relevance** of a trial. For example, using a **placebo control** in conditions where patients typically do not respond to existing treatments can provide a clearer demonstration of the new treatment's efficacy. However, in trials involving **life-threatening conditions**, the use of a placebo can pose significant **ethical dilemmas**. In such cases, ICH E10 advocates for the use of **active treatment controls** to ensure that patients are not denied access to effective therapies. Ethical concerns surrounding placebo use are particularly pronounced in trials for conditions such as **cancer** or **HIV**, where withholding treatment could lead to significant harm. ICH E10 addresses these issues by recommending that researchers carefully balance the **scientific need** for a placebo control with the **ethical**

responsibility to protect patient welfare. Additionally, the guideline discusses the **clinical and regulatory implications** of choosing different control groups, highlighting that the wrong choice can lead to **misleading results** or **delays in drug approval**. For instance, trials that use inappropriate control groups may fail to demonstrate the real-world benefits of a new treatment, leading to **underpowered** studies that are unable to detect meaningful differences between the experimental treatment and the control.

22.5 ICH E11 – Clinical Investigation in Pediatric Populations

The **ICH E11** guideline provides a comprehensive framework for conducting clinical trials in **pediatric populations** (patients under the age of 18), ensuring that new therapies intended for children are tested for both **safety** and **efficacy**. Pediatric clinical trials are essential because children are not simply smaller adults; their physiological and metabolic profiles differ significantly, meaning that drugs that are effective and safe in adults may not behave the same way in younger patients. ICH E11 emphasizes that therapies specifically intended for children must be thoroughly tested in pediatric populations to ensure that they meet the necessary standards of care. The guideline sets out to address the gaps that historically existed in pediatric drug development, where many therapies were approved without being properly tested in children, leading to uncertainty about the correct dosage or potential side effects. By following ICH E11, sponsors can generate the required data to support regulatory approval for pediatric use, ensuring that children have access to safe, effective, and appropriately dosed medications.

Designing **pediatric trials** presents a unique set of challenges that differ from trials conducted in adult populations. One of the most significant issues is determining **age-appropriate dosing**, as children's metabolic rates and **drug absorption, distribution, metabolism, and excretion** (ADME) processes vary depending on their developmental stage. For example, infants, toddlers, and adolescents may require different formulations or doses of the same drug to achieve therapeutic efficacy without causing harm. ICH E11 encourages sponsors to conduct **pharmacokinetic** and **pharmacodynamic** studies in different pediatric age groups to establish safe and effective dosing regimens. Another key consideration in pediatric trial design is obtaining **informed consent** from guardians or parents, as children cannot legally consent to participate in clinical research. This process must be handled with care, ensuring that parents fully understand the risks and benefits of the study before agreeing to enroll their child. Additionally, ICH E11 highlights the need for **age-specific safety monitoring** due to the potential for different **adverse events** in pediatric patients compared to adults. For instance, children may be more prone to certain side effects like growth suppression or developmental delays, requiring long-term follow-up in trials.

The **ethical challenges** of involving children in clinical trials are a major focus of the **ICH E11 guideline**. Conducting research on vulnerable populations such as children raises significant ethical considerations, including the importance of ensuring that trials are conducted in the **best interest of the child**. One ethical principle emphasized by ICH E11 is obtaining **assent** from children when appropriate. While children cannot provide formal consent, they should still be given age-appropriate explanations about the trial and asked for their **assent** to participate, particularly in cases involving older children or adolescents. The guideline also stresses the importance of using **pediatric-specific endpoints**, which may differ from those used in adult trials. For example, trials for pediatric asthma medications may focus on **lung function** or **quality of life** metrics that are more relevant to children. ICH E11 also ensures that trials are designed to minimize unnecessary risks to pediatric participants, in line with international ethical standards. Several **pediatric trials** have led to the approval of life-saving therapies for childhood diseases. For instance, clinical studies conducted under ICH E11 principles were crucial for the development and approval of **pediatric vaccines** and treatments for childhood cancers, such as **leukemia**. These trials helped establish safe dosage regimens and identified potential long-term side effects, leading to treatments that have significantly improved survival rates and quality of life for children with these conditions.

CHAPTER TWENTY-THREE

Biostatistics in Clinical Research

23.1 Key Biostatistical Principles

Introduction to Biostatistics

Biostatistics is an essential element in the field of clinical research, ensuring that data collected during clinical trials are analyzed and interpreted in a manner that adheres to scientific principles. The role of biostatistics is foundational because it provides the tools necessary to quantify treatment effects, assess potential risks, and make predictions based on the data gathered from participants. Without the proper application of biostatistical methods, clinical trial outcomes could easily be prone to bias, misinterpretation, or uncertainty, leading to misleading conclusions about the efficacy and safety of new therapies. The rigorous use of biostatistical techniques enables researchers to maintain objectivity, ensuring that the results are reliable and meaningful for decision-making in healthcare. Through these methods, biostatistics not only validates the trial outcomes but also ensures that they can be generalized to broader populations with accuracy and precision.

The importance of biostatistics lies in its central role in evidence-based medicine. It forms the backbone of the analysis used to determine whether new treatments are both effective and safe for patient use. For example, when a new drug is being tested, biostatistics helps determine whether the drug provides significant improvement in patient outcomes compared to existing treatments or a placebo. By evaluating and analyzing the data from clinical trials, biostatisticians can measure the drug's impact, identify any associated risks, and ensure that the conclusions drawn are based on solid, empirical evidence. This type of data-driven decision-making is critical for regulatory bodies like the FDA or EMA when deciding whether to approve a new drug for public use. Biostatistics not only helps in identifying the magnitude of the drug's effect but also plays a vital role in ensuring that the analysis is conducted fairly and transparently, which is crucial for maintaining public trust in clinical research.

To achieve these goals, biostatistics employs various tools and methods that are vital to understanding trends, making predictions, and confirming statistical significance. These include **descriptive statistics**, which summarize data patterns; **hypothesis testing**, which helps determine whether observed effects are real or due to chance; and **regression analysis**, which identifies relationships between variables. Each of these methods is applied with precision to ensure that the conclusions reached are valid and that the results can withstand scrutiny from the scientific community. For instance, hypothesis testing helps researchers decide whether a treatment has a significant effect or whether the observed differences could be attributed to random variation. By using such statistical tools, clinical trials become a reliable source of evidence, allowing researchers to draw accurate and useful conclusions from the data.

Core Principles

One of the core principles of clinical trial design is **randomization**, a process that ensures participants are assigned to treatment groups without bias. Randomization is essential because it helps ensure that the treatment and control groups are comparable at the start of the trial, reducing the potential for external factors to influence the outcomes. By randomly assigning participants, researchers can minimize confounding variables, such as age or pre-existing conditions, which might otherwise skew the results. Randomization not only enhances the internal validity of the trial but also increases the likelihood that the observed effects are truly attributable to the treatment under investigation, rather than to other unrelated factors.

Another critical principle in clinical research is **blinding**, which involves concealing treatment assignments from participants, researchers, or both. **Single-blind** studies keep participants unaware of which treatment they are receiving, while **double-blind** studies ensure that neither participants nor researchers know which treatment is being administered. Blinding is used to prevent bias that might arise from expectations or preconceptions about the treatment. For instance, if participants know they are receiving the active treatment, they might report better outcomes simply due to the placebo effect, rather than the actual efficacy of the drug. By maintaining blinding throughout the study, researchers can ensure that the results are driven solely by the treatment's effects, rather than by psychological or observational bias.

Sample size determination is another crucial aspect of clinical trial design. Determining the appropriate sample size ensures that the trial is capable of detecting a statistically significant difference between treatment groups if one exists. Larger sample sizes increase the trial's **statistical power**, meaning there is a higher probability of detecting a true effect. However, excessively large sample sizes can lead to unnecessary costs and complexity, making it essential to strike a balance. A well-calculated sample size allows researchers to detect clinically meaningful differences without expending more resources than necessary. For example, if a trial is underpowered (i.e., has too few participants), it may fail to detect a true treatment effect, leading to a **Type II error**, where an effective treatment is incorrectly deemed ineffective.

The concept of **statistical power** is vital for understanding the reliability of a clinical trial's results. **Statistical power** refers to the probability that the trial will detect a treatment effect if one truly exists. A commonly accepted level of statistical power is **80%**, meaning that there is an 80% chance of detecting a significant difference between treatment groups if such a difference exists. Low statistical power increases the likelihood of missing a real effect, leading to incorrect conclusions about the treatment's efficacy. In trials with low power, even if a treatment works, the study might not provide enough evidence to demonstrate that effectiveness, which can delay the approval of potentially life-saving therapies.

Examples of Key Concepts

The **p-value** is a statistical measure used to determine whether the results observed in a clinical trial are statistically significant. A **p-value** of less than **0.05** typically indicates that the observed effect is unlikely to have occurred by chance, with a probability of less than 5%. For example, in a clinical trial testing a new drug, a **p-value** of 0.03 would indicate that there is only a 3% chance that the results are due to random variation, suggesting that the treatment likely had a real impact. The use of p-values helps researchers assess whether the differences between treatment and control groups are meaningful and not merely the result of random fluctuations in the data.

Another essential biostatistical tool is the **confidence interval (CI)**, which provides a range of values within which the true effect size is likely to lie. A **95% confidence interval** means that if the trial were repeated 100 times, the true treatment effect would fall within the calculated range in 95 of those trials. Confidence intervals offer more information than p-values alone by showing not only whether the result is statistically significant but also providing insight into the **precision** of the estimate. For instance, in a trial investigating the effect of a diabetes medication on blood sugar levels, a **95% confidence interval** for the reduction in blood sugar might range from **1.5 to 3.0 mmol/L**, indicating that the true reduction in blood sugar lies within this range with 95% confidence.

Hypothesis testing is another fundamental concept in clinical trials. It is used to test an assumption about a population parameter. The **null hypothesis (H^0)** typically assumes that there is no difference between the treatment and control groups. If the data suggest that the null hypothesis is unlikely, it is rejected in favor of the **alternative hypothesis (H_1)**, which posits that there is a significant difference between the groups. For example, in a cardiovascular trial evaluating a new drug, researchers might test the null hypothesis that the drug has no effect on reducing heart attacks. If the trial shows a statistically significant reduction in heart attacks, the null hypothesis would be rejected, and the alternative hypothesis—indicating that the drug reduces heart attack risk—would be accepted.

These biostatistical principles form the foundation for ensuring that clinical trials are conducted rigorously, with the results providing valid and reliable insights into the safety and efficacy of new treatments.

23.2 Application in Clinical Study Design

Biostatistics plays a central role in the design of clinical trials, ensuring that the study is scientifically sound and capable of producing valid and interpretable results. The application of biostatistical principles is essential to addressing key clinical questions, as it provides the framework for structuring the trial in a way that minimizes bias, controls for confounding variables, and maximizes the accuracy of the results. Without the application of biostatistics in the design phase, a clinical trial may produce data that are difficult to interpret or unreliable, ultimately compromising the ability to make informed decisions about the safety and efficacy of the intervention being studied. A well-designed study that incorporates biostatistics is more likely to generate results that can be replicated and generalized to the broader population. This ensures that the conclusions drawn from the trial are both scientifically valid and relevant to real-world clinical practice, which is critical for regulatory approval and the successful adoption of new treatments.

Randomization is one of the most important biostatistical techniques applied in the design of clinical trials. It involves randomly assigning participants to different treatment groups to reduce the potential for **selection bias**, which occurs when certain participants are more likely to receive one treatment over another. By ensuring that participants are randomly assigned, researchers can ensure that the treatment groups are comparable at the start of the trial, reducing the likelihood that external factors (such as age, gender, or disease severity) will influence the outcomes. Randomization enhances the **internal validity** of the trial by making it less likely that observed differences between groups are due to pre-existing characteristics rather than the treatment itself. In addition to randomization, **stratification** is used to ensure that specific subgroups within the population, such as those defined by age or disease severity, are evenly distributed between the treatment arms. Stratification ensures that these important variables are balanced across groups, further reducing the risk of confounding and making it easier to detect true treatment effects within subpopulations of interest.

Another critical aspect of trial design that relies heavily on biostatistics is the determination of **sample size** and **power calculations**. The sample size of a clinical trial is crucial because it directly impacts the **statistical power** of the study—the probability that the trial will detect a treatment effect if one truly exists. A trial with too few participants may fail to detect a clinically significant difference, even if the treatment is effective, leading to what is known as a **Type II error**. For instance, if a clinical trial testing a new cancer therapy has insufficient power due to a small sample size, the results may incorrectly suggest that the therapy has no effect, when in reality, it may be highly effective. Biostatisticians calculate the appropriate sample size based on several factors, including the **expected effect size** (the magnitude of the difference between treatment groups), the desired **significance level** (usually set at 0.05), and the required statistical power (typically set at 80%). These calculations ensure that the trial is designed with enough participants to reliably detect a meaningful difference, if one exists, while avoiding the unnecessary inclusion of excess participants, which would increase costs and complexity without providing additional value.

For example, in a trial investigating the effect of a new antihypertensive drug, biostatisticians may calculate that a sample size of **300 participants** per group is necessary to detect a **5 mmHg reduction in systolic blood pressure** compared to the placebo group, with 80% power and a significance level of 0.05. If the trial is conducted with a much smaller sample size—say, 100 participants per group—the study might lack the statistical power to detect this reduction, even though the drug could be genuinely effective. In this scenario, a trial with insufficient power could lead to a false conclusion, delaying the approval and availability of an effective treatment. Proper sample size calculations ensure that clinical trials are designed to yield meaningful results that can inform clinical decision-making, regulatory approvals, and future research.

23.3 Statistical Methods for Data Analysis

In clinical research, statistical methods play a crucial role in analyzing the data collected during trials, allowing researchers to draw valid conclusions about the effectiveness and safety of treatments. The choice of statistical method depends on the type of data being analyzed, the research question, and the design of the study. Different **statistical techniques** offer tools for summarizing data, testing hypotheses, and identifying relationships between variables. Broadly, these methods can be categorized into **descriptive statistics**, which provide a summary of the data, and **inferential statistics**, which allow researchers to make conclusions about a population based on sample data.

Descriptive statistics help summarize the main features of a dataset, providing an overview of important measures such as the **mean**, **median**, **standard deviation**, and **range**. For example, in a trial testing a new drug for reducing blood pressure, descriptive statistics might reveal that the **mean reduction** in systolic blood pressure was 8 mmHg, with a **standard deviation** of 2.5 mmHg, indicating the degree of variation in the treatment effect across participants. Descriptive statistics are foundational for understanding the basic characteristics of the dataset before moving to more complex analyses.

Inferential statistics, on the other hand, involve making predictions or inferences about a population based on sample data. Common methods include **hypothesis testing** and **confidence intervals**, which are used to determine whether the observed effects in a trial are statistically significant. For example, a **t-test** might be used to compare the mean blood pressure reduction between the treatment and placebo groups, allowing researchers to infer whether the new drug's effect is significantly different from the placebo. **Parametric tests**, such as **ANOVA (Analysis of Variance)**, are commonly used when the data follow a normal distribution, whereas **non-parametric tests**, such as the **Mann-Whitney U test**, are applied when the data do not meet the assumptions of normality.

The **selection of the appropriate statistical method** is critical and depends largely on the type of data being analyzed. For instance, if the data are **categorical** (e.g., success vs. failure), researchers might use a **chi-square test** to determine whether there is a significant association between treatment and outcomes. In contrast, if the data are **continuous** (e.g., blood pressure, cholesterol levels), parametric tests such as **t-tests** or **ANOVA** might be more appropriate. The choice of method also depends on the study design. For example, in a **randomized controlled trial (RCT)**, researchers often use regression analysis to adjust for confounding variables, ensuring that the observed effect is due to the treatment rather than other factors. Failing to select the correct method can lead to misleading conclusions, such as underestimating or overestimating the treatment's effect. Therefore, biostatisticians carefully evaluate the data type and study design to ensure that the chosen methods align with the research objectives and produce reliable results.

A common example of statistical methods in action is the use of **Kaplan-Meier curves** in **survival analysis**. This method is used to estimate the survival probabilities over time in clinical trials where the outcome is the time to an event, such as death or disease progression. Kaplan-Meier curves are particularly useful in **oncology trials**, where they can illustrate differences in survival between treatment groups. For instance, a trial comparing two cancer treatments might show that patients in the experimental group had a higher probability of survival at 12 months compared to those in the control group. By analyzing the **hazard ratio** and conducting **log-rank tests**, researchers can determine whether the survival differences are statistically significant.

Another example is the use of **ANOVA** when comparing the means of more than two groups. For instance, in a clinical trial testing multiple doses of a new medication, ANOVA can be used to compare the mean response across the different dose groups to determine whether there are significant differences in treatment effects between them. If ANOVA reveals a significant result, post-hoc tests, such as **Tukey's HSD**, can be applied to identify which specific groups differ from each other.

The application of statistical methods in clinical research ensures that the data are interpreted in a scientifically sound manner, providing the evidence needed to support the development of new treatments. By choosing the correct methods and applying them rigorously, researchers can confidently draw conclusions that inform regulatory decisions, clinical guidelines, and future research.

23.4 Interpretation of Clinical Trial Data

Interpreting clinical trial data is a critical process that determines the success of the research and its implications for patient care. A robust **data interpretation framework** allows researchers to make sense of the statistical results obtained from a clinical trial and draw meaningful conclusions about the treatment's **efficacy**, **safety**, and **comparative effectiveness.** When interpreting clinical trial data, several key statistical measures play a crucial role, including **p-values**, **confidence intervals**, and **effect sizes.** Each of these helps researchers quantify the strength of the observed effects and assess whether they are likely to be genuine findings or the result of chance.

The **p-value** is one of the most widely used tools for determining whether the differences observed between treatment groups are statistically significant. A **p-value** of less than **0.05** is typically used as the threshold for statistical significance, meaning that there is less than a 5% chance that the observed difference occurred by random chance alone. However, while a statistically significant p-value suggests that the treatment effect is unlikely to be due to chance, it does not provide information about the **magnitude** of the effect or its **clinical importance**. That is where **effect sizes** and **confidence intervals (CIs)** become critical. The **effect size** measures the strength of the treatment's impact, giving a sense of how large or small the treatment effect is. For example, a clinical trial for a cholesterol-lowering drug may show a statistically significant reduction in LDL cholesterol levels with a **p-value of 0.02**, but the effect size would tell us how much cholesterol levels actually dropped, allowing us to understand the clinical importance of the result. Additionally, **confidence intervals** provide a range of plausible values within which the true treatment effect is likely to fall, offering more insight into the **precision** of the estimates.

When interpreting clinical trial data, it is crucial to differentiate between **statistical significance** and **clinical significance**. Statistical significance, typically indicated by a **p-value** less than 0.05, tells us whether the observed effect is likely to be real rather than due to chance. However, it does not necessarily imply that the effect is large enough to make a meaningful difference in patient outcomes. **Clinical significance**, on the other hand, refers to the **practical importance** of the treatment effect—whether it is large enough to improve the health and quality of life of patients. For example, in a clinical trial for a weight loss drug, a reduction in body weight of 0.5 kg may be statistically significant with a **p-value of 0.04**, but such a small reduction is unlikely to be clinically meaningful for patients seeking substantial weight loss. Conversely, a large reduction in body weight, such as 10 kg, would likely be both statistically significant and clinically significant, indicating a meaningful benefit for patients. Researchers must always consider both the statistical and clinical significance of trial results when making conclusions about the effectiveness of a treatment.

Another essential aspect of data interpretation is understanding how to handle **uncertainty and variability** in the results. Clinical trials often involve variability in patient responses, making it critical to account for this when drawing conclusions. **Confidence intervals** are useful tools in this regard, as they provide a range of plausible values for the treatment effect, giving a clearer picture of the **precision** of the results. For example, if a clinical trial shows that a new antihypertensive drug lowers systolic blood pressure by an average of **8 mmHg**, with a **95% confidence interval** ranging from **5 to 11 mmHg**, this suggests that the true reduction in blood pressure is likely to fall within that range. The **width** of the confidence interval reflects the level of uncertainty—narrow intervals indicate more precise estimates, while wider intervals suggest greater uncertainty. Understanding the **variability** in the data helps researchers assess how confident they can be in their findings and whether further research is needed to refine the estimates.

CHAPTER TWENTY-FOUR

Key FDA Guidelines for Clinical Research

The U.S. Food and Drug Administration (FDA) is a critical regulatory authority in the domain of clinical research, providing guidelines that ensure the safety, efficacy, and quality of pharmaceuticals and medical devices. The FDA's guidelines are essential for guiding the design, conduct, and reporting of clinical trials, ensuring that new treatments meet rigorous standards before they are approved for public use. This chapter aims to elucidate the key FDA guidelines that shape clinical research, providing a comprehensive overview of their implications for researchers, sponsors, and regulatory bodies.

The FDA's guidelines cover a wide range of topics critical to clinical research, including the requirements for conducting trials, the responsibilities of investigators and sponsors, and the criteria for data reporting and safety monitoring. These guidelines are designed to protect participants, ensure the integrity of clinical trials, and facilitate the development of effective new therapies.

One of the central guidelines issued by the FDA is the Good Clinical Practice (GCP) guideline, which outlines the standards for the design, conduct, and reporting of clinical trials. The GCP guidelines ensure that trials are conducted with the utmost respect for participants and that data is reliable and accurately reported. This includes provisions for informed consent, protocol adherence, and the handling of adverse events.

Another crucial set of guidelines pertains to the New Drug Application (NDA) process, which provides detailed instructions on the submission requirements for new drugs. The NDA process is comprehensive, requiring extensive data on a drug's safety and efficacy from clinical trials, as well as information on its manufacturing and labeling.

The FDA also provides specific guidelines for the conduct of clinical trials involving special populations, such as pediatric and geriatric patients, to ensure that their unique needs are addressed. Additionally, there are guidelines for clinical trials involving medical devices, including the requirements for premarket approval and postmarket surveillance.

Understanding these FDA guidelines is crucial for all stakeholders involved in clinical research. Researchers must adhere to these guidelines to ensure compliance and to facilitate the successful development and approval of new treatments. This chapter will explore the major FDA guidelines, their application in clinical research, and their impact on the overall drug development process.

24.1 CFR 21 Part 50: Protection of Human Subjects

CFR 21 Part 50 is a key regulation under the U.S. Food and Drug Administration (FDA) that outlines the guidelines for protecting the rights, safety, and well-being of human subjects involved in clinical research. This regulation serves as the foundation for ethical clinical trials, ensuring that all individuals participating in studies are treated with respect and dignity. At its core, Part 50 aligns closely with the principles of **informed consent** and **ethical treatment** in research, mirroring international standards such as the **Declaration of Helsinki** and **Good Clinical Practice (GCP)** guidelines. These regulations are intended to ensure that participants are fully informed of their role in the study, including the risks, benefits, and alternatives before they agree to take part. By enforcing these principles, the FDA seeks to protect participants from harm and ensure that their decision to join a study is voluntary and based on a clear understanding of the research procedures involved.

One of the central provisions of CFR 21 Part 50 is the **informed consent process**, which is a critical component in safeguarding the autonomy of participants. The informed consent document provides detailed information about the study, including its purpose, duration, procedures, potential risks and benefits, and the rights of the participants, including their right to withdraw from the study at any time without penalty. The process of obtaining informed consent is not merely about having participants sign a form; it is about ensuring that they fully understand what they are consenting to. The FDA mandates that informed consent be obtained in a language understandable to the participant, free from complex medical jargon that could hinder comprehension. Furthermore, for **vulnerable populations** such as children, pregnant women, or individuals with cognitive impairments, the regulation requires additional safeguards. In these cases, legally authorized representatives may provide consent on behalf of the participant, but researchers must still ensure that the participants themselves are involved in the decision-making process to the extent possible. For example, **assent** from children is required in addition to parental consent, ensuring that even minors have a say in whether or not they participate in the research.

The **Institutional Review Board (IRB)** plays a crucial role in ensuring compliance with CFR 21 Part 50 by reviewing and approving all clinical trial protocols before the study begins. The IRB is responsible for evaluating whether the trial adheres to ethical standards, particularly in relation to participant safety and the informed consent process. Each IRB is composed of individuals with diverse backgrounds, including scientific and non-scientific members, who collectively assess the potential risks and benefits of the study. They ensure that any foreseeable risks are minimized and that the potential benefits justify the risks involved. In 2022 alone, IRBs across the U.S. reviewed thousands of clinical trials under these guidelines, reflecting the extensive oversight required to protect human subjects in research. The IRB also continues to monitor ongoing trials through periodic reviews, ensuring that the study continues to meet ethical standards and that any adverse events or changes to the study protocol are reported and handled appropriately. Should a trial fail to meet these standards, the IRB has the authority to suspend or terminate the study.

The importance of CFR 21 Part 50 extends beyond the protection of individual participants; it also ensures that clinical research is conducted in a manner that upholds public trust in the scientific process. By mandating rigorous standards for informed consent and continuous oversight by IRBs, the regulation helps maintain the integrity of clinical research, ensuring that studies are conducted ethically and that the data generated are reliable and credible. Through these provisions, CFR 21 Part 50 plays a fundamental role in the advancement of medical knowledge while safeguarding the rights and welfare of those who participate in the research.

24.2 CFR 21 Part 54: Financial Disclosure by Clinical Investigators

CFR 21 Part 54 is a regulatory guideline established by the FDA to ensure transparency in clinical research by requiring clinical investigators to disclose any financial interests that may have the potential to affect the objectivity of their research. This regulation is crucial in safeguarding the integrity of clinical trials, as financial interests can introduce biases that may influence the study's outcomes. Clinical investigators, who are responsible for conducting the research and ensuring the safety and efficacy of new treatments, must remain objective and impartial. If their financial ties to the sponsor or other entities involved in the trial are not disclosed, it can lead to conflicts of interest that jeopardize the credibility of the study. By mandating financial disclosures, CFR 21 Part 54 ensures that sponsors, regulatory authorities, and the public are fully aware of any potential conflicts, allowing them to assess the reliability of the study's data. This emphasis on transparency is integral to maintaining trust in the clinical research process and protecting patient safety.

The **disclosure requirements** outlined in CFR 21 Part 54 are comprehensive, covering a range of financial interests that could impact the objectivity of the research. Investigators are required to disclose any **equity ownership** in the company sponsoring the trial, as financial stakes in the company could lead to bias in the way the trial is conducted or how the results are interpreted. Similarly, if an investigator receives **compensation tied to the outcome of the study**, such as bonuses or financial incentives based on the trial's success, this must be disclosed. Such arrangements could create pressure to produce favorable results, compromising the trial's objectivity. Additionally, **intellectual property rights** related to the product being studied must also be disclosed. If an investigator holds patents or stands to benefit from the commercialization of the treatment, this financial interest could influence their decisions throughout the trial, from study design to data interpretation. Failure to disclose these financial interests can result in regulatory action by the FDA, including the rejection of trial data or even the invalidation of the entire study, delaying or preventing the approval of new drugs or devices.

The importance of **transparency** in clinical trials cannot be overstated. There have been numerous instances where undisclosed financial interests led to questions about the validity of the trial data, and in some cases, entire trials have been invalidated, affecting drug approvals. For example, a well-known case involved a clinical trial for a cardiovascular drug where the lead investigator failed to disclose substantial financial ties to the drug's manufacturer. When the undisclosed financial interest was uncovered, the FDA questioned the objectivity of the trial's results, leading to delays in the drug's approval and tarnishing the credibility of both the investigator and the sponsoring company. Such cases highlight the critical role that transparency plays in ensuring that clinical trials are conducted ethically and that the resulting data are trustworthy. By disclosing financial interests, investigators help maintain the integrity of the research and protect the public from potentially biased or manipulated results. This regulatory framework ensures that the data submitted to the FDA are free from undue influence, facilitating the approval of safe and effective treatments based solely on the merits of the research.

24.3 CFR 21 Part 312: Investigational New Drug Application (IND)

The **Investigational New Drug (IND) application** is a critical regulatory step in the development of new therapies, allowing the **legal shipment** and use of experimental drugs in clinical trials before they receive formal approval from the FDA. Without an IND, it would be illegal to distribute an investigational drug across state lines or administer it to human subjects in the U.S. The primary purpose of the IND is to ensure that the drug being tested is safe for use in humans during early-phase clinical trials. By submitting an IND, sponsors (typically pharmaceutical companies or research institutions) are seeking FDA approval to begin testing the drug on human participants, providing the necessary safety and scientific rationale for conducting the trial. The IND safeguards participants' rights and well-being while also facilitating the generation of critical safety and efficacy data that inform later stages of drug development.

An IND application comprises several key components, all of which must provide detailed and reliable information about the investigational drug. One of the core elements of the IND is the **clinical study protocol**, which outlines the objectives of the trial, the criteria for selecting participants, the dosing regimen, and the methods for monitoring and assessing patient outcomes. This protocol is essential in ensuring that the study is scientifically valid and ethically conducted. Additionally, the IND includes **manufacturing information** that describes how the drug is produced, ensuring that it meets high standards of quality and purity. This helps the FDA evaluate whether the drug can be manufactured consistently and safely. Another crucial component of the IND is the **safety data** from preclinical studies, which typically involve laboratory and animal testing. These preclinical studies provide initial insights into the drug's safety profile, such as its toxicity, pharmacokinetics, and pharmacodynamics, offering evidence that the drug is unlikely to pose significant risks to human participants. After the IND is submitted, the FDA has **30 days** to review the application and either allow the trial to proceed or place it on hold if concerns about safety or study design arise.

The role of INDs in drug development is particularly important in **early-phase clinical trials** (Phase I and II), which primarily focus on evaluating the **safety** of the investigational drug in humans. These early trials are essential for determining the appropriate dosage, identifying potential side effects, and gathering preliminary data on the drug's efficacy. The safety data generated from these trials form the foundation for advancing to later stages of development, where larger studies are conducted to further assess the drug's effectiveness and safety. Without the IND process, it would be impossible to ensure that experimental drugs undergo a rigorous, step-by-step evaluation before being made available to the public. In addition, the IND application helps the FDA monitor ongoing trials, ensuring that any emerging safety concerns are addressed promptly. This ongoing oversight is critical for protecting trial participants and ensuring that drug development proceeds responsibly and ethically.

24.4 CFR 21 Part 314: Application for FDA Approval to Market a New Drug

The **New Drug Application (NDA)** is the final step in the regulatory process that allows a pharmaceutical company to gain **FDA approval** to market a new drug in the United States. The NDA is a comprehensive submission that includes all data from **preclinical** and **clinical trials**, along with detailed information about the drug's manufacturing process, quality control measures, and proposed labeling. The NDA serves as the formal mechanism by which the FDA evaluates whether the drug is safe and effective for its intended use and whether the benefits outweigh the risks. Once approved, the drug can be made available to the public for prescription or over-the-counter use, marking the culmination of years of research and development. The NDA is crucial because it ensures that only drugs that meet stringent safety, efficacy, and quality standards are made available to patients, protecting public health.

An NDA must include several key components, each of which plays a vital role in the FDA's decision-making process. One of the most important components is the **clinical trial results**, which provide detailed data from **Phase I, II, and III** trials. These results demonstrate how the drug performs in humans, covering its safety profile, efficacy, and any side effects or adverse events that may arise. Along with the clinical trial data, the NDA includes **proposed labeling**, which specifies the drug's approved uses, dosage, potential side effects, and contraindications. The labeling helps healthcare providers understand how to prescribe and use the drug safely and effectively. Another critical component of the NDA is the **risk-benefit analysis**, where the sponsor presents evidence that the benefits of the drug outweigh its potential risks. This analysis is key to the FDA's decision, as it allows the agency to weigh the drug's therapeutic potential against any safety concerns. After submission, the FDA typically takes **6 to 10 months** to review the NDA, during which time it may request additional data or clarification from the sponsor. The thoroughness of this review process ensures that all aspects of the drug's development and intended use are carefully evaluated before approval is granted.

A notable example of a successful NDA is the approval of the cholesterol-lowering drug **atorvastatin** (marketed as Lipitor), which has had a significant impact on public health. The drug's developer submitted an NDA after conducting extensive clinical trials demonstrating its ability to reduce LDL cholesterol levels and decrease the risk of cardiovascular events such as heart attacks and strokes. The FDA reviewed the NDA within the standard 10-month timeframe and approved Lipitor for use in lowering cholesterol, leading to widespread use and making it one of the most prescribed drugs in the world. The success of Lipitor not only highlighted the importance of thorough clinical trials but also showed how a well-documented NDA can expedite the approval process for drugs that offer substantial public health benefits.

24.5 CFR 21 Part 320: Bioavailability and Bioequivalence Requirements

Bioavailability refers to the rate and extent to which the active ingredient of a drug is absorbed and becomes available at the site of action in the body. It is a key factor in determining the effectiveness of a drug, as it influences how much of the drug reaches the bloodstream and how quickly it acts. **Bioequivalence**, on the other hand, is a concept used to compare two drug formulations, typically a **generic drug** and its **brand-name counterpart**. For two drugs to be considered bioequivalent, they must have the same bioavailability, meaning they deliver the same amount of active ingredient into the bloodstream at the same rate and extent. CFR 21 Part 320 outlines the requirements for conducting bioavailability and bioequivalence studies, which are critical to ensuring that patients can safely switch between brand-name and generic medications without any differences in therapeutic effects.

The regulatory importance of bioavailability and bioequivalence studies lies in their role in the **approval of generic drugs**. For a generic drug to receive FDA approval, the manufacturer must demonstrate through bioequivalence studies that the generic version performs similarly to the brand-name drug in terms of **absorption**, **distribution**, and **effectiveness**. These studies are essential because they ensure that the generic drug provides the same therapeutic benefits as the original, without the need for additional clinical trials. By showing that the generic and brand-name drugs are bioequivalent, the FDA can be confident that patients will experience the same outcomes regardless of which version they take. This process helps to ensure the safety and effectiveness of generic medications while making more affordable treatment options available to the public. Bioequivalence studies are also crucial in the context of **interchangeability**, allowing pharmacists to substitute generic drugs for brand-name products without compromising treatment quality.

One example of a bioequivalence study involves **simvastatin**, a cholesterol-lowering drug. After the patent for the brand-name version (Zocor) expired, multiple generic versions were developed. In order for these generics to gain FDA approval, manufacturers conducted bioequivalence studies comparing their products to Zocor. The studies showed that the generic versions had the same bioavailability as the brand-name drug, meaning they were absorbed into the bloodstream at the same rate and extent. Based on these results, the FDA approved the generic versions, allowing them to enter the market. The approval of these generics significantly reduced the cost of simvastatin for patients, demonstrating the public health benefits of the bioequivalence requirements outlined in CFR 21 Part 320.

24.6 CFR 21 Part 812: Investigational Device Exemptions (IDE)

An **Investigational Device Exemption (IDE)** is a regulatory mechanism that allows a medical device that has not yet been approved by the FDA to be used in clinical studies for the purpose of collecting data on its **safety** and **efficacy**. The IDE permits the investigational device to be tested in humans under carefully controlled circumstances, ensuring that the device can undergo clinical trials while complying with regulatory requirements. This is an essential step in the **development of medical devices**, as it provides the data necessary for manufacturers to seek FDA approval later in the process. By granting an IDE, the FDA allows investigational devices to be studied in clinical trials even though they have not been fully evaluated or cleared for marketing. The clinical data generated under an IDE often serve as the foundation for future **Premarket Approval (PMA)** applications or **510(k) submissions**, which are required to bring a new medical device to market.

The IDE application process includes several **key requirements** to ensure that the investigational device is tested in a manner that protects patient safety and adheres to ethical standards. Before initiating a clinical trial with an investigational device, the sponsor must submit a comprehensive **clinical protocol** detailing the study's objectives, design, procedures, and endpoints. This protocol ensures that the trial is scientifically sound and capable of producing valid and reliable data on the device's performance. Additionally, **informed consent** must be obtained from all participants in the study, ensuring that they are fully aware of the potential risks and benefits of participating in the trial. The **FDA's approval** of the IDE is required before the study can begin, as the agency reviews the protocol, safety data from preclinical testing, and the device's intended use to ensure that the benefits of the study outweigh the risks to participants. The IDE is critical in the early stages of medical device development because it allows manufacturers to test their devices in real-world settings, providing valuable insights into how the device functions in patients and identifying any potential safety concerns that may not have been evident in laboratory testing.

An example of a medical device that underwent clinical trials under an IDE is the **Sapien Transcatheter Heart Valve**, developed by Edwards Lifesciences. The Sapien valve was designed as an alternative to open-heart surgery for patients with severe aortic stenosis who were too high-risk for traditional valve replacement surgery. The investigational use of the device began under an IDE, where clinical trials were conducted to evaluate its safety and efficacy in human patients. These studies provided critical data that supported the device's eventual **FDA approval**, making it one of the first transcatheter heart valves to be approved for commercial use in the United States. The IDE process was instrumental in allowing the innovative technology to be tested and eventually made available to a population of patients who previously had limited treatment options.

24.7 CFR 21 Part 822: Post-Market Surveillance

Post-market surveillance is an essential regulatory process mandated by the FDA under CFR 21 Part 822, requiring manufacturers to monitor the **safety and effectiveness** of medical devices after they have been approved and released into the market. While pre-market clinical trials provide initial data on a device's performance, they often do not capture the full range of potential risks, especially those that may arise during **long-term use** or in a broader patient population. Post-market surveillance is designed to bridge this gap, ensuring that any **adverse events**, device malfunctions, or unforeseen complications are detected and addressed in a timely manner once the device is in widespread use. This ongoing monitoring helps to protect public health by identifying any new risks associated with the device and ensuring that corrective actions can be taken if necessary. Through post-market surveillance, the FDA maintains its oversight role, ensuring that devices remain safe and effective throughout their lifecycle.

Manufacturers are required to conduct post-market surveillance by implementing a variety of **surveillance methods**. These methods often include conducting **post-market clinical studies**, where the device is evaluated in real-world conditions to assess its long-term performance and safety. Manufacturers are also obligated to monitor and report any **adverse events** that occur during the use of the device, especially those that could lead to serious injury or death. These reports, submitted through the FDA's **Medical Device Reporting (MDR)** system, allow the FDA to track potential safety issues and take regulatory action when necessary. Additionally, manufacturers may be required to submit **periodic updates** to the FDA, detailing the outcomes of ongoing post-market studies and any safety concerns that have been identified. The combination of these surveillance methods ensures that manufacturers remain responsible for the safety of their devices even after they have been approved for commercial use.

One notable example of post-market surveillance leading to action involves the **DePuy ASR hip replacement device**, which was recalled after post-market data revealed significant safety concerns. The device was initially approved for use based on clinical trial data, but post-market surveillance showed a high rate of **device failure** and **adverse events** such as pain and difficulty walking in patients who had received the implant. The post-market reports also indicated a need for **revision surgeries** due to complications such as **metal debris** being released into the body. As a result of the post-market surveillance data, the device was ultimately **recalled** by the manufacturer, and the FDA issued safety alerts to healthcare providers. This example underscores the importance of post-market surveillance in identifying risks that may not have been apparent during the initial clinical trials and demonstrates how ongoing monitoring plays a critical role in ensuring patient safety after a device has been approved for use.

24.8 FDA Safety Reporting Requirements

The **FDA mandates safety reporting** during clinical trials to ensure that any **adverse events** or **unexpected side effects** are promptly identified, reported, and addressed to protect participant safety. These safety reporting requirements are vital for maintaining the **integrity of clinical trial data** and ensuring that risks to participants are minimized. The FDA's focus on continuous monitoring during clinical trials allows for the early detection of potential safety concerns, ensuring that participants are not exposed to unnecessary harm and that the investigational drug or device's risk profile is fully understood before it reaches the market. This approach is in line with Good Clinical Practice (GCP) standards, emphasizing the importance of immediate reporting of safety issues to enable timely intervention.

There are several **types of reports** required by the FDA during clinical trials, each designed to capture specific aspects of participant safety and the trial's progress. One of the most critical reports is the **Serious Adverse Event (SAE)** report, which must be submitted to the FDA whenever a participant experiences a serious health issue, such as hospitalization, life-threatening conditions, disability, or death. SAEs are particularly important because they can signal previously unrecognized risks associated with the investigational product. These reports must be submitted promptly to allow the FDA to evaluate whether the trial should continue as planned or whether changes are needed to protect participants. In addition to SAE reporting, sponsors are also required to submit **Annual Progress Reports (APRs)**, which provide a comprehensive update on the trial's status, including the number of participants enrolled, any safety concerns identified during the reporting period, and updates on any ongoing safety monitoring activities. These reports ensure that the FDA has a continuous overview of the trial's progress and can intervene if safety issues arise.

The **importance of safety reporting** is evident in numerous clinical trials where early detection of safety concerns led to crucial modifications. For example, in a trial evaluating a new cancer treatment, early SAE reports revealed that participants were experiencing severe gastrointestinal side effects at a higher rate than anticipated. In response to these safety reports, the trial protocol was modified to include **dose adjustments** and more intensive **monitoring** of gastrointestinal symptoms, which reduced the incidence of these adverse events and allowed the trial to continue safely. Similarly, in a cardiovascular drug trial, early safety reporting highlighted unexpected **liver enzyme elevations** in some participants. As a result, the formulation of the drug was modified to reduce liver toxicity, ensuring that the investigational product could be tested further without causing undue harm to participants. These examples underscore the critical role that timely safety reporting plays in ensuring that clinical trials are conducted ethically and that patient safety remains the top priority throughout the trial process.

CHAPTER TWENTY-FIVE

Key European Union (EU) Regulations and ISO Standards

The regulatory environment in the European Union (EU) is integral to ensuring the safety, efficacy, and quality of medical products and clinical research. This chapter focuses on the key regulations that govern clinical trials and medical devices within the EU, as well as the relevant International Organization for Standardization (ISO) standards that further enhance the integrity of clinical research.

The EU has established a comprehensive regulatory framework that includes several key regulations, such as the Clinical Trials Regulation (EU) No 536/2014, which aims to streamline the approval process for clinical trials across member states while ensuring the protection of participants. This regulation emphasizes transparency, requiring the registration of clinical trials in a publicly accessible database and mandating the reporting of trial results. Such measures promote accountability and facilitate the sharing of knowledge within the scientific community.

Another significant regulation is the Medical Devices Regulation (MDR) (EU) 2017/745, which provides a framework for the safety and performance of medical devices. The MDR introduces stricter requirements for clinical evaluation, post-market surveillance, and the overall oversight of medical devices, ensuring that they meet high safety standards throughout their lifecycle. Understanding these regulations is essential for researchers and manufacturers involved in the development and testing of medical devices.

In addition to EU regulations, ISO standards play a crucial role in harmonizing practices and ensuring quality in clinical research and medical product development. Standards such as ISO 14155, which outlines the good clinical practice for clinical trials of medical devices, provide guidelines for the design, conduct, and reporting of trials, ensuring that they are conducted ethically and scientifically. These standards promote consistency across international borders and facilitate the acceptance of data from studies conducted in different countries.

The interplay between EU regulations and ISO standards is vital for achieving high standards in clinical research. This chapter will delve into the specifics of key EU regulations and ISO standards, exploring their implications for clinical trials and medical device development. By understanding these regulatory frameworks, stakeholders can navigate the complexities of clinical research in the EU and contribute to the advancement of safe and effective medical products.

25.1 EU Directives 2001 on Clinical Trials

The **EU Directives 2001/20/EC** marked a significant turning point in the regulation of clinical trials across the European Union. These directives were introduced with the primary aim of harmonizing the regulatory framework for clinical trials within the EU member states, ensuring that all trials are conducted according to strict guidelines related to ethics, safety, and transparency. Before the implementation of these directives, clinical trials in the EU were governed by various national regulations, which led to inconsistencies in how trials were conducted across borders. The 2001 directives sought to address this by creating a unified regulatory system that would not only streamline the trial process but also enhance the protection of participants and ensure high standards of data integrity.

At the heart of the **EU Directives 2001/20/EC** is the concept of **participant protection**. The directive places a strong emphasis on ensuring that all clinical trials are conducted with the **informed consent** of participants. This is particularly important as it ensures that participants are fully aware of the potential risks and benefits associated with their involvement in a clinical trial. The directive mandates that no trial can proceed without obtaining clear and voluntary consent from each participant. In addition to this, the directives underscore the need for trials to be conducted under strict **ethical guidelines**. This involves the formation of **ethics committees** that are responsible for reviewing and approving the trial protocols before the study can begin. These committees ensure that the rights, safety, and well-being of participants are prioritized, and that the trial is scientifically sound and ethically justified.

The **legal obligations** of sponsors are also clearly outlined in the EU Directives 2001/20/EC. Sponsors are the entities responsible for initiating, managing, and financing clinical trials, and they must comply with the regulatory requirements set forth by the directives. This includes submitting **detailed trial applications** to the relevant regulatory authorities in each member state where the trial is to be conducted. The applications must include comprehensive information about the trial's objectives, methodology, and risk assessment. The directive also mandates that sponsors maintain **data integrity** throughout the trial process. This means that all data collected during the trial must be accurate, reliable, and verifiable, ensuring that the results can be trusted by regulatory bodies and the broader scientific community.

One of the most significant impacts of the **EU Directives 2001/20/EC** is the way it has simplified the **authorization process** for conducting clinical trials within the EU. Prior to the implementation of these directives, sponsors often faced numerous administrative hurdles when trying to conduct trials in multiple EU countries, as each nation had its own set of regulations. The directives have streamlined this process by introducing a **single application procedure**, which allows sponsors to submit one trial application to multiple countries simultaneously. This has not only reduced the administrative burden for sponsors but has also made it easier for researchers to conduct **cross-border clinical trials**. In turn, this has facilitated the development of new treatments and therapies, particularly in cases where large, diverse populations are needed to generate robust clinical data.

The EU **Directives 2001/20/EC** were a major step forward in creating a more cohesive and efficient clinical trial landscape within Europe. By emphasizing the importance of **ethics**, **participant protection**, and **data integrity**, the directives have ensured that clinical trials conducted in the EU are held to the highest standards of safety and scientific rigor. The streamlined regulatory framework has also facilitated greater collaboration between EU member states, allowing for more efficient and effective research that benefits both patients and the scientific community.

25.2 EudraLex Volume 3 – Scientific Guidelines for Medicinal Products

EudraLex Volume 3 serves as a comprehensive guide for the **scientific development, approval, and regulation** of medicinal products within the **European Union (EU)**. These guidelines are vital for ensuring that all medicinal products meet the necessary standards of **quality, safety, and efficacy** before they are approved for use in the EU. The importance of these guidelines cannot be overstated, as they play a crucial role in protecting public health by ensuring that all medicines are rigorously tested and evaluated before reaching the market.

The **scope of EudraLex Volume 3** covers various stages of drug development, starting from **preclinical studies**, through **clinical trial design**, and continuing into **post-market surveillance**. Preclinical studies are the first step in the development process and are critical for assessing the initial safety profile of a medicinal product. These studies, usually conducted in **animal models**, help researchers understand how a drug behaves in a living organism, identifying potential toxicities, pharmacokinetic properties, and the mechanism of action. EudraLex Volume 3 provides detailed guidance on how these studies should be conducted to ensure the collection of reliable and accurate data that can be used to justify proceeding to **clinical trials** in humans.

For **clinical trial design**, EudraLex Volume 3 offers guidelines on how to structure studies in order to generate robust data that can demonstrate the **safety** and **efficacy** of a new medicinal product. The guidelines emphasize the need for trials to be scientifically sound and ethically conducted, with appropriate safeguards to protect participants. The guidelines also cover **trial endpoints, statistical methodologies**, and how to manage **adverse events** during trials. Additionally, the guidelines ensure that the results are reliable and reproducible, which is critical for regulatory approval. After a product is approved and reaches the market, **post-market surveillance** becomes an essential component of EudraLex Volume 3. This phase ensures that any long-term or rare side effects, which may not have been evident during clinical trials, are identified and addressed swiftly. The guidelines include detailed requirements for **pharmacovigilance** and **risk management plans**, which help in the continued monitoring of the product's safety profile once it is available to the public.

EudraLex Volume 3 also aligns closely with **global regulatory standards**, such as those established by the **International Council for Harmonisation (ICH)**. The **ICH guidelines** set out internationally accepted principles for the testing and regulation of medicinal products, with a focus on ensuring the **harmonization** of pharmaceutical regulation across different regions. By adhering to these global standards, the EU ensures that its medicinal products meet international benchmarks, facilitating the approval and use of European medicines in non-EU countries and vice versa. This alignment helps **reduce duplication of efforts**, enabling faster and more efficient drug development processes on a global scale.

Several specific sections of **EudraLex Volume 3** are particularly noteworthy, especially those relating to **biological medicinal products** and **biosimilars**. The rapid growth of **biotechnology** in recent decades has led to significant advancements in the development of **biologics**—medicines derived from living organisms. Given their complexity, biologics require special regulatory attention to ensure their **safety**, **quality**, and **efficacy**. EudraLex Volume 3 provides comprehensive guidelines on the production and evaluation of biological products, addressing the unique challenges that arise in their development. Furthermore, as **biosimilars** (biological products similar to already authorized reference products) have become increasingly important in reducing healthcare costs and increasing access to therapies, the guidelines have evolved to include specific regulations on their approval. This ensures that biosimilars meet stringent standards of **comparability** to the original product in terms of safety, efficacy, and quality.

EudraLex Volume 3 plays a pivotal role in shaping the regulatory landscape for medicinal products in the EU. By providing detailed guidelines across all stages of drug development, from preclinical studies to post-market surveillance, it ensures that only the highest-quality products reach patients. Furthermore, by aligning with international standards and addressing the evolving challenges of modern drug development, particularly in the field of biotechnology, EudraLex Volume 3 remains an essential resource for ensuring the **safety** and **efficacy** of medicines in Europe and beyond.

25.3 EU Annual Safety Report (ASR)

The **EU Annual Safety Report (ASR)** is a crucial regulatory requirement for any ongoing clinical trial within the European Union. Its primary function is to **monitor and assess the safety profile** of investigational drugs throughout the trial process, ensuring that the benefits continue to outweigh any potential risks. The **ASR** provides a systematic and standardized way of reviewing safety data collected over a **12-month period**, enabling both sponsors and regulatory bodies to evaluate the **risk-**

benefit ratio of a drug in development.

The **purpose of the ASR** is to document all safety-related data from clinical trials conducted in that particular year. This report is submitted to the **regulatory authorities** in the EU, ensuring that they are kept fully informed about the ongoing safety of the drug in question. It serves as a critical tool for identifying trends in **adverse events** that may not have been immediately apparent during the early stages of a clinical trial. By regularly compiling and analyzing the safety data, the ASR ensures that the trial remains ethically sound and that **participant safety** is maintained at all times. The report also serves as an early-warning system, flagging any emerging safety concerns that could necessitate modifications to the trial design or, in severe cases, suspension of the trial.

The **ASR** is instrumental in identifying **adverse events** and monitoring whether the **risks remain acceptable** as the trial progresses. This is particularly important in **long-term trials**, where the cumulative effects of a drug might lead to delayed or unforeseen adverse reactions. **Adverse drug reactions (ADRs)**, which are unintended and harmful effects resulting from the use of the drug, are systematically recorded and analyzed in the ASR. In addition to ADRs, the report places a strong emphasis on **serious adverse events (SAEs)**, which include life-threatening conditions, hospitalizations, or permanent disabilities resulting from the trial. Monitoring these adverse events on an annual basis ensures that participants are not exposed to **unacceptable levels of risk** and that any emerging issues are quickly addressed.

One of the critical aspects of the **ASR** is the inclusion of a comprehensive **risk-benefit assessment**. This assessment balances the known risks of the investigational drug against its potential benefits, determining whether it is still justifiable to continue the trial. The ASR not only looks at the number and severity of adverse events but also examines the **frequency and pattern** of these events across different trial phases and participant groups. If the risks start to outweigh the benefits, the regulatory authorities may recommend halting the trial or modifying its design to minimize further risks. Conversely, if the benefits remain substantial and the adverse events manageable, the trial can proceed as planned.

The **specific data** included in the ASR is exhaustive and provides a detailed overview of the trial's safety profile. This data includes the total number of **adverse drug reactions (ADRs)**, a breakdown of **serious adverse events (SAEs)**, the duration of these events, and any interventions required to manage them. Additionally, the ASR may include **comparative analyses** across different trial sites or participant demographics to identify patterns that may not be evident in smaller data sets. By aggregating this data annually, the ASR offers a comprehensive view of how the investigational drug is performing from a safety perspective and provides regulatory authorities with the information they need to make informed decisions.

25.4 ISO 14155: Clinical Investigation of Medical Devices

ISO 14155 is an internationally recognized standard that provides a framework for conducting **clinical investigations of medical devices**. This standard is designed to ensure that all trials meet the highest levels of **good clinical practice (GCP)** and adhere to strict **ethical standards**. By following ISO 14155, clinical investigations are conducted in a manner that prioritizes **participant safety**, ensures **data integrity**, and adheres to **regulatory requirements.**

The **scope of ISO 14155** is broad, encompassing all aspects of clinical trial design, execution, and reporting for medical devices. This standard places a strong emphasis on **participant safety** throughout the trial process, ensuring that the risks are thoroughly assessed and minimized. The standard also focuses on ensuring the **ethical conduct** of trials, mandating that participants provide informed consent and that their rights are protected throughout the study. In terms of **data reliability**, ISO 14155 ensures that the methods used to collect, analyze, and report data are scientifically sound and transparent, allowing for accurate and verifiable results that regulatory bodies and sponsors can trust.

ISO 14155 lays out specific requirements for the **design of clinical trials** for medical devices, ensuring that these trials are structured in a way that promotes the collection of high-quality data while protecting participants. One of the key components is the integration of **risk management** into the study design. Before the trial begins, potential risks associated with the medical device are identified, assessed, and managed to ensure they are within acceptable limits. This risk management process continues throughout the study, with ongoing **safety monitoring** to detect any emerging issues that could impact participant safety. The standard also mandates that participants must provide **informed consent** before enrolling in the trial. This process ensures that participants fully understand the potential risks and benefits of the trial, as well as their rights as participants, including the option to withdraw from the study at any time without penalty.

ISO 14155 aligns closely with the **EU Medical Devices Regulation (MDR)**, which governs the approval and post-market monitoring of medical devices in the European Union. By adhering to ISO 14155, clinical trials of medical devices meet the rigorous standards set forth by the **MDR**, ensuring that devices are both **safe** and **effective**. This alignment facilitates the regulatory approval process by ensuring that trials meet both **quality standards** and **ethical requirements**. The MDR requires that all medical devices undergo thorough clinical investigation before they can be approved for use in the EU, and ISO 14155 provides the specific guidelines for how these investigations should be carried out. This ensures that trials are not only compliant with EU regulations but also align with international best practices, which is particularly important for companies seeking approval in multiple markets.

CHAPTER TWENTY-SIX

Bibliography

1. International Council for Harmonisation of Technical Requirements for Pharmaceuticals for Human Use (ICH).
   ICH E6(R2) – Guideline for Good Clinical Practice. ICH Harmonised Guideline, 2016.
2. European Medicines Agency (EMA).
   Guidelines on the Investigation of Bioequivalence. London: European Medicines Agency, 2010.
3. U.S. Food and Drug Administration (FDA).
   CFR 21 Part 50 – Protection of Human Subjects. Washington, D.C.: U.S. Department of Health and Human Services, 2019.
4. World Health Organization (WHO).
   Handbook for Good Clinical Research Practice (GCP): Guidance for Implementation. Geneva: World Health Organization, 2005.
5. Council for International Organizations of Medical Sciences (CIOMS).
   International Ethical Guidelines for Health-related Research Involving Humans, 4th ed. Geneva: CIOMS, 2016.
6. U.S. Food and Drug Administration (FDA).
   CFR 21 Part 312 – Investigational New Drug Application (IND). Washington, D.C.: U.S. Department of Health and Human Services, 2019.
7. Central Drugs Standard Control Organization (CDSCO).
   Good Clinical Practice Guidelines for Clinical Trials in India. New Delhi: Ministry of Health and Family Welfare, Government of India, 2016.
8. International Council for Harmonisation of Technical Requirements for Pharmaceuticals for Human Use (ICH).
   ICH E8 – General Considerations for Clinical Trials. ICH Harmonised Guideline, 2019.

9. Nuremberg Military Tribunals under Control Council Law No. 10. *The Nuremberg Code (1947)*. Trials of War Criminals before the Nuremberg Military Tribunals. Washington, D.C.: U.S. Government Printing Office, 1949.
10. U.S. Food and Drug Administration (FDA). *CFR 21 Part 314 – Applications for FDA Approval to Market a New Drug*. Washington, D.C.: U.S. Department of Health and Human Services, 2020.
11. European Commission. *Directive 2001/20/EC of the European Parliament and of the Council on the Approximation of the Laws, Regulations and Administrative Provisions of the Member States Relating to the Implementation of Good Clinical Practice in the Conduct of Clinical Trials on Medicinal Products for Human Use*. Official Journal of the European Communities, 2001.
12. National Commission for the Protection of Human Subjects of Biomedical and Behavioral Research. *The Belmont Report: Ethical Principles and Guidelines for the Protection of Human Subjects of Research*. Washington, D.C.: U.S. Government Printing Office, 1979.
13. World Medical Association (WMA). *Declaration of Helsinki – Ethical Principles for Medical Research Involving Human Subjects*. JAMA 310, no. 20 (2013): 2191-2194.
14. U.S. Food and Drug Administration (FDA). *FDA Guidance for Industry: Acceptance of Foreign Clinical Studies*. Washington, D.C.: U.S. Department of Health and Human Services, 2020.
15. International Organization for Standardization (ISO). *ISO 14155 – Clinical Investigation of Medical Devices for Human Subjects – Good Clinical Practice*. Geneva: International Organization for Standardization, 2020.
16. European Medicines Agency (EMA). *Volume 9A of the Rules Governing Medicinal Products in the European Union – Pharmacovigilance for Medicinal Products for Human Use*. London: European Medicines Agency, 2012.
17. Indian Council of Medical Research (ICMR). *Ethical Guidelines for Biomedical Research on Human Participants*. New Delhi: Indian Council of Medical Research, 2017.

18. Central Drugs Standard Control Organization (CDSCO). *Schedule Y of the Drugs and Cosmetics Act – Requirements and Guidelines for Permission to Import and/or Manufacture of New Drugs for Sale or to Undertake Clinical Trials*. New Delhi: Ministry of Health and Family Welfare, Government of India, 2019.
19. U.S. Food and Drug Administration (FDA). *CFR 21 Part 812 – Investigational Device Exemptions (IDE)*. Washington, D.C.: U.S. Department of Health and Human Services, 2021.
20. European Medicines Agency (EMA). *EudraLex Volume 3 – Scientific Guidelines for Medicinal Products for Human Use*. London: European Medicines Agency, 2018.
21. World Health Organization (WHO). *Operational Guidelines for Ethics Committees that Review Biomedical Research*. Geneva: World Health Organization, 2000.
22. U.S. Food and Drug Administration (FDA). *CFR 21 Part 822 – Post-Market Surveillance*. Washington, D.C.: U.S. Department of Health and Human Services, 2021.
23. International Council for Harmonisation of Technical Requirements for Pharmaceuticals for Human Use (ICH). *ICH E10 – Choice of Control Group in Clinical Trials*. ICH Harmonised Guideline, 2000.
24. European Medicines Agency (EMA). *Annual Safety Report (ASR) for Clinical Trials Conducted in the European Union*. London: European Medicines Agency, 2015.
25. Global Harmonization Task Force (GHTF). *Clinical Evidence – Key Definitions and Concepts for Medical Device Trials*. GHTF Study Group 5, 2012.
26. World Health Organization (WHO). *WHO Handbook on Clinical Trial Registration: A Platform for Responsible Clinical Trial Data Sharing*. Geneva: World Health Organization, 2015.
27. U.S. Food and Drug Administration (FDA). *FDA Guidance for Industry: Pharmacovigilance and Risk Management Programs*. Washington, D.C.: U.S. Department of Health and Human Services, 2005.
28. European Medicines Agency (EMA). *Guideline on the Data Monitoring Committees*. London: European Medicines Agency, 2005.

29. World Medical Association (WMA).
Ethical Principles for Medical Research Involving Human Subjects – The Helsinki Declaration (1964-2013). Ferney-Voltaire: World Medical Association, 2013.
30. International Council for Harmonisation of Technical Requirements for Pharmaceuticals for Human Use (ICH).
ICH E7 – Studies in Support of Special Populations: Geriatrics. ICH Harmonised Guideline, 1993.
31. U.S. Food and Drug Administration (FDA).
Financial Disclosure by Clinical Investigators: Guidance for Industry. Washington, D.C.: U.S. Department of Health and Human Services, 2013.
32. Global Harmonization Task Force (GHTF).
Clinical Evidence for Medical Devices – Key Definitions and Concepts. GHTF Study Group 5, 2007.
33. U.S. Food and Drug Administration (FDA).
Guidance for Clinical Trial Sponsors: Establishment and Operation of Clinical Trial Data Monitoring Committees. Washington, D.C.: U.S. Department of Health and Human Services, 2006.
34. Indian Council of Medical Research (ICMR).
National Ethical Guidelines for Biomedical and Health Research Involving Human Participants. New Delhi: Indian Council of Medical Research, 2017.
35. National Institutes of Health (NIH).
NIH Policy on the Use of a Single Institutional Review Board for Multi-Site Research. Bethesda: National Institutes of Health, 2016.
36. European Medicines Agency (EMA).
Guideline on Good Pharmacovigilance Practices (GVP): Module V – Risk Management Systems. London: European Medicines Agency, 2012.
37. International Council for Harmonisation of Technical Requirements for Pharmaceuticals for Human Use (ICH).
ICH E4 – Dose-Response Information to Support Drug Registration. ICH Harmonised Guideline, 1994.
38. U.S. Department of Health and Human Services (HHS).
The Common Rule: Federal Policy for the Protection of Human Subjects. Washington, D.C.: U.S. Department of Health and Human Services, 2017.

39. World Health Organization (WHO).
Global Strategy on Human Resources for Health: Workforce 2030. Geneva: World Health Organization, 2016.
40. U.S. Food and Drug Administration (FDA).
CFR 21 Part 320 – Bioavailability and Bioequivalence Requirements. Washington, D.C.: U.S. Department of Health and Human Services, 2020.
41. Central Drugs Standard Control Organization (CDSCO).
Clinical Trials Rules, 2019 (India). New Delhi: Ministry of Health and Family Welfare, Government of India, 2019.
42. National Institutes of Health (NIH).
NIH Policy and Guidelines on the Inclusion of Women and Minorities as Subjects in Clinical Research. Bethesda: National Institutes of Health, 2001.
43. U.S. Food and Drug Administration (FDA).
FDA Guidance for Industry: E6(R2) Good Clinical Practice. Washington, D.C.: U.S. Department of Health and Human Services, 2018.
44. World Health Organization (WHO).
Guidelines for Good Clinical Practice (GCP) for Trials on Pharmaceutical Products. Geneva: World Health Organization, 1995.
45. International Council for Harmonisation of Technical Requirements for Pharmaceuticals for Human Use (ICH).
ICH E11 – Clinical Investigation of Medicinal Products in the Pediatric Population. ICH Harmonised Guideline, 2000.
46. Central Drugs Standard Control Organization (CDSCO).
Guidelines for the Approval of Clinical Trials and New Drugs in India. New Delhi: Ministry of Health and Family Welfare, Government of India, 2017.
47. World Health Organization (WHO).
Ethical and Safety Recommendations for Intervention Research on Violence Against Women. Geneva: World Health Organization, 2016.
48. European Medicines Agency (EMA).
Guideline on Clinical Trials in Small Populations. London: European Medicines Agency, 2006.
49. National Bioethics Advisory Commission (NBAC).
Research Involving Human Biological Materials: Ethical Issues and Policy Guidance. Bethesda: National Bioethics Advisory Commission, 1999.

50. National Institutes of Health (NIH).
NIH Policy on Dissemination of NIH-Funded Clinical Trial Information.
Bethesda: National Institutes of Health, 2016.

www.ingramcontent.com/pod-product-compliance
Ingram Content Group UK Ltd.
Pitfield, Milton Keynes, MK11 3LW, UK
UKHW062310290726
14090UKWH00018B/989